RED
DESERT
SKY

John Lomax III was raised in Texas and is the grandson of pioneering folklorist John Avery Lomax. He has been a nationally published US music journalist since 1967; his work has also been published in Europe, Asia and Australia. He is author of *Nashville: Music City USA* (1986) and co-author of *The Country Music Book* (1988). He presently writes regular columns for *Country Music International* in London and *Country Music Update* in Gympie. John is also an artist manager and has represented Townes Van Zandt, Steve Earle and The Cactus Brothers. He began representing Dead Ringer Band in 1996.

RED DESERT SKY

The Amazing Adventures of the CHAMBERS FAMILY

JOHN LOMAX III

ALLEN&UNWIN

First published in 2001

Copyright ©John Lomax III 2001

Allen & Unwin
83 Alexander Street
Crows Nest NSW 2065
Australia
Phone: (61 2) 8425 0100
Fax: (61 2) 9906 2218
Email: info@allenandunwin.com
Web: www.allenandunwin.com

National Library of Australia
Cataloguing-in-Publication entry:

Lomax, John, III.
  Red desert sky: the amazing adventures of the Chambers family.

  Includes index.
  ISBN 1 86508 425 5.

  1. Dead Ringer Band (Musical group). 2. Country music
  groups—Australia. I. Title.

781.6420994

Design by Nada Backovic
Set in 12/13.5 pt Weiss by DOCUPRO, Canberra
Printed by Griffin Press, South Australia

10 9 8 7 6 5 4 3 2 1

To my late grandfather, John Avery Lomax, who began the Lomax musical tradition, and to my uncle Alan and my aunts, Shirley and Bess, who carried that torch forward.

To my late mother, Margaret Marable Lomax, and my late father, John Avery Lomax Jr, who passed on the torch and taught me right from wrong.

To my late brother, Joseph Franklin Lomax, who taught me grace and style.

To my son, John Nova Lomax, for carrying on the family musical tradition.

To my daughter, Amanda Margaret Lomax, for starting her own Lomax traditions.

To my daughter-in-law, Jacqueline Wallace Lomax, for having and nurturing the most recent Lomax in our branch of the family, my grandson.

And to that grandson, John Henry Lomax, for simply being a feisty five-year-old.

To Evelyn Shriver for staying the course long enough to light the fuse.

Most importantly, to my sweeet, loving wife, Melanie Wells, for sharing her life with mine and for quietly teaching me to be a better person.

Contents

Acknowledgments

No man is an island and no author single-handedly creates a book. In the case of *Red Desert Sky*, many people played key roles and deserve my heart-felt thanks.

First of all, there would be no book without Bill, Diane, Nash and Kasey Chambers. Their willingness to share the story of their lives and their vital input throughout the project were and are deeply appreciated.

Thanks to a suggestion from Dead Ringer Band's attorney, Brett Oaten, I contacted Sophie Cunningham at Allen & Unwin early in 1999, hoping she would jump at the chance to publish the story of this extraordinary Australian family. I prepared a three-page summary and sent it to her along with a twenty-page account Bill had written, at my urging, back in 1996.

After a few months, Sophie began to share my belief in the project and, midway through the year, Allen & Unwin's contract arrived. My new agent Edité Kroll, engaged at the suggestion of Susan Nadler, helped bring matters to a successful conclusion and work commenced in October 1999.

Alisa Atkins of Antioch, Tennessee then swiftly transcribed the many hours of conversations with the four Chambers which form the backbone of the book. The Chambers family examined *Red Desert Sky* in draft form and made many valuable corrections and suggestions. I completed a working draft in January so the Chambers could get a sense of *Red Desert Sky* prior to the initial deadline. My long-time Australian friend Keith Glass helped me iron out some rough spots, corrected a few stray mistakes and supplied the essay on Australian country music found in the Appendix. Suggestions from my son, John Nova Lomax, and my wife, Melanie Wells, also helped improve the manuscript.

Lisa Taylor of Madison, Tennessee, formatted the text for presentation to the publisher; Suzi Dunn at Office Depot ensured the proper copies were made, and thus *Red Desert Sky* arrived at Allen & Unwin's offices reasonably close to the deadline.

Veteran country journalist Sue Jarvis came onboard as a specialist editor. Her suggestions and corrections improved the text markedly and her encouragement and enthusiasm helped foster my second wind.

Allen & Unwin's Colette Vella then entered my life as in-house editor. Her patience and expertise have been instrumental in ensuring that *Red Desert Sky* completed its journey through the remaining steps in the publishing process and made its way to the reader. I am also grateful to Raf Rouco, who proofread the book, and Nada Backovic and DOCUPRO, who brought their wisdom and skills to bear on the physical presentation of *Red Desert Sky*: their work in typesetting, layout and design has resulted in the beautiful book you hold in your hands today.

In addition to taking several of the photographs, Nashville's John Montgomery of Nouveau Photography provided essential colour scans of photos borrowed from the Chambers family.

My desire to come to Australia was stoked mightily in 1966 and 1967 when I took two college courses in the history of the region, both taught by C. Hartley Grattan, author of the two-volume set, *The History of the Southwest Pacific*. Prior to meeting Dead Ringer Band and the Chambers family, I corresponded with several industry notables, including Nick Erby, Keith Glass and Reg Lindsay; all helped me learn more about the Australian country music world.

I made my first Australian music business deal with Laurie Dunn of Massive Records in 1995 and I am also indebted to him for providing my first air ticket 'down under', in September 1996. Massive employees Kaye Crick (interviewed for the book) and Louise Stovin-Bradford kindly helped me find lodging and ferried me about on that initial visit.

In the intervening years I have been fortunate enough to

return to Australia numerous times. These trips have allowed me to build up a network of contacts, all of whom have, at one time or another, provided sage advice regarding the Australian country music industry and the career of Dead Ringer Band. Their friendship, acceptance and kind encouragement have meant a great deal to me. I hope they will be pleased with *Red Desert Sky;* the time they shared and their insight helped make this book possible!

A pat on the back is due to the following folks: Bob Aird, Glenn A. Baker, B.J. Barker, David Baxter, John Brommel, Michael Chugg, Darren Coggan, Leon Concannon, Shanley Del, Martin Delcanho, Joan, Bevan and Tierzah Douglas, Bruce Elder, Warren Fahey, Jon Farkas, Nick Hampton, Barry Harley, Tony Harlow, Melita Hodge, Max King, Bob Kirchner, David Latta, Jeff McCormack, Gayle Madill, Keith Melbourne, Barbara Morrison, Cathy Oates, Michelle O'Donnell, Chris O'Hearn, Richard Porteous, Gary Rabin, Jason Redlich, Steve Reid, Greg Shaw, Wally Sparrow, Shane and Kathryn Pitt Warren, Worm Werchon and Fred Wild (who shared source material with me from a 1994 DRB road trip).

Lastly, to end at the beginning, words alone can hardly express my appreciation to Bill, Diane, Nash and Kasey Chambers for spending hours telling me about their lives and for trusting me to tell their story to the world. During the more than five years I've known this remarkable family they have taken me into their trust, made me feel a part of their lives and shared their food, home and thoughts. My hope is that they feel *Red Desert Sky* accurately, honestly and vividly portrays their adventurous lives to date.

John Lomax III
May 2001

Prologue

The dark-haired, thirty-six-year-old woman eased out of her bed at sun's first light, crawled over her sleeping husband and slipped outside silently, into the Nullarbor dawn. She yawned, stretched, blew on her hands to ward off the fading night's chill and took a moment to look around her at the limitless landscape of green salt bush, scrubby blue bush and red dirt that encircled her as far as she could see. The sky above her spanned unobstructed to the horizon in a full circle, making her feel she was caught inside a dome, a human frozen to the dark amber Nullarbor Plain.

The glow of the red desert sky in the east was just beginning to fade into daylight, so she started the day's chores. She checked the fire and saw a few coals still glowing so she carefully added small twigs, then larger dry branches from the firewood the kids, Nash and Kasey, had gathered yesterday. They would be up soon and her work day would really begin: cooking, washing, preparing fox skins and overseeing the kids' correspondence lessons.

She put the billy on the fire when the flames began to crackle, relishing a few minutes of solitude as she waited for it to boil. She thought best when she was alone and now she thought of how ironic it was that private moments to herself were hard to get even though there weren't five other humans within 100 kilometres.

Last night's fox shooting had been good but they'd found two separate poisoned baits, proof that other hunters had moved into the area, working with cyanide instead of firearms. They had

On the Nullarbor's fringe, Bill and Diane ponder their options.

fewer pelts than last year and the price the fur fetched was slowly falling.

The warm northern breeze began to pick up, reminding her that soon the Nullarbor would become too hot for them to live there. They would again migrate east, then south across the Plain, back down to their hometown fishing village, to try their luck with the sea during the warmer months. Had it really been nine years since 1977, when the four of them had first come to this forsaken land, in search of foxes and freedom? Nash was thirteen now, Kasey ten. Diane didn't know if she knew enough to give them much more schooling. They needed to be around children their age, to play sports, learn social skills and be involved in peer group interactions.

And what of her and Bill? They'd earned decent money as pub musicians once, until the kids came along, then they had worked to make a go of living a normal, settled existence. They hadn't been able to make ends meet simply by fishing all summer so they'd become nomadic hunters; now the hunting was getting harder and less profitable with each passing year. Maybe, she thought, she and Bill could start a band again, back home. Maybe they could make enough money that way to feed and clothe them all. Maybe . . . oh, who'd ever want to hear some band from the middle of nowhere in South Australia? What was to become of them? The balmy north wind blew harder and the billy boiled.

Introduction

Early in March 1996, Laurie Dunn, founder and Managing Director of Sydney-based Massive Records, went to Nashville to attend the Country Radio Seminar, an annual gathering which brings several thousand radio professionals to town to discuss the state of the industry with record label personnel. CRS is a four-day event stuffed full of panels, speakers and other business gatherings during the days, followed by booze-filled 'schmoozefests' (free eats and alcohol for the radio folks) and artist showcase performances during the evenings.

Laurie and I had done a small licensing deal previously for the Australian issue of recordings made by David Schnaufer, 'America's Dulcimer Champion', a remarkable instrumentalist whose records I had co-produced for my own tiny label, SFL Tapes & Discs. Although we had made our deal about a year before, Laurie and I had never met, so we introduced ourselves over a few beers at the Longhorn Steakhouse, a noted Nashville watering hole near 'Music Row', the heart of the city's multi-billion dollar music industry.

I was trying to establish an export business, selling finished CDs by Nashville-based artists to importers in Europe, Asia and Australia. The meeting went well: I felt Laurie was an astute music business guy with considerable charm. Upon parting, we each presented the other with about a half dozen CDs. In my case they were made by clients I wanted to export in the Australasian market; his CDs were by home-grown Australian country artists or records he had licensed in from the States. I put his stack of platters on the front seat as I buckled in for the ride home, about a twenty-minute drive.

I remember thinking at the time, 'Australian country? Yeah, sure', giggling to myself at the mere thought of what I figured was bush ballad albums made for a tiny label in Sydney competing in the almost $2 billion annual sales juggernaut that American country had become during the huge boom years of the first half of the 1990s. I scooped up a beer for the road, manoeuvred on to the highway, slipped into cruise control and slid the first disc into the player of my trusty 1986 Cadillac.

Still snickering and thinking, 'Australian country? This is really gonna be *bad*' and remembering the Monty Python sketch about Australian wines from the 1970s, I pushed the play button for *Home Fires*, a CD by a family group called Dead Ringer Band.

Homefires

Can you feel the homefires burning
As you ride that white lined highway
Can you feel the homefires burning
Hometown folks I'm not too far away . . .

Darren Coggan © 1995, *Control*

CRACK! KABOOM! Cranial lightning and mental thunder struck as the sweet voice of Kasey Chambers and ethereal family harmonies filled the car with the first verse of the song fellow country singer Darren Coggan had written about them. I was intrigued in less than ten seconds, hooked in about twenty and a complete goner at the half-minute mark. By the time 'Homefires' reached the second chorus, I was singing along at the top of my lungs, pounding the dash in time to the drums, jumping up and down in the car seat, barrelling down the dark highway at 120 kilometres an hour, transported to absolute ecstasy by the music I was hearing. The track is a pure, honest, brilliant fusion of the finest elements of country, folk, rock and bluegrass, dripping with heartfelt harmonies and brilliantly understated production. Dead Ringer Band sounded like a reincarnation of The Carter Family, rocketed forward seventy years in time and given modern instruments. Most of their musical influences were

Home Fires, *Dead Ringer Band's second full-length CD, released in 1995.*

obviously American, yet their sound also bore an unmistakable Australian flavour, lyrically and melodically. In short, Dead Ringer Band—Bill, Diane, Nash and Kasey Chambers: father, mother, son and daughter, respectively—stole my heart in minutes, nay seconds, and have yet to give it back.

This doesn't happen often. In fact, I've been surrounded by music, both live and recorded, for years—first as a listener and since 1967 within the music industry, initially as a journalist then in other roles, including artist management for Townes Van Zandt and Steve Earle. But I had *never* been so enraptured by a recording! I became even more entranced as I listened to the other thirteen tracks. The twenty-minute drive home stretched to almost an hour: I wasn't about to pull into my driveway until I had heard all of *Home Fires*. I got home and eagerly devoured the information in the CD booklet to find out more about this band.

I got in touch with Laurie as soon as he returned, babbling about *Home Fires* and bombarding him with questions about Dead Ringer Band. After a few such chats and a flurry of faxes, he supplied their numbers. So on 25 March 1996, I sent an introductory fax to the Chambers family, describing my interest in their music and my hopes for obtaining a US release for their album. Their reply came back in a few hours (see Appendix A).

And off we went. I was even more fascinated when I learned they had spent slightly over half of the years between 1976 and 1986 living in the extreme outback of Australia, most of it on the near-uninhabitable Nullarbor Plain. Their story sounded like something out of literature—a sort of bizarre, Australian version of *Swiss Family Robinson*. Instead of being shipwrecked on the ocean, the Chambers family had routinely marooned themselves annually on the Nullarbor. This called for further investigation.

During the next five years it has been my privilege to know the four Chambers, initially as clients and business associates (I have represented them in the United States ever since), then as mates. They are honest, caring, decent people with old-fashioned values. For artists, they are extraordinarily other-directed—when they ask you 'How ya goin?', they really want you to tell them what's on your mind. What's more, they listen when you reply.

I had dreamed of going to Australia since I was twelve years old, but until I heard Dead Ringer Band, I had always lacked either a reason or the funds to make such a trip. The chain of events set in motion by their music has enabled me to make seven thoroughly enjoyable jaunts 'down under' so far.

Red Desert Sky relates the life stories of these four remarkable people known professionally as Dead Ringer Band. It is a tale of their amazing adventures on the Nullarbor and in the music industry, two difficult arenas fraught with their own special perils. It details the Chambers' artistic development from being a local band in Southend, South Australia, to becoming the most honoured group in Australian country music. This is a story of survival by a family that has lived by the maxim of playing together and staying together for a quarter of a century. Though I have had a part in their professional development over the past five years, I have tried to submerge that role by presenting as much of the story as possible in their own words: it's their story, not mine.

Every effort has been made to keep this account as straightforward as possible, free from the fluff and puffery too often found in biographies of pop culture figures. I sincerely hope the reader will feel these efforts have succeeded. I also hope that this book will give you a very real sense of who these remarkable four individualists are.

Red Desert Sky was created from source material which includes about twenty hours of interviews and more than five years of faxes, letters and conversations with the various Chambers, published reviews and features from US, European and Australian magazines and newspapers, record company press materials, various books, discussions and correspondence with dozens of people in the Australian and Nashville country music industry. I've also added insights gleaned from my experiences during over thirty years in the music business. The Chambers family saga is the most interesting and unique 'showbiz' story I've ever encountered.

Now, it's time to begin your journey into the lives of Bill, Diane, Nash and Kasey Chambers, four maverick musicians who have forever altered the course of Australian country music.

1

Origins

'Yo ho-ho and a barrel of rum', Bill Chambers' great-great grandfather Jacob must have been singing in 1850 as he rode the shifting waves on Guichen Bay, atop a half-full barrel of grog, bound for the beach at Robe, South Australia. A Swedish seaman, Jake, as he became known, either decided he liked the lay of the land, or maybe he was simply tired of the sway of the sea, so he and the spirits jumped ship after it had stopped for supplies in Robe. The vessel was bound further south still, to Melbourne. The ship weighed anchor and sailed on; Jake and the rum paddled eastward a few hundred metres to alight in the sleepy seaside town, some 370 kilometres south and a bit east of Adelaide. It's not known whether Jake acquired his liquid cargo as a going-away present from a grateful captain or as payment for his months of sea duty or if he simply helped himself. Though no firm evidence exists, one suspects the latter, since sea captains were not generally known for their generosity and common seamen were usually paid at the end of a voyage.

Jake's Australian debut—and this branch of the Chambers line—started auspiciously: that much rum made a fairly decent stake in the mid-nineteenth century. Assuming his barrel contained about 120 litres, Jake had enough to dispense about 2000 servings, a quantity sufficient to keep a smile on the faces of the few citizens of Robe for many months. We can reasonably assume he quickly made friends with the locals.

1

George Lord, an English merchant, was among Robe's earliest settlers in 1846, together with his wife and daughter. In the four years since he had arrived, George had become Robe's most prominent businessman/landowner and the proprietor of the settlement's only hotel, the Criterion, newly completed just in time for Jake's opportune arrival. George and Jake became friends and a short time later Jake became more than friends with George's daughter, Elizabeth, marrying her and becoming the new hotel's manager.

Though the members of this Australian Chambers clan began as innkeepers/publicans, the next three generations all left the security of a steady job and returned to the sea, as fishermen who also became skilled hunters. They also drifted a bit south, settling in the Southend/Beachport/Rendelsham area, forty-five kilometres from Robe—first Jake and Elizabeth's son Charley; then his son Stan, Bill's grandfather; then Bill's dad Eric, soon nicknamed Jake after the family's fountainhead.

Bill: My great grandmother was German. I remember her being quite old, blind when I was a little kid. My sister Julie and I used to sing to her, with my dad. She'd put her hand out and sort of touch me as I was singing. She was totally blind, but she was a tough old lady; she loved music.

Her daughter, Emily Haines, married my grandfather, Stan Chambers, and they settled in her hometown, Rendelsham, where both my parents were born and raised. My dad, Eric, married Judy Stratford. He was eighteen, my mother was sixteen. I was the eldest child. I can still remember my mum's twenty-first birthday.

Bill Chambers was born on 22 December 1950, in Millicent, the location of the nearest hospital to the tiny coastal town of Southend (population thirty back then), which was about sixty kilometres from Mount Gambier. He was born into an unconventional family, even by rural Australian standards.

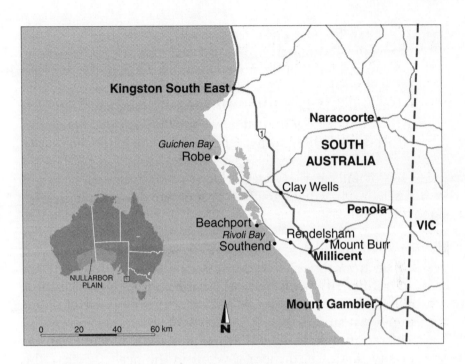

The Beachport/Southend area.

Bill: My dad was a fisherman. Every second night he'd bring a fish home to eat or go out and shoot a wild duck and make stew or something. Even though it sounds a little barbaric now, it was just a way of life to us.

To Bill's knowledge, his dad never held a salaried job—or, for that matter, ever worked for anyone.

Bill: He believes you don't really have to work—you just live, and he lives okay. My grandfather, though, was a hard worker—loading and unloading sailing ships from the age of twelve. He grew chicory and potatoes and, during the war, carrots for the army. He liked to live a simple life.

I used to be very close to my grandpa, Stan. When my sisters and I were small he would dance around the kitchen and sing songs. Usually 'Behind McArty's Mare' or 'MacNamara's Band'.

3

Stan became close friends with Lanky, one of the last surviving Aboriginals from the Buandik tribe. Until they were wiped out by illness and the white settlers, the Buandiks roamed over a territory that extended as far north as the Glenelg River, on the Victoria border. Lanky and Stan spent a lot of time together, hunting and fishing, so my grandfather learned how to live off the land the black man's way.

One of Bill's earliest memories is riding home from school with his mum, a trip of uncertain duration due to a few stops along the way.

Bill: Most of the nights in the wintertime my mum would pick me up from school in an early 1950s Chev. She'd bring the .22 calibre rifle with her and on the way home, she'd shoot rabbits for the dog or for dad to use as lobster bait. Mum would just stop, let the motor run and shoot out the window with a rifle. She was an incredible shot, nineteen out of twenty times, she'd shoot a rabbit in the head. We had this dog, Blondie, and she would jump out the window and go fetch them. By the time we got home, she'd have twenty-odd rabbits.

My oldest sister, Julie, is married to Terry Moran: he owns a trawler and lobster boats. My next oldest sister, Keryn, is also married to a fisherman, Allen Campbell, who also owns a trawler. My youngest sister, Jeanie, is married to a lobster fisherman, Graham Strother. I've also got two other younger brothers, Leigh (married to Sandra) and Jarrod, who are both lobster fishermen as well. They all live in Southend or Beachport, I'm the only one who moved away. They're all a little musical, but they were never keen enough to carry it on.

My oldest brother, Barry, drowned about fifteen years ago: he was lost at sea and never found. He was a fisherman too, just like my father and grandfather. I was a fisherman until I was about twenty-five, but then I decided I wanted to do something different. I guess fishing would have given me a much better financial future, but I don't regret that choice for a moment.

4

I was a real cowboy fan, I loved John Wayne and all the western movies. Occasionally my Auntie Rosalie—she was a piano player—would take us to the drive-in movies. In some of the western movies, they'd have these old-time cowboy singers like Gene Autry or the Sons of the Pioneers, singing these cowboy songs, which I loved. My dad had already sung me the songs, so I already knew them even before I heard them in the movie. I also loved books on shipwrecks: *Robinson Crusoe, Swiss Family Robinson*.

When we were a family growing up, we'd sit along the old fireplace. Mum and Dad would sing sometimes and all us kids would join in. We were a Christian family, so we'd sing a lot of gospel songs.

Bill's mother, Judy Stratford, was an unusual woman, in her own way as unconventional as his father.

Bill: She was brought up in a Christian family, very sheltered, and she once told me that she'd never tasted alcohol in her life and she still says she hasn't. She's never been to Sydney. She loves traditional country music like the old-time hillbilly stuff, but the religion that she was sort of caught up in, the Seventh-Day Adventists, really frowned on professional entertainment. She would stay home at night listening to hillbilly programs on an old AM radio rather than go out and mix with her friends. When one leader of the church heard about this, he immediately paid her a visit to try to talk her into going to Bible College and to 'get a life'. She replied, 'I'm happy where I am. I get more out of listening to my hillbilly music than I would out of college.'

When I was about eight years old, mum purchased a beautiful F-hole guitar for herself, which I still have, but she got tired of guitar lessons pretty soon. She had a book, *The Mel Bay Method*, and she showed me about four chords. I still believe if you've got four chords, you can play most country songs anyway. It's meant to be simple: if you've got too many chords, then you've gone and fucked it up. I found I could play a few songs, but I wanted to learn more.

I went to a guitar teacher. He was an accordion player and he didn't know notes on the guitar. He'd try to show us how it's done on the guitar but it sounded like he wasn't holding his fingers down properly; he couldn't actually play. He could tell when we weren't doing it right, but he couldn't really show us how. I didn't learn a lot from him, to be quite honest, I mainly learned stuff from records. Most of the old record players had 78, 45 and 33 speeds but there was a lower speed again, 16. I never had any records that were meant to be running at 16, but I used to slow the 33s down to 16 or the 45s to 33 and work out the guitar licks. It was slower and you could tell what was going on. Mum and Dad would sing in harmony (similar to the Carter Family), so I desperately tried to play like Mother Maybelle—she's still my favourite guitar stylist.

Bill was never a diligent student; though he stayed in school until he was fifteen, he didn't have a sterling attendance record.

Bill: We lived about thirty kilometres from Millicent, which is where I went to high school. What we would do is catch the bus from Millicent to Rendelsham and for the last fourteen kilometres, Mum would either come and pick me up, or I would ride a push bike when it wasn't too cold and frosty in the mornings. When I did ride my bike, about every second morning I'd miss the bus. I would get up the last straight, it'd be about five to eight and I'd be nearly there and the bus would leave. I would just turn around and ride home happily, whistling all the way.

My dad's still pretty fit. He taught me at an early age to hunt and often told me about the war years—how his father, brother and he would hunt and trap rabbits to survive. They didn't have a regular job like all the other folks around. They owned a bit of land, they would just go out, hunting and trapping rabbits. The survived the war years this way. I didn't realise it at the time, but it must have rubbed off somehow because when I got married and had children, we ended up living the same way.

The emigration of Diane Chambers' great-great-great grand-mother perhaps was not as dramatic as Jake Chambers' onshore arrival perched on a cask of rum, but the story of Diane's origins are certainly romantic. The circumstances were doubtless dramatic enough for the two young lovers involved.

Martha Geracle was born into Spanish royalty in Madrid but her heart led her astray—she ran away with Joseph Doe, a clerk whose lineage was far less grand. She soon bore him a daughter, Jane Doe, Diane's great-great grandmother. The Geracles, doubt-less hoping for a rather more noble 'catch' for Martha, disowned their daughter so the young family travelled to Australia, arriving in the 1840s and settling in the Mount Gambier area, a few years before Jake alighted from his keg on the beach at Robe.

Harriet Pulford, Jane's daughter, was born at Grey, now known as Southend, her daughter, Beatrice Dean (Diane's grand-mother) and Margaret (Dean) Walker (Beatrice's daughter and Diane's mother) were born at Mount Gambier. Thus, Nash and Kasey are fifth-generation Australians on both Diane's side and Bill's.

Diane's mum, Margaret Dean, daughter of Wattie and Beattie Dean, grew up in Millicent but later moved to Melbourne, where she met and married John Forrest. John and his brother Len were orphans who were raised in the Kildonan Children's Home in North Melbourne, and then at the Kilmany Park Boys Farm Home at Sale, east of Melbourne. Afterwards, John joined the Army.

Diane was born on 4 October 1950. Soon afterwards, the family moved to Mount Burr, near Millicent, where her parents separated. Margaret then remarried, to Bill Walker, who thus became Diane's stepfather. (John also remarried, to Monica Whitehead.) Diane, with her mother, stepfather and older sister, Cheryl, then moved to Goolwa, on the mouth of the Murray River in South Australia, where she started school.

Diane: Then we moved again; Mum and Dad bought a small poultry farm with about 1000 free-range laying hens. It was a few kilometres out of Mannum, on the Murray River, northeast of Goolwa. Dad also got a job on a fruit block at Mypolonga, a nearby river town that consisted mostly of orchards so there was always plenty of work available. Dad not only worked there in the early years, he also played football and cricket for Mypo, so much of our social life was with the people from that district. We had many great get-togethers with dances and barbeques, and made lots of wonderful friends who remain close to this day.

Mum stayed home and did the work on the farm; Cheryl and I had to help before and after school. Dad would mix the feed when he came home from work, then go to a neighbour to cart water for the poultry since there was no mains water then. When it was time to vaccinate the chickens against fowl pox we all had to get up very early to get it done before Dad left for work and Cheryl and I went to school. I was never at my best early in the mornings (I'm still not!), so I was pretty grumpy and couldn't see why we had to have stupid chooks! We had to pull some of the downy feathers off the leg so Mum could inject the vaccine. One morning I was a bit slow shucking feathers so I got the vaccine injection job myself! That woke me up for a while.

Cheryl and I used to catch the school bus into Mannum which would have been about fifteen kilometres away. Much to my horror I remember having to walk three kilometres most days and nights to catch the bus and, of course, I thought I was hard done by, having to do that . . . I enjoyed school and I was quite happy going.

When we came home we would go to the sheds and help collect the eggs. After the novelty wore off, I found this really boring so I decided to brighten things up a bit by paiting one of the Beatles' names on each door. As we had a lot of individual sheds in those days there were a lot of brightly painted John, Paul, George and Ringo's along the rows, much to Dad's disgust when the Poultry Adviser or Egg Inspector came calling!

As money became more plentiful, new big cage sheds

were built and life became easier for all of us. Dad and Mum did the farm work and, by then, they had built the number of hens up to about 9000. They added extensions to the house and a swimming pool so our home was always a good spot for the relatives from both sides to come for holidays.

We spent our early school holidays working over on the orchard where Dad worked, cutting apricots for drying, and we really enjoyed earning the money. We had a lot of fun, there were lots of other kids working there also.

Though music was to play a defining role in her later life, Diane made her onstage debut in other areas of the performing arts, going 'on the road' for the first time before she was eight years old.

Diane: Cheryl and I joined Kath Camilleri's dancing school and we would travel around to Mannum and other towns peforming in the concerts. Everyone enjoyed these and Kath put such a lot of time in to teach us and make it all so successful. I think I was in Grade 1 or 2 then and I had a little trouble concentrating intently; I would often still have my back on view when all the other girls would be facing the front! Mum would make all our costumes; Cheryl was very good at dancing, as she was (and is) with everything she took on.

Some years later Diane switched to acting, where she distinguished herself in a leading role during her teenage years.

Diane: I won a trophy in high school for best actress in a play called 'Pandora's Box'. As I had to act very sad and teary, I had the brilliant idea of rubbing Vicks VapoRub all around my eyes to help create the sad effect. What a wrong move that was, as I found out for hours afterwards—maybe it did help me win that prize though!

The thousands of chickens weren't the only animals living on the Walker homestead. One of Diane's saddest memories is of an early four-legged friend.

Diane: We had lots of pets on the farm, including cats, dogs, lambs and rabbits, but my special favourite was my guinea pig. I would spend time with it before and after school, until Mum would call me to get in and do my homework. I vividly remember we had a week of very hot weather when Mum and Dad spent all week trying to keep the chooks alive. I came home from school one afternoon and went to my precious guinea pig and he had died. That was the biggest trauma of my life so far and I fretted for days and wouldn't eat, until I was sat down one day and given lots of comforting advice and told that these things happened and it's very sad, but I couldn't make myself sick and that we could get another guinea pig. I didn't want another one, and didn't have one until many years later.

The Christmas holidays offered a great opportunity for the Walkers to gather with most of the members of their extended families.

Diane: Christmas was always a great event in our lives. The first year we were on the farm we spent it on our own, but after the families from the south east would all come to our house. Mum's sister (Aunty Rene) lived in a big home in Mannum, so between the two homes there was plenty of room for everyone. Some years we would go to Millicent and have one meal with Nanna and Pop Dean and their families, and the other meal with Grandma and Grandpa Walker and their families. We had to get up very early to feed the chooks before leaving on the four-and-a-half hour trip to be there for lunch, and by the time we got home again it would be very late, so Dad would only have a few hours sleep. Then it would be time to get up again and tackle two days' work in one.

Another thing that really stands out in my mind about Christmas was lunch at Nanna and Pop Dean's. Nanna would have a big tree all decorated in her backyard, and we kids were all told that she had a letter from Father Christmas to say that he would come and give out the presents himself. Cheryl, Wayne, Jenny and myself were all at the stage of not quite believing Santa was real, but the little ones were mesmerised when Father Christmas really did come with his bag of presents. I can remember Great Gran Pulford (Nanna Dean's mother) was with us that year too which was a great joy. We older ones were not sure what to think when we were handed our presents and we eyed Father Christmas up and down, and when Wayne got his present he must have picked up on the voice a bit (it was his dad in the costume), then he looked down and saw his shoes—Uncle Jack had forgotten to change them! He opend his mouth and said, 'I know who . . .', and before he could get any more out a couple of aunties grabbed him and took him aside and explained not to spoil it for the little ones. It was a great day. Later Mum and Dad bought a beach house at Southend and everyone would come down there; we would have a huge get-together with a bonfire and a sing-a-long, and Aunty Faye would get everyone laughing with her poetry and yarns.

We had a very close relationship with Aunty Rene and Uncle Ray, and we would stay at their home if there was a school social or anything on that we wanted to go to at night. I remember them taking Cheryl and me to see Billy Thorpe and the Aztecs at the Murray Bridge Town Hall one night. The crowd went back to the hotel where the band were staying and after a lot of yelling and screaming they came out onto the balcony—wow! When we got home from Murray Bridge that night we couldn't even tell Mum and Dad much about it because we had nearly lost our voices from all the screaming and yelling. Aunty Rene and Uncle Ray were a very big part of our lives, being the only other members of our family up this way—we loved them dearly. I look back now and think how patient they were with us as they didn't have any family of their own, but had a very extended one with all the nieces and nephews.

We may not have had much money in our early growing-up years but I'm sure the fun times and happy memories have lasted much longer than money would have.

While strict Christianity was a major part of Bill's childhood, Diane's religious association was on a much more casual basis.

Diane: One of my best friends, Judy Vivian, and her family were Baptist. I used to spend weekends with them and go to church. I found I really enjoyed helping with Sunday school and going along to church. I enjoyed that side of life and learned some of their Christian beliefs.

Bill, for his part, was raised in the more rigid Adventist religious climate.

Bill: They believe in the resurrection and all that sort of thing, but the difference is they believe in worshipping on the seventh day, which they consider is Saturday instead of Sunday. Their holy day runs from Friday evening to Saturday evening. So from Friday sundown to Saturday sundown I was supposed to be devoted to everything Christian. Had to be Christian music. You don't watch television, although we didn't have television anyway so that didn't matter. I didn't even see TV until I was about thirteen years old. But it was always a bit of a drag come Friday night 'cause you couldn't do any of the fun things. But I'm sort of glad, even though I don't go along with all that now. Any sort of discipline is good.

Both Bill and Diane developed an early interest in music, initially from family sing-a-longs, but also from radio and their exposure to church hymns and spirituals. Both became interested in rock'n'roll, country music and folk-rock during their early teens.

Bill: I'd started playing around ten. My mum had a guitar and her and Dad were great hillbilly fans. They'd listen to these old cowboy singers like Wilf Carter, Jimmie Rodgers and Hank Snow, and some of the Australian singers like Tex Morton and Buddy Williams.
   I saw my first real country show when I was seven. My dad took me to see Rick and Thel Carey and I thought, 'That's what I want to be, a country star.'

When I was fifteen years old I went on a holiday into the outback with my grandparents. We were in a little town called Kingoonya, south of Coober Pedy, when it rained hard for a week and it flooded. There were about thirty campers and two tourist buses stuck in town, all staying at an overcrowded hotel. I had my guitar, so on Saturday night I entertained about 200 people, locals and tourists, just me and the guitar. That was the first time I'd ever done anything like that, and it went over pretty well I guess. I sort of thought, 'Maybe I could do this one day.'

As we travelled on to Alice Springs, through the Kimberley ranges and on to Broome, my grandfather would drag me around to groups of other campers in caravan parks, waving his arms, dancing and laughing while I sang and played. Before long we'd have a heap of people around us, listening and singing along.

By the time I went to high school, I was already performing in local concerts. I didn't write songs at this stage, although my father did. My art teacher, Cecil Churchill, was a folk singer. He turned us on to Dylan and Peter, Paul and Mary. I got up in class one day and sang a country song called 'I'll Never Be Fooled Again', which I learned from a Rick and Thel Carey recording.

I remember a couple of the girls came up later and said, 'We loved that, that's incredible, we love your singing.' I think that gave me enough encouragement to keep going.

Meanwhile, over in Mannum, Diane was taking her own first steps into music.

Diane: My stepdad, Bill Walker, and his family used to be singers. When I say singers, it was only around the campfire, or at parties. They used to sing a few old Slim Whitman songs while mum and her sisters would join in.

There was a guy at our high school who had a guitar for sale, so I hounded Mum and Dad until they let me buy it. It was the most atrocious guitar, painted white with a black flower or some such thing on it, but of course I thought it was just wonderful. I started playing around at

13

home, just tinkering away with it on my own. I never had any lessons or anything like that, it was really just a bit of a teenage fad, a fun thing.

'Fun thing' or not, by the time Diane turned fifteen, in 1965, she already was familiar with the songs of her favourite artists.

Diane: I always enjoyed Bob Dylan, Johnny Cash, Donovan, Joan Baez. Peter, Paul and Mary's stuff too. I was a bit more into the folky country thing and a bit of rock'n'roll—Billy Thorpe and the Aztecs, Ray Columbus and the Invaders, Ray Brown and the Whispers . . . back in that era, we were all pushing for peace and freedom of speech. I guess there was a little air of rebellion and attitude that was part of being a teenager in the 1960s. We were starting to talk about San Francisco and the flower people and freedom, trying to express ourselves and thinking we were pretty well tuned in.

I was always a pretty adventurous kid who liked to have a go at anything. It wasn't uncommon for me to get in trouble from my parents. Back in those days we had the bodgies and the widgies and I guess by the way I dressed I was classed as one of them.

One of the movies that stays in my mind is *Easy Rider*. I didn't watch much TV—although we used to always watch *Bandstand* and there was a Kenny Rogers show that we used to watch pretty often, and *F Troop* . . . I loved *F Troop* . . . I still do!

I finished school in Fifth Form [Year 11]—that was as far as I could go at the Mannum school. Back then I always wanted to join the Navy. My mum said I could but only if I took twelve months off to live a bit of the world. But, of course during this time Bill Chambers came along and the Navy didn't seem quite so exciting.

By this time, Bill had already put his career in motion, the compliments by the girls in art class and impromptu outback shows proving enough encouragement for him to take the next step.

14

Bill: I formed a rock and roll band called The Ramblers with my mate Wayne 'Flogger' Dean—he's still a good buddy. The first song I ever sung live was 'Talk Back Trembling Lips', by Ernie Ashworth. One night I heard my voice through a PA system and it just knocked me out, I thought, 'Holy shit, this sounds huge.' It was probably the worst PA in the world, but it was pretty good compared to none.

The Ramblers were Flogger Dean, Dross Topazarkis, Allen Crowe and me. We had three electric guitars and a kit of drums and we were all just bashing away. We all had these horrible guitars, out of tune—we didn't have tuners then—these horrible shitty little amps that were distorting . . . something inside me said, 'This is going nowhere. There is no bottom end.' So I got myself a bass, a Framas, just like Bill Wyman. I really wanted to be a guitar player but somebody had to play bass.

Flogger and I were in class one day and he said, 'You've got to meet my cousin, she likes all this music you like, Bob Dylan, The Byrds and all this weird shit.' So I met Diane about six months later. And he was right, we did have a lot in common.

In a 1994 interview with *Capital News* editor Jon Farkas, Bill recalled first meeting Diane: 'She mentioned that she liked Johnny Cash and Bob Dylan and I said, "that's good enough for me" and I married her.'

Not long afterwards, he got a new inspiration. His music teacher decided to give the class a break from Bach, Brahms and Beethoven; one day he brought in *The Freewheelin' Bob Dylan*.

Bill: When I first heard it, I thought, 'Holy shit, that's really close to the early hillbilly stuff that I listened to.' Sounded like Jimmie Rodgers to me. I could hear the connection, the guitar, his nasally sort of vocal, even though the songs were different and a little more hip. The guy sitting next to me, Brian Bowering, said, 'How come he sounds like that?' [sings

15

a line from 'Blowin' in the Wind' in Dylan's voice]. The teacher said, 'Because he's a drug addict.' I thought, 'Shit, if that's how you sound when you take drugs, I want some.' And suddenly I was just an absolute mad Bob Dylan fan.

I went on holiday with my grandparents, I was sleeping in a swag, in a tent, and I heard Buck Owens and The Buckaroos singing 'Under Your Spell Again' and that changed my whole life again. I'd been listening to The Stones, The Beatles, The Byrds. I'd sort of outgrown the real hillbilly stuff like Wilf Carter and Hank Snow. But I somehow felt there was a music that I hadn't heard yet that I needed to hear. Buck Owens and the Buckaroos had that real modern country sound with that biting, twangy guitar. I just thought, 'My God, that's it, that's what I've been waiting to hear.' I had to find out about Buck Owens—where he got his sound and why he sounded like he did. A couple of years later, I traded in my big arch-top guitar, that I loved, for a Fender Telecaster, which I still own. It's an old, white, faded thing, but it had the Buck Owens sound.

Given that this was 1963, there probably weren't a large number of folks with similar tastes in South Australia.

Bill: I was still in The Ramblers at this stage, but the music they were doing was just shoo-bop, it wasn't what I wanted to do. Every time I mentioned Bob Dylan or The Byrds or something I wanted to do, they looked at me with this blank stare.

One of my classmates, Richie Bowering [Brian's cousin], was also into Dylan and the country music that I had discovered. One day my uncle, Bob Dixon, heard us jamming in the lounge room and said, 'Why don't you practise up and I'll get you an audition for Reg Lindsay's country music show.'

So we went up to Adelaide to audition for Reg Lindsay's *Country Music Hour* and Ernie Sigley's *Adelaide Tonight*. They loved it; they said, 'We want you to perform on both shows straight away.'

It was as if I'd been offered the biggest deal in the world, I thought we'd made it, I was seventeen at the time. We got paid $16 between three guys—Richie, myself and a bass player, Ronald—but they kept him off camera. They came up to us and said, 'Look, he's a good bass player, but he's got a pimply face so we don't want him on camera.'

When Ernie introduced the trio he asked the audience to ring in with suggestions for a name for the then-untitled band. So, after they played the Gosdin Brothers song, 'Hangin' On' and Bobby Goldsboro's 'Molly' ('a horrible disgusting tearjerker,' Bill recalls), Ernie announced the names that callers had suggested. The trio's favourite was The Deerstalkers so, over the next couple of years, The Deerstalkers played all over South Australia, appearing around twenty times on *Adelaide Tonight* and over thirty on Lindsay's popular show. Nevertheless, Bill decided that The Deerstalkers, like The Ramblers, were not destined for stardom.

Bill: I didn't realise that there's a lot more commitment required if you want to make a career in music. So anyway, the whole thing never happened after a while. We didn't get many gigs and we didn't become household names, so I went fishing for a living.

That phase didn't last long, and pretty soon Bill had recruited a new bass player, this one without pimples but with a few other attributes.

After completing high school, Diane had moved back to Millicent and worked at several administrative and retail sales jobs. Her relationship with Bill grew more serious—serious enough, in fact, for him to teach her to play bass so she could accompany him at shows after The Deerstalkers reached the end of their musical hunt.

Bill: I taught Diane the bass because she used to get sick of sitting there and doing nothing while I played. I had a bass with me, had two amps, a guitar and a microphone and I said, 'Look, you can play the bass.' So I spent all that day teaching her the basic chords and we got up that night and performed. That's the only training she's ever had. The amazing thing is, Diane seemed to pick it up right from that moment. She was never a fancy bass player, but she just seemed to know how to follow those basic country songs.

Diane: Just before we got married, with Bill on acoustic and vocals and me playing bass guitar, we would work around our local pub circuit in the southeast. The first time I played live with Bill was at Old Gus's Tavern in an opal mining town, Andamooka. It was a pretty rough little township—the local guys were wild, wild lads. One guy came in with a bucket of opals and just sat it down on the floor and started shouting everybody drinks. He was drinking beer out of a glass boot, a full-size boot made out of glass, and he just got rotten drunk with hundreds of thousands of dollars worth of opals just sitting in that bucket. I'm not sure if he ended up with it by the end of the night, guess I'll never know.

Bill remembers that their repertoire consisted of a mixture of Buddy Holly, Johnny Cash, Donovan, Joan Baez and plenty of Bob Dylan: 'Pretty simple stuff but the crowd loved it. We got paid twenty bucks between the two of us.'

Thus the genesis of Dead Ringer Band began on that raucous night at Old Gus's Tavern in Andamooka, in 1970. The Vietnam War was raging then and the government had just announced a new conscription plan, a fact that played a big role in the bizarre circumstances surrounding Bill and Diane's wedding.

Bill: Anyone whose twentieth birthday fell on a certain date was conscripted and I was one of them. They had to choose them somehow. They gave the date out on TV, you didn't get it in the mail. On the news they said, 'Right, these people are going to Vietnam. Anyone whose birthday's on this date.' You get a letter afterwards but it's a bit of a shock when you're watching the news one night and then they say, 'You're going to Vietnam.' I didn't want to go to Vietnam. I didn't believe in the stupid war and I still don't. I don't think it did any good. It was around September when we heard the news. It sort of upset me, Diane and our families. We didn't know what we were going to do but I knew I wasn't going to war.

Diane and Bill happened to get engaged around that time.

Diane: We were engaged in October, and we were getting married in February. Mum had all the invitations already written up and everything, all the organising was well underway.

Bill: I had written to the Army and said, 'I'm going to be married in February. I need to know what the deal is for married quarters, blah, blah, blah.' I didn't hear anything about it. Then I got a phone call on the 30th of December. It was 1970 and I had just turned twenty. The guy said, 'It's so and so from the Army here. We've had notification that you're getting married before you join the Army.' I said, 'Yeah.' He said, 'If you get married before the end of this year, we'll let you off. We're trying to avoid as many married couples as possible.' And I said, 'The end of the year? It *is* the end of the year, it's the day before New Year's Eve.' He said, 'I know it's a bit late but you've still got time. You can get married today or tomorrow and we won't have you.' I thought it sounded like too good an opportunity to pass up, so I rang Diane up at work and I said, 'You want to get married?' And she freaked out, but I went and picked her up.

Diane: We spoke with the minister, to find out when we could be married, and he said, 'I have to witness your birth certificate seven days prior to marrying you.' We said, 'We haven't got seven days.' He said, 'I can't legally marry you without witnessing it. There's only one person in South Australia that can give you permission, the head of the registered birth, deaths and marriages in Adelaide.' We got on the phone, but couldn't contact him, so we called our local MP, Des Corcoran, and he tried to locate this person, the one person in South Australia who could give permission. We then found out he had gone away on holidays with his family and hadn't informed anyone where he was going. As fate would have it, he was camping with his family and, due to heavy rains, came home early. It was only through the miracle of the rain that his holiday was cut short. We located him and at nine on the morning of the thirty-first of December they rang me at work and said, 'It's all approved, you can get married.'

So then Bill came and picked me up. We raced up to Mount Gambier, found wedding rings, found wedding clothes. My mum and dad lived four hours away, so we rang them and said, 'Do you mind coming down for our wedding today?' We ended up getting married at six that night, about sixty people were at the wedding and we got one present.

2

Early Days in Southend

For a while life was very good for the newly married couple. Bill made a spot of money from fishing in the warmer months, Diane kept her job—she was then with real estate firm Elder's G.M.—and they augmented their income with performances around the area.

Bill: We started playing in the clubs and pubs around Mount Gambier, Millicent, Kingston, Naracoorte, all part of what they now call the 'Green Triangle'. We were doing all right: Diane and I were getting $100 each a gig, that was pretty good back then. We were gigging quite a bit and going along fine, but then Nash came along on 8 May 1973, about three years after we married. We got the name Nash from Crosby, Stills, Nash and Young. Their song, 'Teach Your Children', was no. 1 at the time. That was a great song and I loved the group. People to this day say, 'Do you call him Nash as some sort of tribute to Nashville?' Seems ridiculous really, 'cause it was after Graham Nash. When he was a newborn, we would take him along to gigs. We'd put him in a bassinet behind the bass amp and he would lay there asleep while we played all night, for four-and-a-half hours. There weren't any problems until he was about a year old. He had a mind of his own, which he still exercises to this day.

We used to leave him with my mother and he'd put on a turn. He was quite pissed off that Mum and Dad wanted to leave him home on a Saturday night. But when he'd come he was a pain in the ass, because he'd run around and get into everything. We realised that when you have a one-year-old child, you've got a responsibility, you can't just go and do what you like. So we quit it—that was in the winter of 1974.

Major changes loomed for the Chambers family. They had to find a way to supplement the income they lost by giving up their regular performing.

Bill: It was a funny time because we had made a religious commitment at that time. We stopped doing things like drinking and we got involved in the Seventh-Day Adventist church and lived what we thought was the right way to live. I owned a boat and just barely scratched a living out of cray fishing or rock lobster fishing.

Things were going along okay, but when the winter months came along, we found we couldn't make enough in the summer months to last. Lobster fishing is a seasonal thing: it runs from October to April each year. If you don't make enough in those months, you pretty much can't pay your rent or your car bills, or whatever. So we started shooting foxes around the highways around the area where I lived.

It's illegal to hunt on the highway, but it was the best place to find foxes. They hang around for the 'roos and rabbits that get killed on the road.

I'd take Nash and Diane with me. We'd leave at dark, around seven, and get home about three in the morning. We sometimes drove for all those hours and we'd come home with five to ten foxes. The pelts were worth around $15 each back then.

One night, Nash was two years old, and Diane was pregnant with Kasey. We were out hunting—we had to be careful, because it's really poaching. We would drive along the road with a spotlight, looking for foxes. When we came up to a farmhouse, we'd turn the light off just as we got to the house. As soon as we got past the house we'd turn it on again. If we saw a fox we'd shoot it, jump over the fence as quickly as possible, grab the fox and drive away before the sleeping farmer realised what was going on. Although we were helping the farmers—foxes kill their sheep—nobody likes to be woken by gunshots in their front yard at three in the morning.

One night we drove past a farm house that was quite close to the road. I spotted a fox, so I pulled up, shone the light on him and shot him. Within ten seconds, every light in the house came on, the front door flew open, a guy ran out in his pyjamas, jumped in his ute and screamed down the driveway. I took off—we had a Jeep with a six-cylinder Rambler motor, so it was quite a powerful machine, had a bit of 'get up and go'. I thought to myself: 'I'll leave the fox, we're getting out of here!' So we took off up the road. We hit 140 kilometres an hour on this narrow road, gravel is flying everywhere and we're leaving the guy behind. I suddenly looked at the fuel gauge and realised it was on empty.

Nash was in the back; he was awake by this time. He realised something was going wrong and he was terrified, his little eyes wide open. Diane was in the back. She'd been asleep and I screamed to wake her up. I said, 'This guy's after us and he's pissed off. He's going to catch us 'cause we're running out of fuel. There's a jerrycan of fuel and a hose in the back. You're going to have to open the back door and siphon some fuel into the tank.'

We're going 140 kilometres an hour on this back road. She's pregnant. I know it sounds crazy but it's true. She's never siphoned petrol in her life. So I said, 'All you have to do is put the hose in the jerrycan and suck until the petrol comes out.' The fuel inlet was just around the corner from the back door of the jeep and she could reach it by leaning out. By this time we were losing power and the farmer was right up behind us. So Diane opened the back door and started siphoning petrol. Then our jeep just totally died and came to a grinding halt with no power at all. But then she managed to get the hose in the gas tank, suddenly we caught the new line of fuel and we took off again, leaving the poor farmer in our dust.

We got a visit from the police a week later. Although he didn't charge us, he said it was a pretty stupid thing to do, which it was, and if I was caught shooting in that area again, I'd lose my gun *and* my driver's licences. After that episode I realised that I couldn't keep doing something like that. It was illegal, stupid and I put my wife and kids in danger by acting so irresponsibly.

Bill and Diane began their life together in an extraordinarily picturesque spot. The house, however, had few creature comforts.

Diane: Our first home was a really low tumble-down shack where we paid a dollar a week rent. It had an outside loo. Nothing very glamorous at all but it was our first home so it was pretty special. The walls weren't lined and it was right on the beach so that each morning you'd just look out your window and see the surf.

With their home turf now off limits for nocturnal hunting, drastic measures needed to be taken to make ends meet. Bill's dad was making a decent living from fox hunting up a bit further north. Fox furs were fashionable then and a skilled hunter could average ten foxes a night, or $150—pretty good pay in the early 1970s. Bill and Diane decided to become full-time hunters during the winter months, albeit in a more remote location.

Diane: Nash was eighteen months old and we went out to some of the station country, around Koondoolka and Yarna in the Gawler range. The very first trip was with Bill's sister, Julie, her husband, Terry, and their two kids, Shannon and Donna. Shannon was about the same age as Nash, Donna was a few years older. We had a little hut that we did our cooking in and we slept in tents.

Bill: We would shoot pigeons and galahs, almost anything that was edible. We'd make stew and put in potatoes, carrots and whatever else we could find. We learned to live off the land 'cause you couldn't get to a shop every day.

Bill and fox skins pose with rifle.

It got too hot to live in that area by about November, so they returned to Southend, having done reasonably well. Bill then resumed his fishing career. Thus, in 1976, a pattern was established: summers in Southend, fishing for the bounty of the sea; winters hunting foxes and living off the land, roaming the station country, first around the Gawler and Flinders Ranges, then into the heart of the Nullarbor.

By the time Kasey was born on 4 June 1976—like Nash, in Mount Gambier—the Chambers were just beginning to establish their pattern. It being winter, hunting season, Kasey made her first outback visit shortly after she was born.

Bill: We drove for two days solid and ended up about 800 kilometres northwest of Adelaide in the Gawler Ranges. The hills were dotted with huge rocky outcrops and the creeks were dry and shaded with big gum trees, kangaroos and emus everywhere. By this time we were driving on a dirt track which took us as far west as we could go, back to Koondoolka Station.

Looking out over the Great Australian Bight.

They lived in relative luxury later at Koondoolka Station, north of Iron Knob. After getting permission from the owner, the hunters moved into a tin hut with an open fireplace. Diane learned to bake bread over the open coals and they began a life of living off the land.

Bill: Dick Moulde, the foreman at Koondoolka Station, said that foxes had almost taken over his property and eaten what few sheep he had left. Foxes were introduced to Australia in the eighteenth century and are considered a pest. As their skins were worth about $15 each in the fur trade, it seemed like a good idea for us to become full-time fox hunters.

Diane: We stayed in an old shearers' quarters where it was pretty bare and basic but at least we had a wood stove to cook on. Each night we had to fuel up the generator to give us really dim, dull little lights. My mum and dad came with us then. Dad and Bill would go out shooting every night and Mum and I would stay with Nash and Kasey.

Bill: It was winter in South Australia, 1976. We borrowed money from a friend to purchase two high-powered rifles and a bright spotlight which we mounted on the roof of the jeep and we were ready to go.

Nearly all of our hunting was done at night, so Diane and the two children would sleep in the bunks we built in the back of the jeep while I drove all night, looking for foxes in the spotlight. On an average night I would shoot and skin about twenty foxes, sometimes up to thirty-five or forty.

We spent our days in a two-room tin shack which had nothing inside but a rough table, two chairs and an open fireplace. The roof was full of holes, but as it seldom rained that didn't matter.

Our light was by kerosene lantern only and television or refrigeration were unthinkable luxuries. We were trying to make our home in very barren country. I provided our only entertainment by singing a few old Carter Family songs on an acoustic guitar around the fireplace. I have no doubt that although Nash and Kasey were very young, this extreme way of life left an impression that they still carry with them to this day.

Diane: A bit later on we were way out in the middle of nowhere on Yarna Station. Nobody ever came by. One particular night we heard the sound of a vehicle in the distance, getting closer and then moving further away. It did this for a little while. It's late at night, Mum and I were there with two little kids, we had no vehicle and no lights. The generator had run out of fuel. We were both too scared to go down in the dark, 500 or 600 metres, to refuel the generator with this vehicle driving around. It got closer and closer and we could see the lights: it was a motor bike. We saw it coming along one of the big dirt roads, then up our little track, coming right towards us. We had no lights on, no one would have known we were there. Anyway, were getting very anxious by the time the motor bike pulled up just outside our door. Then we heard the guy hop off and start to walk towards us. So I grabbed the .22 rifle, loaded it and stood by the door, ready to protect my kids. This guy came to the door

Feeding pet kangaroos: Nash (left), 'Yarna' station manager's daughter, Mary-Anne Young, and Bill, holding Kasey.

and I yelled out, 'Who is it? I've got a loaded gun, don't come any closer or I'll shoot.'

And this guy yells out, 'Don't shoot, it's only me, Rodney the rabbit.' It turned out he was a station hand, a guy we knew. With that we let him in and got him to go down and fill up our generator 'cause we were too scared. He stayed and had a coffee with us and a few hours later off he went.

The next morning the owners of the property came up to visit us. We were good friends with them and a visit wasn't uncommon. First thing they said was, 'Ah. Hear you had an intruder last night. No messing with you girls.' And with that the bush telegraph just took it out all over the outback, so we knew we wouldn't have a problem with anyone because we'd pulled a gun on Rodney.

Not long afterwards, the family faced another crisis, one which forced them to realise the precariousness of outback isolation. Little Kasey used to choke a lot, to have trouble breathing, a situation usually resolved by a bit of patting on her back or turning her upside down. She would usually gulp a bit and then resume her breathing.

Diane: That's pretty scary at the best of times, but when you're in the outback, 300 kilometres from the nearest medical centre, it's really scary stuff. One night she was coughing so bad that she was doing this choking thing a few times and she started to turn a little bit blue. We got panicky and scared . . . we normally don't rush the kids off to the doctor for any little ailment, we're pretty independent that way.

We piled Mum, Dad, Nash, Kasey, Bill and myself in the car and took off at 10 o'clock one night to drive on dirt roads for three, four hours to get to Streaky Bay, on the Eyre Peninsula. We tore into town knocking on this doctor's door, at two in the morning. He was a real funny little short fellow, spoke in a funny way like he had a throat problem himself. He said, 'Look, bring her in and I'll see what I can do.' He warmed up the room and checked her for everything all around the throat. When he couldn't find anything wrong with her, he came back out into the waiting room and said, 'The only thing wrong with her is an over-anxious mother. Just take her home.' I knew she'd been having choking fits. I didn't care what any doctor said.

Living in the extreme bush presented perils that city dwellers would never dream of facing. In addition to venomous snakes and poisonous spiders, wild animals like dingoes, feral cats, emus and even kangaroos could be dangerous to toddlers. Smaller animals could also pose problems. Diane shivers even now when she thinks about this episode.

Diane: Nash was always a 'give it a go' kid, always the one to be in trouble and of course, as she grew up, Kasey discovered that if she played up she could get him in trouble and she worked on it. I don't remember which trip it was, but it was on Coondambo Station. Kasey wasn't born so it was one of the early trips. Nash was about eighteen months old. In the outback you'd find lots of meat ants, which are big and black, probably anything from a half-an-inch to an inch in size. Their ant-holes were quite big mounds on the ground with the neck of the hole about half-an-inch in diameter. I said to Nash, 'See those holes? They are full of ants. Whatever you do, you mustn't poke sticks or stones and things down them or you will stir the ants up and they'll get very angry with you.'

I was sitting in our little cabin, and next thing you know Nash started screaming. I looked out the window and he was black, absolutely black up to the waist so you could not see anything of him. It still creeps me today to think of it. I've always hated ants and spiders: they give me a really creepy fear, if I ever got an ant on me I would shudder. I have an absolute fear of ants. But I tore out, grabbed his clothes and just shredded them off him and brushed off the few that were up over his head. It taught him a lesson, but it spooked me for ages after because of my fear of ants, yet I'd gone out and done that. That's when I realised that a mother will do anything for her kids!

Dangers notwithstanding, Bill and Diane Chambers were, and still are, not folks easily deterred from their goal, in this case feeding their family. They'd found that fox hunting paid well enough to get them through the winter, so as soon as the 1977 summer heat waned, Bill went back out to scout the fox population and establish their next base camp.

3

Life on the Nullarbor

Bill returned to Koondoolka Station on his own and remained there for a while. The western end of Koondoolka is bordered by the 'Dingo Fence', built many years ago to stop dingoes crossing from the remote outback into the sheep stations. It stretches for thousands of miles from the east end of the Nullarbor Plain up to Coober Pedy opal fields and way across the desert country to the west.

Professional 'doggers' had laid poisonous baits to kill dingoes, wild cats and foxes, so eventually foxes became quite scarce in the station country of the Gawler Ranges. Almost overnight the Chambers' good living became just a bare existence. So Bill began to look further afield for new fox-hunting territory.

Bill: I heard there were a lot out on the Nullarbor, so I headed out to a place called Ivy Tanks, at the east end of the Nullarbor Plain. There was a little bit of water for washing fox skins—it was pretty putrid-looking water, and there were a couple of dead crows, a dead dingo and a dead wedge-tailed eagle in the tanks. I lived around there for a little while on my own and realised that I could make a living. I went back home and got Diane and the kids and we moved out there when Kasey was almost a year old and Nash was about three. We ended up buying an old caravan 'cause I figured that it was a bit rough, I couldn't take a woman and children out there and just live on the ground.

I remember the day we told Diane's mum and dad we were going to live in the bush for a while. They said, 'You're what?' My family was a little more used to it, but a lot of our friends thought we were crazy. They said, 'You can't do that. You can't bring kids up out in the bush.'

Diane: Looking back now, I can appreciate the fears that they had, but of course at that age we were too young, independent and ready for an adventure.

Bill: We were only in our early twenties, we just wanted to have fun. When we went out there we were about the same age Nash and Kasey are now. We went out to the Nullarbor against all odds and against common sense, really. We didn't intend to stay too long, but we stayed for ten years. Years later, when we started touring as a band, when we hit the road trying to make a living out of music, people said the same thing, 'You can't, it won't happen, you can't do that. You can't just hit the road and expect to survive.' Well we almost didn't, but we survived.

I talked Diane into going out on the Nullarbor for a couple of weeks. At first she liked the idea of going there—she's always had a sense of adventure—but when we arrived at Ivy Tanks on the old highway, she changed her mind. I think she had thought it was a roadhouse or a truck stop, and it had been once, but it was abandoned when the new road was built. All that was left there were these old tanks with a bit of stinking water and no one around for miles. I was quite happy. I was doing what I wanted to do.

The first night we were there she freaked out, almost went hysterical, she was okay really until I went off the road and started driving across the Nullarbor by compass. There were no roads to follow, just the stars or the compass. She suddenly realised we were in the middle of nowhere and no one knew where we were. I think she thought we weren't going to get back alive. She freaked right out, started crying and of course that upset the kids and I ended up calling an early night and going back to camp. We talked about it seriously the next day. She decided to stay and put up with it a little longer. After a week or two, she got used to the idea and we started to like living in an area where we didn't have to answer to anyone. The only time we ever went to town or saw anyone was about every second or third week when we would drive into the Yalata or Nullarbor roadhouse and get some fuel, pick up a few supplies.

With the family Chambers tucked into their caravan near Ivy Tanks on the fringe of the Nullarbor, it seems a good time to reflect on their location and the hazards facing them. The Nullarbor Plain takes its name from the Latin, *nullus arbor*, meaning literally 'no trees'. It encompasses about 300 000 square kilometres, a bit more than the United Kingdom, including Northern Ireland, or the American state of Colorado.

Trees aren't the only thing the Nullarbor lacks; water is another. The area's annual rainfall averages 250 millimetres and it is not unusual for some areas to go several years between showers. Despite the scant rain, the Nullarbor is dotted with subsurface limestone caves formed by rainwater and chemical action over the past thirteen million years. In some spots, you can hear the ocean bubbling beneath.

The Great Victoria Desert and a scrubby wasteland called Maralinga mark the northern boundary. Maralinga is a prohibited area where the British government conducted atomic bomb testing in the 1950s. At the time, no one knew the effect it would have on humans, but years later many locals were seriously affected; it is still dangerous to go near there. The 100-metre cliffs of the Great Australian Bight are the southern boundary of the Nullarbor. A line drawn due south from Ooldea to Yalata forms the Nullarbor's eastern extremity; from there the Plain extends westward about 650 kilometres, across South Australia and several hundred kilometres beyond Eucla, at the Western Australian border.

The Eyre Highway, completed in 1976 and named for colonial administrator Edward John Eyre, the first white person to explore the area and survive, traverses the southern portion, north of the coastline. The only rail line connecting the east and west coasts of Australia, the Indian Pacific route, crosses the Plain about 100 kilometres north of the highway. During one long, lonesome section, the railway stretches for nearly 500 kilometres without a bend—the longest straight section of train line in the world.

Bill: We thought originally that Koondoolka was isolated, but that was civilised compared to this. On the sheep station we had access to water, a shack to live in and other folk to talk to, sometimes. On the Nullarbor we had to carry water in drums, we slept under the stars and we often never sighted another soul for weeks. There were very few roads so most of our travelling was done cross country by compass course or by studying the stars. We relied particularly upon the Southern Cross to help us navigate the direction in which we were heading. What roads there were were covered with large boulders that would tear off the differential or the fuel tank of an average family car within a few minutes. The rough stony terrain found on the Nullarbor is really only suited to the high clearance and rugged build of a four-wheel drive vehicle. We eventually built a heavy-duty trailer to haul our camping gear and shooting equipment. The trailer also enabled us to carry enough drinking water for three weeks and about eighty gallons of fuel.

Nullarbor settlements are sparse—in fact, the only 'towns' are situated either along the Eyre Highway or on the rail line, which parallels the original highway through the Nullarbor. One of the largest of these settlements, Cook, is home to around seventy people, mostly fettlers, railroad workers. The settlements along the Eyre Highway—Yalata, Nullarbor, Koonalda, Border Village/Eucla, Madura and Cocklebiddy—are on average about eighty kilometres apart and consist of a store/petrol station/ restaurant/bar/motel complex. Population density is among the lowest on earth, huge chunks are marked on maps as 'uninhabited', the remaining one-fifth or so averages a population density of 0.03 people per square kilometre. That works out to about 1800 people spread over 300 000 square kilometres. To put this into perspective, an average of 1660 cars, trucks and buses cross the Sydney Harbour Bridge every fifteen minutes. The Nullarbor is such an arid, desolate, forbidding area that virtually no one lives beyond the few settlements.

Bill: Most of the Nullarbor is very stony with dry, hard soil that's a rich red colour. However, red sand dunes covered in mallee trees (low scrubby gums) border the eastern and northern edges. You need a four-wheel drive vehicle to venture into the dunes and even then we found we would spend many hours digging ourselves out of the sand 'bogs' we became stuck in. Nash and Kasey would search the dunes for Aboriginal spear heads—we still have hundreds of them, some perfect specimens, stored safely at home, along with large stone axe heads, grindstones and boomerangs. These are not modern mass-produced boomerangs but genuine artefacts left behind centuries ago by the original people who roamed this land.

Mobile phones weren't available in the late 1970s—even today, most of the Nullarbor is out of range. Radio reception during the day is poor, spotty even after dark. Thus, if you run into trouble off the road or rail line in the Nullarbor, you are on your own. The chances of someone happening by are extremely remote.

Bill may have felt at home on the Nullarbor, but Diane was not so pleased at first. Her first few weeks out there were not a happy time.

Diane: Medical problems, breakdowns, running out of water—life was unbelievably precious. As a mother you're a lot more aware of those things in case something goes wrong. You had to respect—incredibly respect—what you were caught up with. Yeah, that first time I was really frightened, because I was responsible for two small lives.

She was sound asleep during one of her first nights on the Nullarbor when she was awakened by a pounding noise, a sound that kept getting closer and louder as its source neared their small caravan.

Diane: It turned out to only be a kangaroo bounding past, but it frightened me to hear this pounding going by.

We would go shooting at night, it's flat but there were lots of little tufts and salt bushes and rocks and things that create shadows so that a lot of the time you couldn't see the caves. Some were small, some were just big, huge holes, gaping holes in the earth. Most of the time I would drive. Bill would be standing on the front seat with his body through the hole we'd cut in the roof, working the spotlight. Your mind is not totally focused on one thing. You're focusing on kids in the back, you're focusing on driving over rocks, over bushes, you still had to be very cautious, because even though Bill was standing on the seat up through the top of the roof, he had deadly weapons. We couldn't allow for an accident in a vehicle.

I remember sometimes nodding off to sleep when Bill took a turn at driving. If we were travelling cross-country in an area where we weren't getting any foxes, we'd high-tail out and move on quickly to another area. One particular night we had done this. Bill was inside driving and I was sitting in the passenger seat, nodding off with the kids in the back. I heard him say, 'Shit, that was close.' That woke me out of my noddiness. I sat up and looked out my side window and we'd just gone past this great big cave, just a huge hole in the ground, and then as I looked forward, there was another enormous one just ahead of us. It was quite scary, as we could very easily just drive down those caves. I was always terrified that I would drive down one at night. That would be the end of us. No one would ever know where we were or ever find us.

Bill: They're just these huge holes, some of them are fifty to 100 feet wide by sixty to eighty feet deep, huge holes in the ground, no warning at all. Although we didn't end up driving down any, we had a few close scares.

That was the Chambers' domain, a 300 000 square kilometre playing field of salt bush, rocks and blue bush, with submerged limestone caves lurking in the shadows of the plain, like hidden ocean reefs on the high seas. A flat landscape dotted with dull green bushes amid red soil stretches to the limits of vision in every direction. A vast sky, a colossal blue dome, spreads above, encompassing you and everything in the world within its azure boundaries. There are no mountains, no rivers, meadows, trees or grass—only the Nullarbor.

Caves weren't the only subterranean dangers the family faced.

Bill: On the Southern side of the Nullarbor near the beginning of the Great Australian Bight, the country is a little more sandy. That's where thousands of hairy nose wombats make their home. They dig burrows so deep and large a vehicle could almost disappear into one. In fact, one night we did. I was driving along, not watching too carefully when the side of the jeep fell into the edge of a huge wombat hole and tipped over on its side. Diane and the kids were frightened but no one was hurt so we all climbed out and spent the next five hours jacking the jeep up and filling the hole a little at a time, then jacking some more. In the end, I guess we did more damage to the wombat's home than anything else.

Though the Chambers family only lived on the Nullarbor during the cooler months, it could still get pretty hot even then. Bill recalls the thermometer climbed to 47 degrees Celsius, only cooling down to about 35 degrees at night. Overnight temperatures sometimes fell to the freezing point.

Diane: We did experience all weather—nights would get very, very cold. It didn't rain much but that was always a pretty miserable time 'cause all we could do was sit in the vehicle or else inside the little trailer wagon we had. Then we'd have to try to dry everything and that would get a bit tedious.

Bill at Disappointment Cave near their first Nullabor camp. Caves such as this were one of the deadly nocturnal surprises the hunters faced.

When you go to the Nullarbor—a long journey from just about anywhere except Ceduna, the eastern gateway—you'll enter the region's vast, unrelenting nothingness beginning about an hour's drive westward. There are no landmarks, it's like being at sea, beyond the sight of land.

But there's really more out there—a lot more—than meets the eye at first. And if you go to the Nullarbor and spend six months every year there for ten years, as the Chambers family did, you'll find life aplenty even in that forbidding, forsaken land.

Some of the wildlife—kangaroos, wombats, emus, foxes, rabbits, lizards, turkeys, wild horses, donkeys and camels—didn't pose a serious threat to the family. Other life forms, however, could be deadly.

Bill: Sometimes we never sighted a tree or wood of any kind so one night when I spotted a dead tree, I decided to carry it with us until we made camp at daylight so we would have firewood. I threw the log on the roof directly across the hole above our heads. We travelled this way for about five hours. When I dragged the log off to get ready to build a fire, a snake slithered out, obviously a little angry at being disturbed from his home. It was a western taipan, all the more deadly considering how easily it could have found its way through the hole in the roof on to the front seat.

According to standard reference sources, mortality from the bite of a western taipan approaches 100 per cent unless antivenin is administered. Death occurs within minutes. Several other varieties of poisonous snakes live on the Plain, a few capable of inflicting fatal bites, though none can kill you with the dispatch of the snake which had just spent five hours just above their heads.

Nash: There are lots of dingoes in certain areas. They're very strange creatures. Some are extremely timid, yet others would be quite curious. I remember a few occasions when we'd be sitting around the campfire eating dinner and a dingo that had probably never seen a human before would walk up and stand a couple feet away from us, just sort of look around at us and the fire and then walk off.

   When we'd shoot foxes we'd skin them and hang them on hooks on the front end of the vehicle until it was time to stop and skin them. Occasionally dingoes would come up and try to drag the foxes off the bullbar. The only way to stop them would be to shoot them. That's why we believe Lindy Chamberlain's story [about a dingo stealing her baby, Azaria]; we've lived out there and seen what dingoes can do. We have no doubts at all that a dingo took her baby. We've seen dingoes haul off twenty, thirty pound foxes, easy, they're very strong. They often hunt in packs. I don't think they'd ever attack a healthy, full-grown man but if you were injured, with a broken leg or something and they were in a pack and hungry, I reckon they'd have a go at you.

Bill: Many nights we've been awakened by the blood-curdling howls they make when they call to their mates. One night while I was asleep in my swag I woke up and there was a dingo standing over me, staring down at my face in the moonlight.

Nash: There's quite a few feral cats out there, they're mongrel things. They grow really big—probably three, four times the size of a domestic cat, about the size of a fox. They're huge, really strong, they often kill wildlife just for the hell of it. We used to hunt them as well; at times their skins were worth a bit of money, though not as much as fox skins.

Bill: We had a black poodle called 'Licorice', 'Licky' we called him—he thought he was human. He had to do everything the family did: he ate when we ate, he slept when we slept, lots of times he would drape himself over me while I drove. One night as I watched him hunt rabbits in the headlights of the jeep, he managed to disturb a wild cat from a clump of bushes. Licky turned to run but the frightened cat sprung onto him and dug his claws into his rear and just hung on. I laughed so hard I woke the family. We watched poor, terrified Licky run at least 200 yards with that snarling cat stuck on his behind.

Other life forms incapable of inflicting mortal or serious wounds also ranked as major nuisances, the most annoying being the omnipresent flies. 'Whoever ate the most food, ate the most flies. They were so thick you could accidentally eat them some-times,' Bill remembered. Kasey recalled this aspect of Nullarbor life: 'I've seen a couple of photos of dad trying to smile with flies covering his face and he can't do it.'

Fortunately, it can get quite windy on the Plain, a circum-stance that blows away the flies. But those breezes presented their own set of difficulties.

Diane: The wind is the one thing that can wear your nerves down. It was probably the worst thing to affect my moods because I was continually cooking on an open fire. I'd be there turning something in the frypan or stirring something in the camp oven and the wind would blow the flame, so you'd move to the other side. You soon learn not to get down-wind. And then the wind would flip around and blow in your eyes and Nash would hit Kasey over the head or something and then she'd be screaming, I'm getting smoke in my eyes and trying not to burn dinner. Yeah, you do get a little stressed at times.

Not all of the dangers the family faced were natural ones. Some hunters used other methods to kill foxes, including one hazardous to all life forms.

Nash: There was one guy that started poisoning them, laying cyanide baits around. We were totally opposed to that. When you're fox shooting, it's not written in stone, but each fox hunter has a certain area he works. Generally the other fox shooters stay away and work their own area but this guy didn't care about that; he was often in our area poisoning. One time the family with us, Val and Gary Chambers, were travelling down to get supplies. Gary came across a dead fox and one of these baits. He bent down to have a look at it and the wind sort of swirled. He got a sniff of this cyanide and he started to go all funny and he thought he was dying. Cyanide is really terrible stuff, I've heard of people having a bloody nose for five days just from smelling traces of it.

Keeping themselves relatively clean was not an easy task for the Chambers. The nearest facilities—roadhouses on the Eyre Highway or in one of the tiny settlements along the rail line— were miles away, so the family had to improvise in that regard as they did in so many other areas of their lives.

Diane: We had to carry what we called our wash water. Sometimes we'd get it from an old tank somewhere, sometimes we'd pull into the railway siding, to people's houses. Actually if we did that, they'd always let us use their showers, which was a total luxury, or we'd sometimes get water from a dam somewhere. After a rain, if there were puddles, you'd have to fill up your wash-water container with that 'cause you just don't survive without water. Water became the most precious thing in the world. It was gold to us.

41

We'd boil up a big billycan full, our 'wash billy' we called it. It was only used for washing 'cause you'd never know what was in the water, so we didn't use that billy to cook any food or boil the kettle for tea and coffee. When the water had boiled we'd pour it into a large tub and that would be our bath. We would always have a wash at night, just before we were ready to push off for the night's shooting. The kids would have a scrub every night, in just the minimum amount of water. As you can imagine, it was pretty dirty in the outback. They'd just strip off, wash from head to toe, get into their pyjamas and into the bus. That water from our scrubs would then have to be saved and used for washing the clothes. The only time we would throw out water, even dirty water like that, is when we could immediately replace it. When you travel and live out in the middle of nowhere, you have to save every little drop. The kids both learned very, very quickly that water can be the difference between life and death on the Nullarbor. They learned to just pour a tiny bit into a cup to scrub their teeth each morning and at night.

We carried toilet paper and we had what we called a 'johnny stick', a little spade. We would always go away from camp, dig a little hole, do our business, then bury it. Even though there was no one out there, we still didn't pollute the environment. We always had tarps with us so if there was anyone around we could put up a little bit of shelter around us, but there was usually no one around, just the four of us, so it didn't matter—we didn't need privacy. Sometimes if we would camp for a few days in one area and there was a tree around, we'd go to the luxury of getting a few branches and fashioning ourselves some type of toilet seat to sit on, make our own little drop toilet.

After that first year on the Nullarbor, Bill and Diane realised the full extent of the dangers they faced in such an isolated, inhospitable area. Bill recalls that, during some of their Nullarbor years, there were up to nine other groups also shooting foxes but those nine groups were spread out over 300 000 square kilometres. After that first year, Bill's cousin Gary, his wife Val and their kids came out with them. Once on the Nullarbor they split up to hunt in separate areas but kept in touch via CB radio and would get together for social occasions from time to time.

Bill: We camped together sometimes, just for company. We tried to keep in [CB] radio contact so that if anything went wrong with either vehicle, we wouldn't be stranded. We would sometimes see the other hunters from far away—the Nullarbor is so flat you can see a spotlight at night for 100 kilometres or more. Some nights there'd be lights all around us.

Sometimes, when the children's ranks swelled from two to five, they would organise entertainment. 'Val, Gary and their three children, Narelle, Traci and Clint, would sometimes travel with us or we'd camp together when times were right,' Diane remembered.

Kasey: Nash and I would make little plays. We would get them out of books, one was the tortoise and the hare. We would make our own costumes and everything, just use Mum and Dad's clothes and stuff like that. I also remember we did Sherlock Holmes once too, but I think we just made that up. I guess we were born to be on the stage even back then.

Bill: Nash and Kasey would say, 'Mum and Dad, we're going to entertain you. You've got to pay us twenty cents each for the show and you're going to sit on a rock and we're going to put on a concert.' They would pretend there was a curtain, then they would build little props and put on a show by singing a few songs and making out like they were playing the guitar. I guess somehow they wanted to be entertainers. I don't know where they got that from, it was sort of in them somehow.

Concerts were one means of entertainment that broke the monotony of their outback life. Birthdays were another; all five

43

Kasey, Licky and Nash enjoy a Nullarbor birthday 1985.

kids had birthdays during the six to seven months they were on the Plain annually. Those were happy occasions.

Kasey: Mum and Dad would usually take presents out for us kids but when we met up with someone else and found out that they were having a birthday we'd just have to make something up. I remember one time Barry, Dad's brother, and his friend Angus came out to go shooting. Angus had a birthday but we didn't have anything to give him, so we wrapped up anything we could find and gave it to this poor guy: wombat dung, an empty box of matches, an apple, rabbit droppings.

44

Driving on the Nullarbor during the day was also a tough proposition. The limestone caves were easier to spot but caves and wombat warrens weren't the only problems the terrain presented.

Bill: Further north, along the railway line, it gets very rocky. The rocks are so sharp they can rip the side out of your tyre. Punctures are very common, we'd get them mostly from the salt bush. But what's worse is when we'd knock the side out of our tyre with a rock. It's money down the drain, they're not worth repairing. The worst night I remember for punctures was when we were towing the caravan cross-country. We had nine flat tyres in one night. I was a little bit pissed off by morning.

Because we'd be using the starter motor all night and running bright spotlights, car batteries didn't last too long. We'd be lucky if they lasted six months. In the latter years, we carried a 240 volt generator with us for charging car batteries and running electric lights. During the last year or so on the Nullarbor, we even brought a video and a TV with us. We were high-tech hunters in the last couple years of our shooting career.

One can only begin to imagine the difficulty of such a life for two adults, parents of two young children adrift on the Nullarbor. But, what was this existence like for Nash, who spent half the years between four and fourteen living in such isolation, and for Kasey, who was eleven years old before she ever spent a full year living in 'civilisation'?

Kasey: We had pet rabbits while we were out there. Dad would catch them. We would always go for the little ones because they're easier to tame. Dad would shoot just above their ears, being careful not to hit them and they would just kind of sit there. Dad would then jump out of the car and grab them while they were still stunned. All us kids had a rabbit each. We tamed them and took them around with us. After they were tamed we would let them out, not for too long, just play with them around one little area.

When we stopped going out to the Nullarbor we took them home and they had babies, then the babies had babies. We had these generations of rabbits. Some of their names were Jackson, Bourbon Whiskey, Bowie and Winchester—he was named after one of the rifles, he wasn't real happy about that. We also had pet birds at times.

We'd build cubby houses. It's a bit hard to build a tree house without trees, so we'd make them out of rocks or fox boards when dad wasn't using them to dry the skins. We'd sometimes make a little fort and play in that. Nash and I would just play or fight or whatever.

I would help Mum, like little kids do, that kind of 'help out' where it's a really annoying kind of thing. When Mum was baking bread or something like that I would get to mix the dough up.

It wasn't until the last few years that I was allowed to shoot a rifle. Dad was really, really strict about guns because we were around them so much. I was never allowed to touch them without Mum and Dad's permission and supervision. Nash would take me shooting lots of times, hunting for rabbits or wild pigeons for dinner. He had a slug gun and we would go shoot pigeons or have target shooting competitions. Of course, I never won. Sometimes when we shot something and we came up close, if it was still alive, we had to shoot it again so I would be allowed to shoot it then.

Nash: When we'd buy groceries, once we packed them all into the trailer, there'd be cardboard boxes left over. We used to cut the bottom out so our legs could go through, then we'd make little cars out of them, draw wheels on the side, a steering wheel on the inside and then we'd be cruising around, that used to be one of our major things to do.

I'd often have little pet lizards, little geckos, they were great. We've also had pet rabbits, budgies, canaries and we even had a joey at one stage.

I think Tonka trucks were my favourite toys. I remember playing with my trucks all the time and leaving them behind Dad's parked four-wheel drive. One day Dad said: 'If you keep leaving your trucks there they'll get run over.' Of course, I kept leaving my trucks behind the four-wheel drive and one day Dad accidentally ran over my favourite one. I was around four years old and I took one look at the squashed toy and said, 'I never liked trucks anyway.'

Us kids would often do little, crafty-kind of things to pass the time, we bought some of the toys, we made some and Dad made us a few, carved out of wood.

I remember getting a bow and arrow for my twelfth birthday. I spent weeks practising, then I started hunting rabbits and I even shot a fox one night. It's amazing what we did just to amuse ourselves, just basically anything.

There's hundreds of spiders, trapdoor spiders, they live in a little hole with a door at the opening. As kids we were always poking sticks and fingers down them, all those stupid things that children do. We were very lucky although I do think we were quite responsible most of the time we were out there.

Kasey and I had the job of gathering firewood. We could spend an hour or two just looking for enough wood to cook the evening meal. Sometimes we would come across plenty of firewood, what we call a 'donga'—a small clump of five or six trees, maybe quite a few more. These dongas would be sitting in the middle of nowhere, just a small group of trees with nothing else around for miles.

Though she was too young to become an expert fox shooter during the family's time on the Nullarbor, Kasey did play a useful role during the nocturnal hunting forays.

Kasey: I would go to bed first, in the back of the four-wheel drive, then Nash and then Mum. But nearly every night I would wake after Mum had fallen asleep and sit with Dad while he kept driving and looking for foxes. He would say, 'It's okay if you get up, just don't tell your mother.' Usually Mum or Nash would drive while he was standing up through the hole in the roof, but once they went to bed and he had to drive, that's when I would work the spotlight. It was great, I just loved that.

Dad would tell me heaps of stories then. One was about when he was on the *New Faces* TV show and he sang 'Tennessee Flat Top Box'. He won that week, so he was invited to return and compete in the grand final, along with all the other winners from throughout the year. One of the winners of the other shows just happened to be Paul Hogan—he was obviously an unknown then. Paul Hogan won, dad lost. I asked dad that night, 'What does Paul Hogan do now?' And he said, 'Well, he's a big movie star.' And I said, 'Gee, you really showed him, didn't you dad?'

I was serious, I really thought my dad is *so lucky* because he gets to be a fox shooter and Paul Hogan only gets to be a big movie star, you know. All through that time, when anyone ever asked me what I wanted to do when I grew up, I'd say, 'I want to be a fox shooter.' That was all I wanted to do, be a fox shooter and marry a fox shooter and go out and do exactly what my mum and dad did; that's a little bit different than my lifestyle now, of course.

Nash had bigger and grander plans for his future occupation.

Nash: I always wanted to be a knocker, a guy that had one of those big cranes with the big steel balls and knocked down buildings. My grandfather, my mum's dad, he even bought me a hardhat, I thought I was pretty cool. But years and years ago we used to be involved in the Seventh-Day Adventist church, back in those days when I was about three or four years old I thought I wanted to be a minister although I'm sort of at the opposite end of the scale now.

Aside from their vehicle, CB radio and more accurate weaponry, Bill, Diane, Nash and Kasey lived much as nomadic hunters have lived for centuries. Get up, forage for wood, get the fire going, cook over the open flames, live off the land, try to keep clean amidst the dirt, flies, smoke and wind, spend the day working and then hunt most of the night.

During their Nullarbor years, the Chambers might often go as long as three weeks without seeing another living soul. Amid such geographic and social isolation, the family welcomed any human contact, be it visits from Gary and his family, trips to gather supplies or bizarre, chance encounters in the heart of the trackless wasteland.

Bill: Most of today's Aborigines are living in towns or on reserves but occasionally we came across them many miles from nowhere, wandering aimlessly, just living on yams and witchetty grubs. A typical party travelling on foot would include the grandfather, usually the leader—they have great respect for age—the parents, half-a-dozen children, a couple of camels and up to fifteen or twenty dogs. The dogs are usually part dingo and on cold nights they sleep with the children to keep them warm.

One day we were driving along the track from Yalata Mission to Ooldea when we came across a broken down old Chev truck with about thirty-five people on the back, it was standing room only. They were so crammed in with kids and dogs that I'm sure many would have fallen off if there hadn't been steel rails along the sides.

They were stranded with no drinking water, over 160 kilometres from Ooldea, no shade, a searing desert sun. The problem was a dead battery so we gave them our spare but it turned out to also be flat.

Then we hitched a rope from the four-wheel drive to the front of the loaded truck. Not one of the Aborigines would get off, they were too scared of being left behind. I gradually got the truck moving fast enough along the stony track for their motor to kick into life and off they went. That road is very rarely used, so if we hadn't happened along they could easily have died.

Six months later on the same track we came across a stranded family standing around an old battered Holden sedan. This time it was a couple about thirty years old with two small children who were wearing absolutely no clothes

49

at all. They'd been without food or water for two days so we quickly found them a loaf of bread and some biscuits, and watched as they madly sucked at our water bottle.

The father said, 'We need oil, bloody car's broken.' I handed him our drum of engine oil but as he poured it in the top of the motor the oil ran out the bottom just as fast. 'Gonna need a lot more oil, boss,' he said. I crawled under the car and saw that a stone had driven a gaping hole through the sump of the motor, so I knew the situation was fairly hopeless.

Our vehicle was already overloaded and cramped for room, but we couldn't leave them there. The father looked on top of the four-wheel drive and said, 'We could ride up there, boss', but his wife wasn't too keen about that idea so we made room inside somehow. We squeezed the two parents in the front seat with Diane and I and the naked children climbed on the bunks with Nash and Kasey. They spent the next three hours running from one end of the four-wheel drive to the other, laughing excitedly while the parents completely ignored the fact that the kids were tearing our vehicle apart and sliding over our beds with their bare bottoms.

As we drove along the rough road they spotted our collection of cassettes and said, 'Got any Slim Dusty tapes, mate? We'll swap for a boomerang.' We swapped two Slim Dusty albums for a handmade boomerang and a carved goanna made from myall wood.

When we reached the railway line near Ooldea, they quickly scrambled out without saying a word, and wandered into a nearby donga.

There are others living on the Nullarbor, some denizens even more unusual and taciturn than the Aborigines who originated there.

Bill: Strange things happen in the outback. One morning about 11.30 I crawled out of my swag and looked out across the desert and thought I was hallucinating. There was a bearded gentleman wearing sandals, with a turban on his head, leading six camels. On the back of the first three camels were three attractive looking women while the last three camels carried their water and supplies. This sight was strange enough but when they got close to our camp they just nodded and walked right on by, gradually getting smaller and smaller until they disappeared over the horizon. Sounds crazy but all four of us saw them so I know I wasn't dreaming. Years later I discovered there are descendants of the old Afghans still living their chosen way of life, operating camel trains out in the remote central and western desert areas.

Such unusual events were highlights of course—occurrences which relieved the tedium of the hardscrabble existence Bill and Diane had chosen for themselves and their children. For the six to seven months they lived on the Nullarbor each year, from 1977 through 1986, their lives settled into a pretty steady but humdrum routine.

Diane: An average day would be hunting at night and camping during the day. The four-wheel drive had bunks in the back, raised off the floor so we could use the underneath for storage. All down one side was a big, long cupboard with a couple of drawers. On top of that was Nash's bunk, which was the length of the side of the vehicle, while Kasey's bunk was stretched across the width. It was actually in three levels: there was our bunk, then Nash's, on top of the long cupboard on the side and Kasey's bed was at his feet, across the back.

We'd head out shooting at night. Kasey would pack it in pretty early, back in the days when she was only a little shaver. Nash was always a bit of an adventure freak and didn't really adhere to nighttime rules of going to bed, so he would be up until ten or eleven, then he would hop in the back and go to sleep. Anywhere from midnight, two or three in the morning, I would climb into the back also and go to sleep. That left Bill driving, working the light and shooting until dawn: this was our night pattern.

In the morning, when the kids started to wake up and make a bit of noise, we would climb out of the vehicle and start our day, leaving Bill to sleep. From there we would gather what wood we could find, often just little twigs from the salt-bush stumps, and light the fire.

Then we'd put water on and sort of start the day with a bit of a scrub—it was only always a mini-scrub, face and hands—and have breakfast. Then it would be time to start the schoolwork. This would start around 10 a.m. We'd do that for a couple of hours; sometimes we'd have a break and then come back to it later, depending on the day's routine and quantity of schooling to be completed.

When we finished school, I'd start doing a bit of washing, boiling the water on the fire and using the scrubbing brush and my hands. After that I'd make bread in the camp oven (a heavy cast iron pot). We'd make a couple of loaves every couple of days, rather than a loaf every day. We used to make our own buns; we had to do everything ourselves.

Bill: I'd get up, the foxes were already skinned, we'd skin them at night, but we'd have to peg them, so if we had a good night fox shooting, we'd spend most of the next day pegging and let them dry in the sun. We'd peg the skins on boards. We usually had about thirty plywood boards about two feet wide and four feet long, the kids would often help me do this. In the early days we pegged the skins with a hammer and nails but we progressed to using staple guns before long. That made the job much quicker, although Nash has painful memories of stapling his thumb to the boards a few times when he wasn't watching carefully.

Diane: By the time Bill would get up for the day the kids would be out of school and roaming around, playing in the rabbit warrens or the wombat holes or making cubbies in the bushes. It was a major treat if one of them ended up with a cardboard box or anything like that, that gave Nash something he could use to make a toy car, or Kasey could make a doll's cradle.

First of all, Bill would have to get all the boards out and set them up from the night before to dry in the sun.

That'd only take a couple days most times out there because we had such dry, windy, sunny weather. But each night you'd have to pack them up and put them in the little trailer, then off we'd move to the next camp. So we'd get them out the next day, set them out to continue to dry, and then pull them off, which meant that we had to go and yank all the staples out. Nash and I would do that often.

Bill: You can peg a skin on each side of the board, so you could peg sixty fox skins at a time. We'd stand them up against the salt bush, we'd lay them on the bush so the air could get around them, if you stack them all up on top of one another the air doesn't get to them, they don't dry properly.

The only problem is sometimes we'd peg the fox skins, go away for the night's hunt, leave them at the camp and come back—it wasn't always easy to find your way back either, 'cause we worked mainly by compass—and the wild cats had gotten into our fox skins, eaten some and torn others. They'd chew on them and rip them. Sometimes, if we didn't get up early enough, the crows would be on them, picking and ripping them to shreds; sometimes a dingo would get in and start chewing on them.

Diane: Nash, of course, would always help, because that's the sort of kid he was. Then we would peg the skins and chuck the carcasses away. Nash would have a go at pegging—he had a go at everything, he ended up learning how to skin, everything. He was eight years old when he started driving, and he learned very early how to handle a weapon, a gun, and respect it. Rules were incredibly strict. Nash and Kasey learned early *never* to touch a weapon without having first asked us and we were there to supervise. Nash became a really good shot. I used to do quite a bit of shooting—I was a pretty good shot—and a little bit later on Kasey did the same. She never sort of got into it as much, but that's probably her girly side, but she was also a lot younger.

This idyllic, if extremely arduous, routine was, however, sometimes interrupted abruptly. Family members are very calm now when recalling dangerous incidents, but their descriptions of occurrences out there recalled Ernest K. Gann's summary of life as an airplane pilot: 'hours of tedium interrupted by seconds of terror'. The Chambers were unexpectedly reminded of the precariousness of their existence one day when they suddenly stared death in the face.

Bill: We were travelling along in the Jeep and it caught fire. Something must have shorted out electronically under the dashboard—sparks and flames were everywhere. Everything went dead. We had no power. I grabbed the water container, the only water container we had, and threw it all over the dash to put the fire out, which it did.

But I suddenly realised I'd panicked and gotten rid of all our drinking water. I had no vehicle in going order and we were miles from anywhere. We had no way to call for help so it looked pretty bad for us.

I had a couple of old jumper leads, jump-starting battery leads. I kept fiddling and fiddling around with them until I finally shorted out the starter motor and got it going again. We got back but you never know what you're going to do under panic conditions.

Running out of water on the Nullarbor will end your life as swiftly as a traffic accident in the city, but instead of hightailing it back home after this terrifying brush with death the Chambers augmented their water storage rules and the family carried on, as Diane relates: 'After that we always carried emergency water, so that once we'd gotten so far down on our main supply we'd go for more. We never touched the emergency water.'

During that close call, the lack of water almost doomed them, but another time too much water put all of their lives in jeopardy.

Bill: It rained very heavily. There's only twice I can remember it raining that much in the ten years. We were trying to get to Cook, the central town on the railway line, to meet the Tea and Sugar Train and get supplies. But it rained and when it rains on the Nullarbor the ground gets very clayey and you can't drive. You just sink down and get bogged. We got stuck in the mud for about two days solid at one stage.

That wasn't all that critical. Because it was raining, there was fresh water lying all around us. We managed to shoot a rabbit or two and we survived on rabbit stew.

The family experienced one of their most frightening nights when they had ranged far afield, to the north of the Nullarbor, in the Great Victoria Desert. This emergency again involved them making a scary low-speed dash to the nearest medical treatment centre.

Bill: Kasey got whooping cough and she just coughed herself crazy and didn't stop. She'd lose her breath but she kept coughing. That was very scary, 'cause sometimes we felt she wasn't going to get her breath and keep breathing. We were about 200 kilometres northwest of Cook, very isolated country—very few people ever go there apart from a few old rabbit trappers. We drove all that night towards Cook. By the time we got there, Kasey was slightly better, so even though we took her to the doctor, it wasn't all that critical by then, but it could have been. The outback is so isolated that if something serious does happen you can die before you get help.

Being in close proximity to deadly weapons also posed a threat to their existence. Gun accidents can happen even to the most experienced hunter.

Bill: I had a mate that shot himself in the wrist, just an accidental shooting but he almost didn't make it. He had to drive himself about fifty or sixty kilometres with a hole shot right through his wrist by a high-powered rifle. It's a pretty scary thing: he went into a state of shock and didn't know what he was doing by the time he got help. He's lucky he got there.

Narrow escapes from dire circumstances were fortunately not the only breaks in their routine. Supply expeditions were, like excursions into town to go to market in days of yore, eagerly anticipated. The Chambers' market, however, was a little bit different: theirs was on big iron wheels, the Tea and Sugar Train, operated by the Indian Pacific Railroad. Following the same 2700 kilometre journey between Adelaide and Perth as the twice-weekly passenger trains which crossed the Nullarbor, the Tea and Sugar Train was the supply link for fettlers and the few other residents of this remote region.

The rail line runs north out of Adelaide and Port Augusta before it starts gradually edging westward, completing its sunward-setting swing just below Woomera. The big steel rail then heads due west, intersecting near Tarcoola with the northward-bound Central Australia Railway line, which links up Coober Pedy and Alice Springs. It is well over 1200 kilometres due west from Tarcoola to Kalgoorlie, the only city of any size between Port Augusta and Perth. Once a week the Tea and Sugar Train makes this run, fitted out with supplies instead of passengers, a mobile general store which brings the outside world to the people of the Nullarbor.

Diane: The Tea and Sugar Train would stop at all the little sidings, the maintenance camps along the railway. It's like a whole carriage of a train, done out like a supermarket, of course on an incredibly minute scale. We'd get a little basket when we went into the carriage, then we'd go through rows and rows and get what we wanted. If we knew we were coming back to meet that train the next week—we sometimes did and sometimes didn't, because we didn't know where we would be—we could order fresh fruit, meats, things like that and they would bring up the special order for you.

The Tea and Sugar Train was always a highlight for the kids, because they'd get their pocket money, and they were allowed to buy a comic and an ice cream every time we hit the train. That was like really, really something special to them.

Red Desert living

Kasey: Nash and I were allowed to get a lolly, an ice cream and a comic book. So we just spent our whole time—because it wasn't very often, once every couple of weeks—we would spend the whole time while Mum was getting all the groceries making sure we chose the *good* comic. We had to read that comic for the next two weeks. We used to read Donald Duck, Ritchie Rich and Archie, of course.

Diane: Every six months, what they'd call a 'special' Train would go through. That was the same principle as the Tea and Sugar Train but it had more carriages. You could buy books, cutlery, TVs, stereos, bedding, every sort of thing—that was the only way the fettlers could get household goods and clothes. That train was quite a treat.

Kasey: Nash and I were allowed to buy some really, really good toys on that one. They didn't really have toys and stuff on the Tea and Sugar Train, it was mostly groceries and a couple of little things. I can only remember one Special Train and I bought myself a truck. I could have had anything on the whole train and I bought myself a *truck*. It had a trailer and a racing car on the back. Nash got a tomahawk and he's still got it.

I remember the casey trains—that's like a little carriage but it's open, it's what the people use who work on the tracks. It's about a quarter the size of one carriage. I got very excited every time we saw one of them: 'There's a casey train, it's my train, it's my train!'

Diane: The train became a really good friend to us. It was a real comfort—somehow it was a connection with society again, to see that train go across. Sometimes they would throw out a newspaper. It might be weeks old, but we were very excited about reading some news from the world beyond.

Bill: Kasey and Nash would get a major thrill when they would put the coins we had given them on the track before the train came past. Then they'd run over, pick them up and

Everyone loves a ride on the casey train, somewhere west of Cook, 1981.

talk excitedly about the squashed coins. We always did teach them the value of money.

Kasey: Because it's so flat, you'd see a train coming from miles away. Nash and I would get up and run as fast as we could to go and try to catch the train. When they saw us out there, they always honked twice, that was the exciting thing of the day.

The Tea and Sugar Train was also their educational link: when they caught up with it, Diane would collect and drop off Nash and Kasey's correspondence lessons. They'd do their lessons out in the open, or if it was too cold or windy, the young students would work on their assignments in the trailer, amid the water, food and fox skins. Now and again, an interesting diversion would appear, gifts literally from above.

Bill: The Nullarbor's covered with these weather balloons: they used to send them up to various places. Because we could see for miles, we'd see these things shining over in the sun.

Kasey: That was so exciting. I remember Nash and I fighting over who got it. We'd tease the other one 'cause they didn't have one.

Diane: Kasey'd do something to hers to do with dolls and Nash would probably shoot an arrow in his. Otherwise, all they had to play with was just sticks and stones and rabbit holes.

Although Bill and Diane had given up their performing career for fox hunting on the Plain and fishing on the sea, music remained in their lives, playing a major role in their mental survival during their months in the harsh Nullarbor environment. Nash and Kasey didn't know it at the time, but their parents were quietly planting a musical seed within them during those years in the bush.

Bill: We had a little bit of radio, at night, through the day you couldn't get anything. We'd pick up Tamworth sometimes, 2TM. We listened to Nick Erby's Hoedown, and sometimes we'd get Sydney. Occasionally we heard something good on the radio, but most of the time we just had our tapes at night. I still remember some of the tapes we bought from the Tea and Sugar Train: Tanya Tucker, Bobby Bare, Kenny Rogers. I'd make up tapes at home for the kids to listen to: Merle Haggard, Marty Robbins' *Gunfighter Ballads*—Nash still talks about *Gunfighter Ballads*.

But the best times we had were just sitting around the campfire with a guitar. I would sing these old Carter Family songs, I'd sing gospel songs, I sang Hank's [Williams] songs, Gram [Parsons] and Emmylou [Harris] songs, Jimmie Rodgers songs. I suppose my kids didn't know what it was all about then, but it had some influence 'cause they're still doing those same songs now.

Diane: Any night we had off due to bad weather or an illness that kept us in camp, Bill would play his guitar. We'd sit around the campfire singing folk, country, gospel and some old rock'n'roll tunes. Towards the last few years of our nomadic life, we hunted rabbits for butchers to sell for human consumption—this lifestyle allowed us the luxury of a permanent camp. It was then that we brought with us our electric guitars and amplifiers, tele and video, and set it all up in a tent as our music room.

There were two other families camped near us during this time. The first was Val and Gary Chambers and their three children, Narelle, Traci and Clint—this is the family who worked with us on a number of occasions and who we had most to do with during our Nullarbor years, being gypsies themselves. The second family was Marlene and Chris Bradley and their two children, Melanie and Jeremy. Marlene played the accordion and the kids would make their own instruments from sticks, rocks, saucepans and buckets. With 'not a soul' around for hundreds of kilometres and no sound restrictions, we certainly had some fun times with plenty of happiness and laughter.

Nash: The earliest strong influences that I can remember are Don Williams' album *I Believe In You* and a lot of Emmylou Harris' early records, Gram Parsons, Merle Haggard, the things that Mum and Dad used to listen to. Dad always sang 'Tennessee Flat Top Box', Merle Haggard's 'Sing Me Back Home'—Dad's done that one for years. The very earliest song I can remember we used to all partake in was 'Daddy Sang Bass'. I always did the 'momma sang tenor' part and then Kasey would sing 'me and little brother would join right in'. We were tone deaf back then, we couldn't sing for shit.

We'd always get dad to sing 'Saddle Boy', the song we sang for the Slim Dusty tribute album [in 1998]. That's the other old one that I remember. It's all a bit hazy to me. I was probably four or five back then.

Kasey: That's the earliest thing I can ever remember singing on my own. I would do the 'me and little brother would join right in', that one line in that one song, that was my line. We sang a lot of gospel songs: Mum and Dad were a lot more heavily into that back then.

I remember listening to a lot of Emmylou Harris, a lot of Amazing Rhythm Aces—they were one of the main artists I remember listening to out there—a lot of Dan Fogelberg. The first album I bought out there that was my own, because everything else was always Dad's tapes, it was *Father Abraham in Smurfland*. Before I ever got a tape myself, Nash bought Michael Jackson's *Thriller* when that first came out. He was rubbing it in to me that he had it and I didn't. We listened to country music back then, we kind of grew up on it, but when we got the chance to buy a tape, we would sneak out and buy the 'cool' music of that time. Nash was rubbing it in that he was so lucky, 'cause he got this new tape that when you listened to one side the other side rewound and that no one else's did that. Of course I believed it and was really jealous.

Rather than relying on random encounters during the nocturnal hunting, Bill had learned to lure his prey by making a fox whistle and to emulate the sounds made by a squawking bird, a wounded or dying animal. Sometimes the family would just drag a freshly dead carcass they'd found or killed behind the vehicle, like trolling on the ocean. They'd get back to camp, turn on the spotlight and fire away, developing the accuracy to hit foxes at up to 400 metres with a .17 caliber or a .222, or rabbits at 100 metres, shooting with a smaller caliber .22.

Their cassette player came in handy then when they realised they could incorporate recording technology in their hunting trips. Kasey recalled that advance in their technique: 'In the last few years Dad would have speakers on the outside of the vehicle. He taped himself whistling so he didn't have to whistle all night. We'd turn the tape on and it just whistled, then the tape would turn over.'

Bill: One time I was back home. We were getting ready to go out for another year and me and my dad had made my whistle tape but we decided to make another one. So we took the tape recorder down to the chook shed, picked up a chook and squeezed him a reasonable amount, until he got to squawking. So we had this chook on tape—in fact I've still got it. It worked but I couldn't put up with the sound of this mournful chook in the throes of being squeezed. It was just a little too sick to accept so we stopped using it. But we didn't hurt him, we just squeezed him.

Kasey: Just squeezed him 'til he screamed.

Bill: It doesn't take much to make a chook squawk.

In some instances, the Chambers family didn't pack up and make a new camp each day. Sometimes they were able to stay for days or even weeks in one spot, to enjoy a semblance of a 'normal' life out there in the midst of nowhere.

Bill: Both those times that it rained a lot, the low areas in the Nullarbor filled up with water so we had lakes. That gave us somewhere handy to do our washing, somewhere to get fresh water. These lakes lasted for a month or more. That was quite a change, it meant we didn't have to travel too far for fresh water. Because there were fresh lakes, there were a lot of wild ducks flying around, so we had some fresh meat too.

On other occasions, the nomads would venture south for a break on the beach, setting up shop on a shore with access to the sea. Everyone fondly remembers those breaks in routine, and in diet, but they also found adventure and faced peril on those occasions as well.

Bill: Anything you're doing, you eventually need a break. Since we were shooting and hunting at night, we were having a late night every night. The earliest we would ever get to bed would be one in the morning and sometimes it was five or six, after daylight. We'd need a break so we used to go down to the Great Australian Bight, on the southern edge of the Nullarbor, and go fishing.

It was quite a treat to catch some mulloway, salmon, tommy ruffs or garfish. The problem in the early days was we didn't have a 'fridge, so we would get the fish and salt them, hang them on wires down a rabbit hole or something, light a fire on the other end and smoke them. Then we had smoked, salted fish. They'd keep anywhere up to three weeks that way, even in the heat.

Diane: It was a treat to head to the coast, camp a few days down on the beach, then we'd have fish soup, fish patties, fish stew; it was great the first couple of days, then fish would wear pretty thin. But the kids would have a wonderful time, playing and swimming.

Bill: It was great to relax and try something different. Fish sure tasted good after we'd been living on rabbit stew for months. On one trip we met a couple called Wendy and David who lived at Mundrabilla Station, about 70 kilometres west of Eucla. They invited us to to stay for a few days at their home. It was an interesting old homestead, nestled right beneath the escarpment on the edge of the Nullarbor. The house was very old. It had huge, thick walls built from natural stone, had square holes right through the walls every few yards. During the daylight we could see quite clearly, which gave us a good view outside. We were intrigued by those holes but never asked about them.

As darkness settled in we sat back and enjoyed their hospitality and the evening meal. When bedtime came, they led us out to a cold, dark room back behind the house.

There were no windows, the cold wind whistled in under the roof and howled through these square holes in the wall. I thought to myself, 'If there is such a thing as a haunted house, then this is it for sure.' Diane said nothing, but I'm sure she felt it too as we lay there trying to go to sleep. We left the kerosene lantern burning as we didn't want to be in total darkness, but that only made things worse: the flickering light made the ghostly shadows move and dance across the room. Every time the wind howled and the old house creaked we jumped in fright. We barely slept at all the whole night.

The next morning at breakfast, David said, 'How did you sleep? Did you see any ghosts during the night?' I could feel the skin on my neck prickle but I tried to sound calm as I said, 'No, why do you ask?' David and Wendy then told us that the holes in the wall were cut many years ago by the family who built the homestead. They were used as rifle holes to shoot the Aborigines who attacked the homestead on many occasions. Apparently both parties believed the land belonged to them and the white family developed such a hatred for blacks that they would either shoot them on sight or hang them, in the meathouse out back, where we had been all night. The story goes that the wife came home one day with her children and found her husband's severed head staring at her from the oven of the stove!

We thanked David and Wendy for their hospitality and left that very day. Sleeping on the ground under the stars might be rough, but that seemed to be much more inviting than another night in Mundrabilla Station.

Diane: We camped on the beach. At other times, if we came across areas where there was water, we'd want to stay awhile. Water was such a luxury, and we had the freedom then to use a bit of water to wash our clothes. We didn't have to wash and recycle the water. I remember one year—I don't even know where this was—but we came across this lake. Of course we started filling up our water tanks and we saw these funny little things going into our wash water. We'd be washing our clothes and we'd find that we'd have one of these little 'goobies', as we called them, scrubbed up among our trousers or something. We found out later when we went looking for information at Ayers Rock that they are outback shrimp. We had no idea what they were but they dried up in the mud and were non-existent for up to thirty years until the rains came, then they came to life. The kids would just splash around in the lake having a great time.

Nash: Another time we went into a place called Shark Bay on the west coast of Australia, and camped on the beach. We went into a local shop there and said, 'Can we swim and snorkel here? Is there any problem with sharks or anything?' They said, 'No, no problems at all.' That night, when we were fishing off the beach we caught a little shark. Then the next day we were about 100 metres out, it was only about waist deep, then the water dropped down about twenty feet all of a sudden. There was lots of coral and stuff there. Dad and I were snorkelling, I was about eight years old, and this shark, probably about an eight-footer, came out of the blue and went straight for me, with his mouth open. I kicked him in the nose with my flipper and tore off on to the beach, swimming there as fast as I could. Dad's out there still waiting for all the bubbles to clear to see where I am and here I am, already standing on the beach. I wasn't waiting around for him! I didn't sleep well that night.

The Chambers didn't confine their roaming to simple side trips to the seashore. On a few occasions during the off season, they embarked on longer excursions as they sought to see as much of Australia as they were able to with the time and money available.

Bill: When it was too hot to be on the Nullarbor, we would often just go on a holiday. We had such a good year on the foxes one year, I remember going home with twenty-odd thousand dollars in cash stuffed in my jeans pocket. Twenty thousand dollars is probably not a lot of money in somebody's book, but when it's in your jeans and it's a big bulging wad of notes, it feels pretty good. We felt that we'd done well enough to go on a holiday that year.

We bought a new caravan and went travelling around Australia for the summer months. Even though it was hot, we went north, to Darwin, Broome and the Kimberley, went everywhere we felt like 'cause we'd made enough money and we felt we'd worked hard enough. So we took the kids away from school again.

Diane: It was around four months, I think, just home schooling and holidaying as we travelled around. We went back down western Australia, right round to end up back home. We were always taking off on little bits of holidays and trips whenever we had a few spare dollars and time. We had already travelled around Victoria, we'd travelled around New South Wales, we actually did a couple of shooting trips up through there to get ourselves around and have a look and to earn our expense money. We did a Queensland trip with my mum and dad one year, covered a fair bit of ground there, so between those trips and performing tours we've been fortunate enough to have travelled all of Australia, including Tassie.

In the mid-1980s, outside forces caused a change in the Chambers' lives and hunting strategy. More people in the fox hunting trade were using poisonous baits. 'The fox fur industry had hit an all-time low, mainly because of the environmental movement, people protesting against furs and wearing fur coats. The last couple of years we were shooting rabbits for a living,' Nash recalled.

Bill: When we were rabbit shooting, the only consolation was that since we were shooting them for meat, they had to be kept in a cold chiller with a diesel motor. We kept the chillers going all the time and occasionally we'd actually get in there for a while, with the dead rabbits, just to cool down. One year the guy that was bringing the rabbits brought up a heap of watermelons and put them in the chiller and we had cold watermelon—that was a bit of a treat.

Living on the Nullarbor for extended periods is both difficult and dangerous, but life out there offered tangible and intangible rewards. On the tangible side, the Nullarbor provided a living for the Chambers family. The income from those autumn and winter sojourns usually was sufficient to carry them through the spring and summer; sometimes it was enough to permit them to take vacations and travel throughout Australia. But the intangible aspects of their Nullarbor experience have meant more in the long run to Bill, Diane, Nash and Kasey.

Diane: It was was enlightening to the heart to see the country after rain. You could almost watch the green come up before your eyes. This dry, parched and barren land just waits and thirsts for a tiny raindrop, then up come the most magnicent wildflowers and rich, green grasses—you can literally see it and feel it. Because there are no luxury elements or exotic distractions out there, this beauty becomes so special—it's like watching a miracle take place. Wildflowers cover the ground with all shapes, sizes and colours—yellows, blues, purples, pinks and whites—and green grasses grow tall enough to hide a fox or kangaroo. Or little trailer and camp homes were surrounded and filled with bunches of wild-flowers. Wildlife also became abundant during these times as their survival became easier.

Lying in our swags under the stars, and being engulfed by the tranquillity of the still nights—these are the memories of a peace and contentment that can only be experienced through the solitude and isolation of the Nullarbor. I loved this and the open spaces, the family unit and the happiness it gave us—I've always been a very family-minded person. As cruel and hard as the outback is and can be, there was a closeness to God and creation. I think it was a great way of life for the kids, and I know Bill and I certainly enjoyed our time there. Nash and Kasey didn't know they were missing out on anything—therefore, they weren't missing out! They had all the love they could possibly get—we did so much together. We became aware of values and beliefs that we would never have been exposed to in a normal suburban life. It bround out survival in us all—both individu-ally and as a family—and it taught us strength, adaptability and a belief in ourselves and life. It gave us a grounding to cope with the hard and sad times that were to greet us along the continuing journey of life.

Kasey: I think I'm lucky. Like I have some people saying, 'Gee you would have been pretty deprived being out there', but I think it's the opposite. I think I'm a lot luckier than most other kids who grow up with the normal life kind of thing.

Nash: Some people, I guess, would have that sense and fear of loneliness and I suppose we might even now if we were out there for a length of time, but back then it was just a very peaceful existence. You lived your life as you wanted, went wherever you wanted each day.

The Nullarbor sort of has certain things that affect you more in an emotional way than a material way. We've seen some magnificent sunsets and sunrises and a couple of times at night, we've seen meteors shooting across the sky. I remember seeing one huge meteor, it was like a ball of fire, moving real slowly—it probably took five minutes to go across the sky. There were all these sparks and stuff flying off behind it, it was quite spectacular. As kids we used to find these things called tektites, little pieces from meteorites that fell out of the sky. They look black but they're actually really dark green.

One night Skylab dropped out of the sky, about sixty kilometres away from us. The whole world was watching and we didn't even know what was going on. Then the next day we saw all this traffic, all these vehicles out on the Nullarbor. That was very weird because we just didn't see anybody for days, even weeks, and all of a sudden there's dozens of cars and trucks whizzing around.

The stars were amazing, magnificent. The only other place that I've seen stars similar to that is Norfolk Island. Just after dark, us kids would lay down on the ground and just look at the stars. We'd often see satellites moving and shooting stars. It was absolutely magnificent to see the sky out there.

Bill: There's always reports of UFOs, all over the world, but the Australian version is called the Min Min lights. There's all sorts of weird sightings of them everywhere. One night about thirty kilometres west of the Nullarbor Roadhouse, we saw some very, very strange lights like that and a few nights later we spoke to someone who saw the same lights. Another one of the fox shooters saw them, and he was scared out of his brains.

Diane: It looked like an airstrip: it was all lit up and we saw the landing lights. It looked really weird. We didn't get too close, but we kept driving and it gradually disappeared.

The Chambers' years of 'wintering' six months on the Nullarbor, 'summering' at Southend or holidaying about the continent wound down when outside events and the growth of the children brought an end—temporary, as we shall see—to the nomadic ways of the family.

Bill: In about the mid-1980s fox furs became unfashionable. it wasn't cool to wear furs. Now imitation furs are even more fashionable than real furs, so I guess it became uncool to wear animal skins wrapped around your body.

Nash was about twelve years old and we realised he had to have a high school education. Even though Diane had brought them so far with their correspondence schooling, she realised that high school was another level, and she didn't feel up to carrying that on. So we decided we had to go back to Mount Gambier or Southend and give our kids a little bit more of a normal education.

We could see the writing on the wall: the skin prices were dropping and I think we were getting a little sick of living like that. When we lived on the Nullarbor we didn't have a proper shower. We would try and wash when we could; sometimes we washed in a bucket, when we had enough water. Sometimes we would rig up some sort of a shower where I had a water container rigged up on the roof of the trailer with a hose for a shower nozzle. We would just jump under that in the cool breeze and have a quick shower. It was pretty damn cold when the weather's cold,

Kasey enjoys a luxurious bush shower.

but it was better than nothing. Even though we learned a lot and had so much fun doing all that, we got a little sick of roughing it.

So we moved back to Southend and decided to try to live a normal life. Even though we never talked about it too much, I think both Diane and I felt a little guilty—we felt that we'd kept our children away from civilisation for long enough. We thought living out there was good for them and I still don't regret it, but at the same time there was a little voice in me saying, 'You're not being fair to your children. They need to see normal things as well.'

Diane: We thought perhaps it might only be until things picked up with the fox hunting, but of course they never did pick up.

4

Southend Again: A Song for Slim

The Chambers family returned to Southend in 1986 and attempted to settle into a more normal existence. Nash and Kasey were enrolled in school, Bill went back to try to wrest a living from the sea and Diane worked to set up their household in a stationary location.

Diane: I think the kids adapted easier than Bill and I did to going back to suburbia and, so to speak, 'normal life'. I've always enjoyed my own space, and although I can mix with people and socialise, I still like time out for me.

Nash and Kasey slipped in fine—kids are so adaptable. There was an independence and a strength and a confidence in them, I think from being raised in such a close family unit. They adapted quickly at first to school and being in a classroom environment.

After that, though, neither of them stuck very well to high school, so maybe we did put too much of a gypsy spirit in them. Nash was used to schooling with freedom, then all of a sudden he had to deal with school with discipline and full days. On the Nullarbor we covered a day's schooling in a couple of hours because we didn't have to break for lunch or recess. I wasn't tending to thirty-five kids in a class, so we could cover their lessons in far less time. That was probably a bit more of a battle for them, but as far as their actual schooling went, they coped pretty well.

They weren't the best attenders so maybe that outback freedom and gypsy spirit which was born and nurtured in them did cause them problems in settling into the rigidness of formal schooling.

Nash came to us one day when he was fourteen and said he wanted to leave school. He'd been doing his fair share of 'wagging' school—at that age, kids don't find school the most trendy place to be. So I said, 'Sure, if you want to leave school, get yourself a job and you can leave.' The very next day he went straight from high school into the main street and knocked on almost every door looking for work. He got a job in a grotty old fish factory and I thought, 'Okay if you're prepared to take that sort of work, it's your choice. You can leave school.' The next day he did.

Kasey sort of followed her brother's footsteps, which is quite a trend with the Chambers clan. None of the Chambers, including Bill and his brothers, sisters and cousins, have a reputation for sticking with school, or abiding by school rules—they've always been free-spirited people in that sense. Kasey was continually wagging school. She'd drive us mad: the school would ring up and say, 'Do you realise Kasey's not here today?' We'd say, 'No, she went on the bus.' Then we'd have to ring Nash at work, tell him 'She's wagged again' and ask if he knew where she might be since he knew all the wagging spots. So we'd traipse into town, get her and either drop her back at school or bring her home. She was really, really good and settled with primary, but she never adapted to high school. She just didn't like the work side of it.

Kasey: I had a whole lot of friends that I hung out with at school who were really good kids, then I had this other group that I would wag school with. I'd skip a week at a time. I don't know how I ever thought I'd get away with it. Of course, the teachers are going to ring my parents and ask, 'Why hasn't your child been here for a whole week?' I went through that whole stage: Mum and Dad didn't know what to do with me, they were at their wit's end about it.

I was just in my rebellion stage, this is normal for a

thirteen-, fourteen-year-old girl. All I wanted was to be cool. It was the unhappiest time in my life; when you're a teenager it's the most confusing time you'll ever go through. The first ten years of my life, I remember I was really happy, on the Nullarbor and when we used to come home from the Nullarbor. We'd have school holidays and Christmas holidays and we'd often just travel around Australia. That was great. The last five or six years of my life have been just unbelievable, great years, all this good stuff has happened. But I just hated it at high school. Once I even ran away from home. It was just horrible. But my parents were great. I think back now and I had the best parents out of all of my friends. They obviously cared about me a lot. I was allowed to do a lot of things, but when they wouldn't let me do any one thing I wanted, I would absolutely crack into tears, make a big deal of it, run away from home.

I hitch-hiked to Mount Gambier once. I got a lift with a truckie, which isn't very smart for a thirteen-year-old girl. I met up with this street guy and I hung out with him for the whole day, I didn't even stay overnight there. Then I ran into my auntie who lives in Mount Gambier, so when Mum and Dad realised I was missing they rang everybody they knew, my auntie being one of them. They came up and picked me up. This guy that I was with, I was saying, 'No, I want to come and live with you', that kind of thing. He lived on the streets, didn't have a house or anything and he did the big lecture: 'You've got a great family and you should go home, you don't want to end up like me.' So I went home.

When they weren't in school or busily wagging it, Nash and Kasey began to develop an interest in popular music. Nash recalls his first concert was a Peter, Paul and Mary show in Mount Gambier when he was about eight. 'Then I remember seeing Brian Cadd, Max Merritt—he had a big hit song, "Slipping Away". Being a teenager, I'd go more for the Black Sorrows and Jimmy Barnes, AC/DC.'

Like his father, Nash was also influenced by American music,

Diane, Kasey and Bill in pre-DRB days, circa 1985.

though in his case it wasn't country acts that attracted his attention.

Nash: I remember seeing Fleetwood Mac in Adelaide. That was my first major concert and my inspiration to do music. We never expected to get to the level they have but it was very inspirational to see them up there with such a huge show. I saw Billy Joel—I wasn't even a huge fan, I only went because the girl I was seeing was a fan but it was a fantastic show.

Kasey: The first big concert I ever saw in my life was Brian Cadd and Max Merritt, in Mount Gambier. It was the most unbelievable thing I'd seen, the atmosphere of a live concert. I didn't get into them heaps musically after that or anything but it was a really amazing experience. Tommy Emmanuel was even more amazing, I didn't know that there were people who could hold a crowd for that long, a couple of hours, just playing guitar. He had Virgil Donarti on drums, he's one of the best drummers in Australia.

We started to go to a lot more concerts after that. We saw Jimmy Barnes, Melissa Ethridge—I really enjoyed her show, I'm a big fan. I sang a couple of her songs back then: 'Sleep While I Drive' was one, Trisha Yearwood did it later on . . . We didn't get to see a lot of country acts, they didn't come down there [to Southend] and we didn't travel away to see gigs 'cause we were always working our own shows.

Nash: In some ways leaving the Nullarbor was good for me, and in some ways it wasn't. As I got older I wanted to spend more time with other kids, go to high school and do normal things like play footy. But that outback life and travelling around was pretty much all we'd known up until that point. For ten years that was our life, so I had sort of a mixed reaction to settling down.

Dad and I used to continue doing a lot of fox shooting, though. I remember I'd go out shooting with him at night and once I got tired or it was late, I'd fall asleep in the back of the car and he'd keep shooting; we'd end up back home in daylight. Then I'd get up, climb out of the car and go to school. Occasionally we'd go away for a two-week trip up north, back where we used to hunt. It wasn't quite on the Nullarbor.

With hunting no longer their principal revenue source, Bill sought other work to provide for his family. Lobster fishing brought in a bit of income but it wasn't as lucrative a business then as it has become today. He tried his hand at filleting fish and wholesaling them as well. Times must have got really tough because he even attempted to become a bricklayer and later tried to become a welder, but he didn't last long with either of those trades. He and Diane also started playing a few gigs around their home area but both felt they needed something more stable than music to provide their livelihood. So around 1988 they decided to open a fish shop. Thus The Trawl Net was born.

Diane: Fresh seafood it was, right on the foreshore at Beachport. We bought the fish off the cray fishermen and the trawlers, but we sold mostly to the tourist trade. The locals caught their

own or it was given to them; it was against the grain to
actually buy fish in a shop.

After having a go at a life without music, Bill and Diane realised
that they could earn a few dollars by resuming their pub performing now that the kids were older. The second genesis of the group
we know today as Dead Ringer Band began around 1987.

Bill: We were just a pub band. We liked country music, but we
        didn't do all country, we did a bit of rock. We'd play
        anything that people yelled out for. At first we had a singer,
        Robert Lesslie, and a sax player, Colin Potter. They were
        both Scotsmen. If you get two Scotsmen. in a band when
        you're doing a lot of pubs and clubs and they give them free
        beer—well, it was not a good match but we had so much
        fun and never stopped laughing . . . We would hire a
        drummer, anyone we could get—matter of fact, B.J. [Barker]
        was one of the first drummers we hired, but back then we
        couldn't get him full-time 'cause he played in a heavy rock
        band. [Barker now drums for both Dead Ringer Band and in
        Kasey's group.]

In 1987 Bill made his debut as a recording artist, some
twenty-two years after he had begun his music career singing in
outback caravan parks. Of course, technically he was already a
veteran of the recording process, having prepared his fox whistle
and chook choking tapes. Although not heretofore known as a
songwriter, he wrote the music and lyrics for all but two songs
on that first album, with Diane penning those and holding down
the bass duties. A traumatic incident triggered Bill's writing hand
into motion.

Bill: I always wanted to write, I used to listen to Hank Williams
        songs and think, 'they're great songs' and I was a great
        Kristofferson fan when he became big. When my brother
        died, it really changed my life. I started writing songs about

things that I felt—I guess it's a release somehow to express your feelings, so I started writing. I remember hearing my dad sing songs he'd written: they were sort of folk songs about the town we lived in, the characters that I grew up with and the fishing.

Kasey: *Sea Eagle*, that was the first album. It was just after Barry (Dad's brother) drowned, so a lot of the songs were written about that. Mum also wrote a couple of the songs, and Dad wrote 'The Wreck of the Geltwood' about a shipwreck found just out of Southend that no one knew about. Barry was one of the people who rediscovered it while diving one day. Most of the songs are about the southeast of South Australia—'Early Days at Robe'. Some were about Beachport. He was doing some of those songs in the gigs as well.

Diane's black and white *Sea Eagle* cover shot pictured Bill walking alone, barefoot, on a deserted beach, staring down at the wet sand. Nash, all of fourteen at the time, made his recording debut on *Sea Eagle*, playing drums on two cuts, including the closing track, 'Northern Highway', re-recorded six years later for Dead Ringer Band's first full-length CD, *Red Desert Sky*. Credited as Bill Chambers, the cassette-only release presented their pub band in full glory: sax, banjo, pedal steel and mandolin backing up Bill on electric and acoustic guitar, dobro, lap steel and harmonica.

Despite Bill's country leanings, *Sea Eagle* today sounds more like a folk-rock album than a country effort. Listening to it thirteen years later, it's clear that Bill had potential aplenty: his guitar and dobro lines, then as now, are clean and clear, smack in the pocket, uncluttered by fancy runs full of extraneous notes. His melodies, though a trifle generic by modern standards, are nonetheless catchy and listenable. There's a marvellous sense of place about *Sea Eagle*: the lyrics detail locations and events familiar to the few hundred residents of Beachport and Southend. Those two coastal towns and the larger Robe, where the Chambers clan had first set foot in Australia, were the subject and/or the setting for all save one of the album's eleven songs.

These songs plainly show the makings of a fine songwriter.

Here's a glimpse from 'Early Days at Robe', sung to a melody similar to Marty Robbins' 'El Paso':

Early Days at Robe

. . . Early days at Robe, settlers and old pioneers
Their stories are written on history's page
Stained with blood, sweat and tears
Early days at Robe, seen many a storm through the years
We're sailing tonight with your ghosts from the past
We're the sons of the old pioneers . . .

Bill Chambers © *1987, Gibbon Music*

In a way, *Sea Eagle* served a couple of other purposes. It was as if Bill and Diane were saying, 'Hey, we're back from the Nullarbor. We've had our outback fling and now we've returned to the nest.' Underscoring the point, in the uptempo 'Town Where I Was Born', Bill sings:

. . . I never want to leave the town where I was born
It harbours many memories of times when I was young
There's happiness and heartache and things long gone
I never want to leave the town where I was born . . .

Bill Chambers © *1987, Gibbon Music*

Sea Eagle also offered palpable proof to Nash and Kasey that music could be more than just singing around the house, at the pub or around a campfire. Music could also result in a tangible product, a document of place and time. Even more importantly to a family in the midst of a major career change, *Sea Eagle* was also a saleable item. Ironically, with a price of $15, the cassette sold for exactly the same price as a fox skin fetched in their Nullarbor heyday. Bill recalled selling about 500 copies over the next few years.

While the albums's first ten songs, all firmly set in their home region, doubtless reassured their families and friends of their intent to remain in the area, if anyone listened closely to Bill's last song,

'Northern Highway', they would have probably been able to predict the family's upcoming peregrinations.

Northern Highway

Well it's midnight on the open road
Lonely desert plains calling me back home
Seems a long time since I was there
Nothing really on my mind
Just some things that I left behind,
Try to tell myself I don't really care

Wish I was on that great Northern Highway
Leaving these cities far behind
Where the plains drift with sand
And the mountains meet the sky
I miss that Northern Highway tonight . . .

Bill Chambers ©*1987, Gibbon Music*

Diane: Back in those summer days, after we'd closed the fish shop in the evening, we'd set up the music gear in the front, right on the beach foreshore, and just start playing. All the tourists and the locals would come around, and we'd end up having a great night. We plugged into the electricity from our shop and within half an hour most of the town folk and holidayers would be nestled around us on their chairs or blankets. On nice, hot summer nights with not much entertainment around, it was a perfect setting. We started to do that quite often, it was really enjoyable and it was appreciated by the locals.

Kasey: The whole town would come and we'd send around the hat. We didn't make much money but we used to like doing it. Lots of times, Trev Warner would come down from Adelaide and play, and bring his son, Kym, as well. I just remember it being the best night—except for when I had to get up on stage and sing, I just wanted to run around with my friends the whole time.

I did my first gig when I was nine, or I could have been

ten. It was at our local club. A club down there is just one room, with a little bar and maybe a pool table. Mum and Dad had started Dead Ringer Band with two other guys, Robert Lesslie and Colin Potter. Caddie Ellis was my best friend, we spent a lot of time in our bedrooms just singing along to tapes and stuff like that. One minute we'd be singing along to whatever was in the Top 40 at the time—really bad music, Tiffany and stuff like that—then we'd be singing along to an Emmylou Harris song. Of course, at that time in our lives, we couldn't tell the difference between them.

We were in the lounge room one night and we came out and said, 'We're going to sing this song.' We sang the theme song to the TV show, *Charles in Charge*. Dad said, 'Oh, hey, we've got a gig this weekend at the club, why don't you girls get up and sing a song?'

We learned 'Time After Time', the Cyndi Lauper song, and 'Walk of Life', by Dire Straits. It was probably the worst thing you'll ever hear in your life. We were terrible, but we had fun. We had been telling everybody, all our friends—we were one of the only bands in Southend and there wasn't a whole lot else to see down there, so everyone came along. Caddie and I dressed in the same outfit, did our hair the same and got up there to sing these songs. We just stood there the whole time, our faces didn't move or anything. I remember it being the scariest thing.

Caddie and I started singing regularly after that. We would get allocated about five songs at every gig that we were allowed to do. Lots of times, we weren't even allowed to stay in the pubs. We'd have to come in, sing our songs and then go because the gigs went so late—we were only ten or eleven then. Caddie's mum, Bev, would often pick us up. Sometimes we would be allowed to stay all night and after we'd sung our five songs, we'd fall asleep on the side of the stage—two kids sprawled out.

We used to sing 'Cow, Cow Boogie', 'More About Love', (later recorded on the *Home Fires* album), 'Trouble Again', by Karla Bonoff, a lot of Top 40 songs, a lot of The Bangles' songs, a couple from Dire Straits. We used to do a lot of old songs too: 'My Boyfriend's Back' and 'Whenever a Teenager Cries'—what a shocker—as well as a couple by Emmylou [Harris].

We did Tina Turner, AC/DC, that sort of stuff because that was what people wanted to hear in the pubs. I used to sing more of the country songs. Caddie had a real gutsy, rock'n'roll voice so she used to sing all the rock'n'roll songs. She was a really good harmoniser; she'd never been brought up with music or anything, she only knew music through me, except for singing at Bible studies and hymns, which we all used to do. Caddie just started singing harmonies one day. She didn't know how she did it, I couldn't sing harmonies to save myself, so I used to sing a lot of the lead. Caddie would sing harmonies to me because she was the only one who could do it.

Then Dad brought out an album called *Kindred Spirit*. Caddie and I got to sing on that one because we were really starting to be part of the band by then. We sang the title track, [Cyndi Lauper's] 'Kindred Spirit'; we learned it from her album and it's really a real country song. We also sang 'Louise', by Paul Siebel.

Nash: When we came back to civilisation full-time, Mum and Dad started a band. They were rehearsing and their drummer rehearsed sometimes but he didn't really want to be in the band. He'd leave his drum kit set up at our house, so when the rest of the band would rehearse I'd just jump on it and bash away. I learned a little on his kit and eventually I bought my own drums. It was a shocking set—we used to call it the boat anchor, that's about all it was good for. I thought it was cool back then, it was my first kit. It was huge. I couldn't really play, but I thought having a big drum set was the main thing a drummer needed—at one stage I had a fourteen-piece rig.

I played drums for probably three or four years, then towards the end of that period I started to sing a few songs, not very well but . . .

According to lore, the group was named by friends who kept remarking about how much Nash and Kasey were 'dead ringers' for their parents. No one remembers the exact year the name became attached to them, though early 1991 seems likely. Kasey believes the name came from a different source.

Kasey: I think it was named fairly well from the start. Everybody put some names in a hat, I remember one of them was Taddy and the Poles, so we're pretty glad that one didn't get picked . . . although Hootie and the Blowfish did alright, you can't argue with that.

    I loved playing in the band and all of my friends thought I was so lucky, but sometimes if there was a school disco or something like that, I wasn't able to go 'cause I had a gig. Caddie and I got $12.50 each per show. We thought that was huge. Our friends thought we were so lucky because we had a job.

Nash: The first song I learned and sang by myself was 'Sloop John B', an old folk song that the Beach Boys recorded. God I'm sick of it now. We did the Georgia Satellites' 'Hippy, Hippy Shake', mainly classic rock'n'roll; 'Wild One', the Johnny O'Keefe song; 'Doctor, Doctor', Robert Palmer; Billy Joel's 'You May Be Right'. We'd throw a few originals in, but generally it was just cover songs: 'Thank God I'm a Country Boy', 'Blue Suede Shoes', 'Till I Can Gain Control Again'.

Bill: We did a bit of everything in those days: 'Old Time Rock and Roll', with Colin on the sax, Creedence, Eagles, Carl Perkins, Elvis, Johnny Cash.

Bill and Diane's pub band may have been primarily performing cover material, but when it came time to record again, Bill wrote twelve of the fifteen songs. *Kindred Spirit*, another cassette-only effort, was issued in 1991, also credited as a Bill Chambers release. Additionally, it marks the first recording to feature all four members of the Chambers family. This time Nash played drums throughout, sang harmony and took lead on one selection, 'Rockin' the Blues'. As usual, Diane kept the pulse on bass. Kasey made her first recorded vocal appearance, singing a passable but tentative version of 'Louise', but doing a better job with the title cut, backed by Caddie's harmony. *Kindred Spirit*, unlike *Sea Eagle*, was built around the Chambers family: Colin Potter on sax and fiddler Hank Groot were the only others to play on the album (though Robert Lesslie did sing one selection, a song of his called 'Voices in the Wind'). Bill manned acoustic and electric guitars, 'pull string slide guitar', dobro, mandolin, banjo, autoharp, harmonica on one track and a bit of bass.

One close listen to the songs on *Kindred Spirit* would be enough to convince any reasonable person that the Chambers planned a return to their nomadic ways. The only song with a local reference in the title was 'Beachport Holiday', an Amazing Rhythm Aces-inflected selection that was lyrically centred around the phrase 'I'm wastin' my life away on a Beachport holiday'. The album opened with 'Wish Me Well', a song of goodbye if there ever was one. 'Livin' on the Land' followed, a tune that could very well have been the family's theme song from their Nullarbor days.

Livin' on the Land

You better pass around the billy boys
We're back out on the road
You've gotta roll your swag, it's time to go
You can fill the water bottle
And pack the frying pan
We're heading for the desert
Livin' on the land

I can still recall the good times
The songs we used to play
The stories we picked up along the way
Like a train going nowhere
We held a Gypsy's hand
A life with no tomorrow
Livin' on the land

Chorus
We'd gaze along the railway line
As the train pulls out of sight
Stand around the campfire, talk long into the night
To think those days are gone now, well it's more than I can stand
Nothing comes close to it, livin' on the land
Nothing comes close to it, livin' on the land
Nothing comes close to it, livin' on the land

You better pass around the billy boys
I can hear the desert call
You've gotta roll your swag, it's time to go
Maybe we can capture
What we once held in our hand
And set our spirit free
Livin' on the land.

Bill Chambers © *1991, Gibbon Music*

Kindred Spirit presented a marked musical growth from 1987's *Sea Eagle*. Bill's growing confidence as a singer, writer and instrumentalist is evident. This second effort evidenced more country influences and would today probably be classed as an album which draws heavily from the traditional side of the music, from the gospel-bluegrass of 'Shelter Me' right on through the proto-1950s rock of 'My Guitar Don't Pay the Rent' and eighteen-year-old Nash's debut as a vocalist, the Memphis-soaked 'Rockin' the Blues' featuring his nifty harp run.

While Kasey's performance on 'Louise' gave little hint of the gifted singer she was to become a few years later, her take on the closing selection, Lauper's title cut (by Jules Shear), presented a singer of considerably more confidence. You can hear her beginning to try on some of the deeper shadings and keen, breathy 'catches' in her voice which have become two of her vocal trademarks.

Steady touring throughout the region helped propel the group, by now named Dead Ringer Band, to six honours, including three first-place finishes, in the 1991 South Australia Country Music Awards, an extraordinary achievement for a band with just one homemade tape to its name and a performing radius only about 160 kilometres from their Beachport/Southend base.

An even more amazing achievement loomed ahead and, like showbiz breaks often do, this one came out of the blue.

Bill: I was working in Beachport when my uncle, Kev Chambers, came in and said, 'Bill, Slim Dusty's live on the radio right now.' Australia was suffering from a horrific drought, it had been for a few years, and Slim was saying he was looking for a song for the farmers: 'If anyone's got any songs out there, send them in.'

Within ten minutes I had written 'Things are Not the Same on the Land'. I got home, walked in the door and Diane started speaking and I said, 'Don't say anything, I've got this song in my head, I've got to record it right now.' So I rushed into our bedroom/practice room/studio—it was such a small house it was the only spare room—and I recorded the song. It was just a rough demo, but I sent it to Slim and about three or four weeks later he called at six in the morning. Slim was a bit of an idol of mine, my dad used to sing lots of his songs. Because I'd spent a lot of time in the outback previously, I was fully aware of his work and I'd always admired him, even though I knew he was quite different from the American hillbilly stuff that I grew up hearing.

He said, 'It's Slim Dusty here, I love your song. I'm going to record it.' It was a big thrill, probably one of the biggest thrills of my lifetime. Then he recorded it, it went to number 1 on the charts and about December of 1991, Terry Hill, who worked at *Capital News*, rang me and asked, 'Are you coming to Tamworth this year?' I said, 'No, I've got a job.' I was working in a fish processing shop then. He said, 'Well, you should come 'cause your song's been nominated for the Golden Guitar Awards' and I said, 'What are you talking about, how can it be nominated? I haven't sent anything.' He said, 'EMI, Slim's record company, presented it to us and we voted it one of the top five for Song of the Year. It's been nominated for a Golden Guitar.' I said, 'What's a Golden Guitar?' He said, 'Well, it's something pretty good.'

Bill and Slim Dusty, 1993.

He sort of laughed but I was serious—I didn't know what a Golden Guitar was, didn't have a clue. All I knew was I like country music; the Australian country music *business* was totally foreign to me. I laughed a bit and he said, 'No, I'm serious. This is a good thing. You've got to come.' I didn't realise at the time but he was trying to tell me that I was going to win so I really should go there. So we decided to go to Tamworth.

Unfortunately, neither Dead Ringer Band lead singer Robert nor sax player Colin wanted to make the fifteen-hour one-way drive from Southend. By this time, Nash and Kasey were performing regularly with the group, so the four Chambers decided they would travel to Tamworth and perform as a family band.

Diane: Some of the local families rallied round and sold a certain amount of fish and lobsters, that gave us the funds to be able to go 'cause we couldn't afford to ourselves. Then we couldn't get accommodation, but at the very last minute Avis and Bill Wright, from Renmark, who had been going to Tamworth for years, had to cancel due to ill health. So we took their accommodation at the Acacia Motel but we have remained good friends ever since.

We busked a lot on the street that year because we had nowhere else to perform. We'd booked in at such a late stage, and we really didn't know anything about Tamworth anyway.

Bill: We tried to get a gig but no one wanted to hear about a family band from South Australia, so we went busking. But we had a big crowd. It was estimated that there were well over a thousand people there both nights we busked on Peel Street. That was the year they started bringing in sound restrictions on the street performers. There was a guy walking around with some sort of hilarious little meter, measuring the volume. He came along to the Dead Ringer Band gig and stood up, walked right up to us in the middle of a song, so we eventually had to stop. He said, 'My meter says you're too loud.' I yelled out at the crowd, 'This guy says we're too loud' and the crowd just went crazy. They yelled, 'No, you're not, play some more', so he was laughed off the stage and walked away with his tail between his legs. We had a quite good Bose PA system that was cutting through pretty well. We had a big crowd, so we had to pump it out. When we passed the hat around, we made more money than we would have made if we'd been in a scheduled show in a club. So we thought perhaps we were on our way.

Diane: We busked a couple of nights in front of the Commercial Hotel on the corner of Peel Street, and had the biggest crowds any buskers had ever drawn in the streets of

Tamworth, or so we were told. We thought we'd made it big time, we took over $800 when the hat came back after being passed around the audience. When we counted it later, we thought, 'Whoa. Music, this is it, we can really make some money out of this.' Little did we know what was ahead of us.

What was immediately ahead was Bill's surprising Song of the Year Golden Guitar victory at Tamworth's premier event, then known as the Australasian Country Music Awards. 'Astonishing' win might be a better description for the then-unknown Chambers was chosen for the Award over established songwriters and stars John Williamson, Graeme Connors and Alan Caswell plus 1992's phenomenal newcomer, Keith Urban.

The folks back home prepared a hero's welcome for the family. When the foursome completed the gruelling drive from Tamworth, they were greeted by an old guitar, painted bright gold, standing in their yard. Inside, their home was gaily decorated, with balloons, streamers and congratulatory messages throughout, and a golden-guitar shaped cake accompanied by champagne.

Bill: It was a real surprise to win Song of the Year. We were just thrilled to be nominated, so to actually win was pretty special. I was naive enough to think after we won that we could make a living at it; we thought we were *on our way* to becoming stars. We didn't realize how much hard work and how much, aside from music, is involved in actually running a career. We had no idea, we thought we'd made it.

I think winning the award went to my head a little bit. I thought now there'd be no looking back, I didn't realise you've got to win a lot of awards, and you've got to have a lot of recognition from a lot of different sources. You've got to continually impress people for a long time before you're actually recognised. I didn't understand that—I was totally naive, every step of the way. That's why we kept going, because we were naive; if we'd realised what's involved in being professional entertainers, we would have given up long ago.

5

A Matter of Time

The winds of change swept over the Chambers family like a gale blowing in from the ocean. Bill's surprise victory and their substantial collections from Peel Street busking sessions provided encouragement for Dead Ringer Band to make major changes in their lives.

Bill: We went home, sold our fresh fish shop and hit the road. We were gonna be country music stars. Kasey was still in school but she was wagging a lot. Finally the headmaster rang one day and said, 'I want to have a talk with you.' Diane and I went to the school and he said, 'Kasey's causing us a few problems. She's just not interested in schoolwork, all she wants to do is sing and write songs. I honestly think she'd be better off leaving school and doing full-time music if that's what she wants to do.' We thought, 'Alright, that's it. We'll take her out of school and do music full-time.'

   She was only fourteen and you can't leave school legally until you're fifteen (it's compulsory until then), but apparently the headmaster overruled that. So we hit the road.

Nash: I don't know how we survived. I didn't have anything to do with the business side back then—Mum did all that. We just lived on the road and camped out. We would turn up in a town and say, 'Hey, do you need a band?' Generally they didn't, so we were doing gigs for $150; occasionally we

*Kasey's round shades and Nash's headband became hallmarks of
The Dead Ringer Band's style in the early 1990s.*

would get a good paying show for $600. I just don't have
any idea how we survived. We did it the hard way: we were
doing four-hour gigs back then, mainly cover songs with a
few originals. There definitely wasn't any spare money lying
around back in those times. But it was really fun back then
because we weren't doing music at all as a career-type thing.

I love music, I'll always be involved in music no matter
what happens in my life, but back then the real fun was in
playing: we didn't have to worry about record companies
and our image, success, album sales or promotion—any of
that. We were just up there, getting pissed, playing songs
and having a good time. I often miss that now in music, but
you can't take your career to a larger level unless you do
take it seriously and treat it like a business. When you do it
as a full-time profession thing, it does take a lot of the fun
out of it.

In the early days we started playing around South
Australia—three, four hours from home: Adelaide was
about four hours north of Southend. Eventually we started

moving outward, doing short runs—a week or two into New South Wales and Victoria; we were mainly just playing hotel pubs then. Mum was doing all the booking and all the organising.

There's a support staff, or crew, behind the scenes of every successful touring act; about this time, Worm Werchon, a Southend neighbour and sometime fisherman, entered the lives of the Chambers family.

Kasey: Just before we started going away, when I was about thirteen, Worm and I started going out. We went out for about three years, so he started coming on the road with us. Then Worm and I broke up, but we still stayed really good friends. He just kept coming on the road with us, so he became our roadie and lighting tech member and has been ever since.

Diane: He's the fun member of the crew, the stabiliser. So often he'd be the one who'd release the family pressures that would creep in on the road, lighten things up for us all. He's just got a beautiful heart, a special heart. I can't imagine life without Worm. While we were all a unit of four as a family, Worm truly became that fifth finger on the hand. He became, he still is and will always be, part of our family.

Bill: That year at Tamworth, we met Keith Melbourne who had previously managed Buddy Williams, Wayne Horsburgh and Ray Kernaghan [Lee's father], all successful artists. He heard us busking on Peel Street in Tamworth, then he rang us after we got home, and said, 'I think you guys can do something. I want to be your manager.' Of course as soon as he'd said he'd worked with Buddy and Ray, I thought, 'This guy's actually done something in country music, maybe he could help us.' We took him on as our manager and he began booking gigs for us while we hit the road. We didn't even have a mobile phone, so sometimes we were weeks away from home and Keith couldn't get in contact with us until we rang in. We didn't stay in touch often enough, because we were always getting our wires crossed: sometimes we went to the wrong town, sometimes Keith sent us to the wrong town—it was a bit of a shambles, and we nearly starved.

Sometimes we'd get to a town and learn the gig had been cancelled. We had no money, and no way to buy food or fuel to get anywhere, so we'd have to beg for a gig, even if it was $100 between the four of us. Sometimes we played for even less, next to nothing just so we could get to the next town. We did that for about a year, a year and a half, and we realised we were going everywhere but getting nowhere.

By this time, the Chambers had learned that if they were going to be country music stars they needed to make a record, both to promote themselves and to sell at the shows. The first true Dead Ringer Band album, not counting the two Bill Chambers cassettes, was a prophetically titled EP, *A Matter of Time*, a four-song CD released in 1992.

Bill sang and played electric and acoustic guitars, Nash supplied drums and some vocals, Diane was on bass and Kasey sang. The family also enlisted the help of a couple of their Adelaide picker friends, Trev and Kym Warner, to add fiddle, banjo and mandolin, and brought along Beccy Sturtzel (now Beccy Cole), a future Star Maker winner, to play rhythm guitar and add backing vocals.

Bill: Beccy was a member of Dead Ringer Band for about six months. She was a valuable member, she taught us about entertaining, getting out there and having fun with the crowd. She's a great entertainer and she taught Kasey a lot, but it only lasted for about six months and we were back as a family band.

Kasey: Beccy was touring around with us, which was great fun. I loved it. She was really, really good to have in the band. Musically, I probably learned more off her than just about anybody 'cause at that stage in my life I was very impressionable. Bec is a great performer who really knows how to work a crowd, and she taught me to sing harmonies. Obviously, throughout my life, I learned more from my dad than anybody musically, but Beccy was a *major* influence during that stage—just having her in the band taught me a lot about singing and working a crowd and because she was in the band, subconsciously it made me kind of compete and want to be a better singer. And she really, really helped me to learn how to talk to a crowd. Then she left the band and went and did her own solo thing.

We grew apart for a few years; we hardly ever saw each other because we went off touring at that stage and Beccy went off to do her own thing. We'd still stay in touch, but we were like best friends during the time we were in the band and then we just didn't see each other, I didn't see a lot of anybody at that time 'cause we were touring away and playing music.

When we both ended up in Sydney, years later, we became best friends again and we have been ever since.

Bill: We met [Adelaide luthier] Brian De Gruchy in 1990 but didn't become friends with him until about 1992. He built a guitar and a mandolin that we used on *A Matter of Time* and we've used his instruments ever since—guitars, dobros, he even built a bass especially for Diane. I counted up the other night and we've got thirteen De Gruchy instruments in our two bands. The word's gotten around now and lots of people play De Gruchy guitars: Graeme Connors, Beccy, Tommy Emmanuel, Troy Cassar-Daley, Trev and Kym Warner, Darren Coggan and Mike McLellan, to name a few.

A Matter of Time featured one original song—the title cut, written by Nash—followed by two songs also penned by Australian writers. One of these, 'Diamantina Drover', was a bush ballad classic; the other, 'Poor Ned', recounted the sad saga of outlaw Ned Kelly. The only American song they recorded, 'Strong Enough to Bend', written by Nashville tunesmiths Beth Neilson Chapman and Don Schlitz, was a number 1 country single for Tanya Tucker in the United States in 1988.

Kasey edged into the spotlight a little bit more on the EP, singing the lead vocal on 'Diamantina Drover' and 'Strong Enough to Bend' while Bill sang the title cut and everyone joined in to lament the demise of 'Poor Ned'. While Kasey's vocal is good on

'Diamantina Drover', she shines on 'Strong Enough to Bend', imbuing the song with innocent huskiness and dusky shadings, shyly showing off the growing power and sparkling clarity she was developing in her voice.

The precise, skilful instrumental work of the Warners, together with Beccy's on-the-mark harmonies, added an additional level of polish to the sound of the new band. It was the first time they had recorded in a 'big-time' studio (they cut in Adelaide), the first time they had hired a professional producer (Eddie Sikorski) and the first time they had utilised accomplished side-men who played as brilliantly as the Warners.

Nash emerged into the spotlight as well, both as a vocalist and a songwriter. Suddenly, in the year since his adolescent-sounding 'Rockin' the Blues', his voice had matured into a man's. With his title cut, Nash also showed that Bill wasn't the only one in the Chambers family with songwriting chops. 'A Matter of Time' was a song that both looked back autobiographically and set the tone for the family's ambitions:

A Matter of Time

. . . *With a part-time job there wasn't much I could afford*
Rented out apartment, living on the second floor
Needed better, I know, but all I had to give
Was a string of broken hearts and a rundown place to live
But I'll live my dream, It's a matter of time
It's a matter of time before I walk away and leave it all behind
I'll live my dream, it's a matter of time . . .

Nash Chambers © 1991, Gibbon Music

Bill: That EP was financed by Terry and Julie Moran (and our credit card). It was just something to sell at gigs; it didn't really get much radio airplay.

For eighteen months we nearly starved and just travelled around. We had a lot of fun, but Kasey got the flu all the time 'cause we were camping in tents: we couldn't afford motels. Venues wouldn't give us a motel room—in fact, sometimes we couldn't even afford a caravan park, so we would camp in the scrub, in the trees outside of town, buy

*The photo used for the cover of Dead Ringer Band's first album,
A Matter of Time (1992).*

a loaf of bread, a can of baked beans, go down the road, just sit there and eat it, we couldn't afford real food or a caravan park. I'm serious: we were very poor, but we loved it. It got into our blood so we just kept doing it, and we believed in ourselves. Kasey and Nash improved the more gigs we played, she started writing songs and I started to think that both her and Nash had a knack for writing, so I thought maybe something would happen one day.

With their EP available, Dead Ringer Band had a useful tool for promoting themselves, although at that point everyone in the family was basically clueless when it came to approaching powers in the industry and key figures in the media.

The black-and-white front cover presented the four Chambers alone in a field, outside Southend, each looking pretty grim, amidst knee-high weeds. The back cover picture showed them in a similar field, though with bushes and ruts from a rudimentary road behind them. While not as desolate as the Nullarbor, the background depicted four people alone, in the middle of nowhere.

Bill: I don't think we had any idea about either a direction or a sound then. We weren't thinking about what Dead Ringer Band should sound like; we were just recording songs that appealed to us. We had a fair bit to learn, but looking back now, 'Strong Enough to Bend' had a sound. It was semi-bluegrass, a cross between bluegrass and country, with harmonies and nice guitar picking. I think that's when we started to think, 'Yeah, that's the sound that we've got to pursue' so we tried to bring out that sound a little more as we went along.

'In for a penny, in for a pound' is the old saying, and so Dead Ringer Band—perhaps from determination or stubbornness, or maybe because they didn't know what else to do—decided to make another CD, this one a full-length album instead of a four-track EP.

Diane: The money we were able to save from that EP was used to start our next one. We've never been very good at managing our finances—basically we're hopeless that way.

It was exciting simply because it was a new era of life for us, from being pretty much nomads, gypsies, wanderers, loners, we were starting to mix with society and other people. It was an adventure in itself and again there were challenges of learning and surviving a whole new lifestyle for us. We were on the road again, this time musically. I do believe our early days on the Nullarbor certainly conditioned us to being able to live, cope and work with one another in such close proximity.

6

Red Desert Sky

Dead Ringer Band decided to make a full album because they realised that albums were more marketable than singles. They recorded *Red Desert Sky* over a six-month period, when they could afford it.

Bill:　We were reasonably proud of the album. Looking back, it was a learning process—I don't know if it was money really well spent. We made it in a studio that was new to us—they'd never made a country album before; the engineer had never worked on a country project, so we were all learning. We finished it up and it sold reasonably well at gigs.

Bill may casually dismiss *Red Desert Sky* today—indeed, the whole family are quite modest, even self-deprecating, about their achievements—but the album, produced by the band and Eddie Sikorski, was a big step forward for them. *A Matter of Time* wasn't a bad recording, but the sparkle, the shine, the *lustre* of *Red Desert Sky* made the EP seem duller. The musical benefits of steady live performances had manifested themselves into a tighter, more focused folk-country sound.

As before, Trev and Kym Warner added adroit touches, their playing twining around Bill's customary tasteful picking to shape a fine record with a much more defined sound and more polished instrumental passages. The overall flavour is country-rock, delicately spiced with folk and bluegrass touches.

Two more extremely exciting elements set the new album apart from the EP: the extraordinarily rapid progress Nash and Kasey had made during the previous year; and the fact that the group's distinctive family harmonies had begun to take shape. This new album plainly marked Nash and Kasey as professionals and clearly flagged the band as an act to watch. Indeed, reviewer Brian Howard of *Capital News* praised the group and *Red Desert Sky* in November 1993: 'this new release should consolidate their popularity. Top Shelf.'

But the most significant development was Kasey's new maturity and assurance as a lead vocalist. It was if she just stopped and said to herself, 'Okay, I'm sixteen now: no more tentative little girl. I'm a young woman so I'm gonna sing like one.' Billed as 'Kasey Jo Chambers', she sang lead on six of the album's thirteen vocals, shining particularly on their remake of 'Sweetest Gift', a venerable gospel song which had been a US country hit for Linda Ronstadt and Emmylou Harris back in 1976. There's a truly transcendent moment in Dead Ringer Band's version, near the end. The instrumentation drops away so they finish with thirty seconds in close-harmony acapella. Kasey's vocal simply soars with sweet visceral power.

Despite, the musical achievement represented by *Red Desert Sky*, however, Dead Ringer Band was still battling to survive on a practical, day-to-day level.

Bill: Nash and I wrote 'Road to Nowhere' when Beccy was in the band. She, Diane and Kasey had all gone to bed after a gig in the Adelaide Hills. Nash and I sat up with a bottle of port and started messing around with the guitar and we came up with that song. There's no doubt it reflects our years on the Nullarbor—anyone who's been across the Nullarbor, past the West Australia border, will know it really is a road to nowhere: every mile's somehow the same and it just stretches into the distance. When you get over the next rise, it's the same again; nothing changes. But there's a beauty about it that we were missing; it was a part of our lives for so long. That's why we wrote the song. We were also right in the middle of our lean years: we weren't making any money, we were hardly making enough to feed ourselves and we felt

Red Desert Sky, *Dead Ringer Band's first full-length CD released in 1993.*

like the band was on a road to nowhere as well. Reality had just started to set in: we realised that becoming country music stars involved more than hitting the road and doing gigs. It was a bit of a shock. I reckon 'Road to Nowhere' was where we found ourselves at that time.

'Road to Nowhere' kicked off the album, with Kasey on lead, singing what seemed to be their new theme song with feathery, velvet-like vocal touches and a poised grace that belied her sixteen years:

Road to Nowhere

Just another endless highway
Another night on the road
Somewhere to lay this body down
And drive away the cold

Each town looks the same now
Faces in the crowd
But you'll never find a home there
Till you turn your life around

Chorus
Feels like I'm on the road to nowhere
Lookin' for a place to call my own
Feels like I'm on the road to nowhere
A road to nowhere, a rolling stone
Five hundred miles tomorrow
In the morning I'll be gone
Just another lonely highway
Somewhere else to sing my song

Don't know what lies before you
What you've got until it's gone
Have you made the right decisions
Are they right or are they wrong

Bill and Nash Chambers © *1993, Gibbon Music*

By now Dead Ringer Band were a lot more savvy to the ways of the music industry, so they sent copies of the new record to the various record labels most active in the country field. Aided by the efforts of manager Keith Melbourne, this time Dead Ringer Band attracted the attention of a key music veteran, Warren Fahey, the maverick operator of Larrikin Records and a great supporter of all styles of indigenous Australian music. Music journalist and promoter Keith Glass recalls meeting with Fahey in his office: 'He was playing *Red Desert Sky* when I walked in. He said, "I'm going to sign this band, what do you think?" I told him I thought they were great and he should do it.' The first 500 copies of *Red Desert Sky* were sold by the group as cassettes on their own label, Larrikin then licensed the album, created a fresh, new striking red and yellow cover and rereleased it on CD and cassette in November 1993.

From a songwriting perspective, *Red Desert Sky* represented another giant step forwards for the band. Bill wrote or co-wrote

Larrikin Records promotional shot, 1993.

five of the songs; Nash, aged nineteen during the recording, was involved with three; and Kasey made her recorded song-writing debut with four selections, including 'Power of the Land', a moving statement about the intangible, emotional value of the earth beneath our feet.

Thus the family advanced from penning just one song on their four-track EP to writing about 80 per cent of *Red Desert Sky*. The album included just three covers, a fine reworking of the US country classic 'Ashes of Love', 'The Sweetest Gift', with those evanescent family harmonies, and 'Itchy, Twitchy Spot', their take on Billy Ray Cyrus' worldwide hit, 'Achy Breaky Heart'. The original songs directly reflected their years of outback isolation on the Nullarbor, a life described by Fahey in the liner notes as 'a rather parched version of *Swiss Family Robinson*'.

Bill: I think Diane and I and the children were really missing the Nullarbor by then. We were in a totally different lifestyle: we were travelling around, we were in there dealing with the public all the time, arguing with venues and agents. We were realising that our situation was quite a different thing from the life we'd become accustomed to on the Nullarbor. I think we probably started missing the outback—it was such a part of our background and we'd spent eleven, twelve years as a family, totally isolated from the rest of the world. All those years weren't uninterrupted—we spent some time back home and some time on holidays—but the majority we spent in the bush, so we missed it.

We still do. Even to this very day we talk about it a lot. We sometimes wish we could simply turn back the years and do it all again. So a lot of the songs reflected the time we spent out there. I remember the night Kasey wrote 'Power of the Land'. We were camped in a tent, outside Balranald. When I heard her working on that I began to realise that she was starting to write songs that were deeper than mine. When she was writing 'Power of the Land', I just listened to it and encouraged her to finish. But as soon as I heard it, I knew that she was thinking about her childhood on the Nullarbor and that she was writing about how she'd grown up and how attached she really was to rural Australia.

Kasey: I was really young when I wrote that song. we were out camping one night in the outback of South Australia. I wanted Garth Brooks to record it, so I sent it to him: Garth Brooks, care of America. I wonder if he got it—he never recorded it, funnily enough!

Power of the Land

Well I was raised on God's good ways
I was taught how to survive
I thought for myself and I knew nothing else
But how to stay alive
They gave me the working hands
They gave me the strength of any man
They gave me the power of the land

That outback sun didn't scare no one
It was the beauty of the land
And a little hard work didn't seem to hurt
Any single man
Their children were their future then
The ones who'd pass it on again
So they gave them the power of the land

Chorus
The power of the land
There's a piece in every man
Don't let it waste away
You're gonna need it someday
The power of the land

Well, the history lies underneath those skies
But the story's never told
Of how they worked for all they earned
Till the day that they grew old
They may not have been the chosen ones
But they became Australia's sons
They all had the power of the land

You can call me blind I sure don't mind
But there's only one real man
It's the Southern one that don't fear no one
It's he who works the land
So take me outback any day
It'll drive these city blues away
Give me the power of the land . . .

Kasey Chambers ©1993, Gibbon Music

Kasey: The first song I ever wrote—I can't remember what year it was, I think 1991—was about Beccy Cole. We first saw her at the Barmera Country Music Festival, I went home after that—we'd gotten to know her a lot over the weekend—and I wrote this song called 'Beccy'. It's *so* bad!

    The next festival we went to was at Port Pirie. Beccy was there. There was a songwriting contest and I'd entered my song. It took me a while to find the courage to play it for anybody. I played it to Dad and Nash first, and of course they said it was really good, but I think they said that so I'd keep trying to write. I entered the songwriting competition; so did Dad. I remember I came first and he came third. I thought that was the greatest thing, but I didn't really write again until a while after that.

Though she had three additional songs on *Red Desert Sky*, 'Power of the Land' was sequenced before the others, up front, in the third slot, following 'Road to Nowhere' and Bill's paean to rural life, 'Born in the Country'.

Nash: I wrote my first song when I was about fifteen or sixteen— it was a terrible song. I did win third prize in the South Australian Country Music Songwriter's Awards. Dad won first prize and this friend of ours, Dave Crombie took second. He wrote a song about Coober Pedy—we used to spend a bit of time fox shooting around that area. We were kinda all like brothers to Dave after that. 'A Matter of Time' was the second song I wrote, but that wasn't all that great, either.

Bill: 'Red Desert Sky' is definitely Nash singing about the Nullarbor. I remember we used to camp in a different place almost every night. Nash and Kasey would wake up the next morning and say, 'Dad, we're on the same camp as we were yesterday', but we weren't: it all looks the same. The Nullarbor can be very stark, quite boring to the eye. There's just flat salt bush plains with nothing on them except rocks

Nash finds a quiet place to rehearse.

and an occasional eagle or a crow circling above. But when the sun goes down, the red sky lights up with a few clouds and it can be incredibly beautiful; usually the wind drops before sundown, and it's just a magic sight. Most nights we would be sitting around the campfire at sunset and that's a picture we'll never forget. I think that's what Nash probably had in mind. It's quite a deep song—it's not just about a sunset, I think it reflects some inner feelings. Nash is quite deep. He doesn't let it out too often, and he feels things that even he probably doesn't like to admit, but you can hear them in his songwriting.

Red Desert Sky

My life's a game that I played wrong
Nothing's the same since you've been gone
Bid farewell when love is lost,
Turn away and count the cost
I have a red desert sky

Chorus
It's just another red desert sky
I'm in a dream, I'll never leave
You want something I'll never be
I still have my red desert sky

I need you to save my life
from a world I can't survive
You felt it was time to leave
In a way I can't believe
I have a red desert sky

It's just another red desert sky
I'm in a dream I'll never leave
You want something I'll never be
I still have my red desert sky . . .

Nash Chambers © *1993, Gibbon Music*

With their second album now in circulation on Larrikin, Dead Ringer Band continued their near non-stop touring. Their performance itineraries for 1993 and 1994 list over 130 appearances each year. With the exception of a few festival dates, these performances consisted of two, three or even four sets per show, meaning that they were then logging 300–500 hours onstage annually, a workload that will certainly lead a band to artistic improvement, provided it doesn't grind them into the ground.

Hitting the road as a country act in Australia entails extensive overland travel. Most of the audience is rural so the group had to range far afield for their shows. Dead Ringer Band performed throughout Queensland, New South Wales, Victoria, Tasmania and their South Australia stomping grounds during this period, ranging from Townsville in the north and Coober Pedy in the west,

Getting in a few songs before the storm.

down to Melbourne in the south. Draw a straight line southwest from Townsville to Coober Pedy, then extend that line due south to the Great Australian Bight and you'll see that Dead Ringer Band's 'territory' during those two years encompassed about a third of Australia's 7 682 300 square kilometres of land area. If we assume each of those 130 shows required an average of 400 kilometres of driving, a conservative estimate considering the vastness of this domain, then the Chambers were covering over 50 000 kilometres annually in their Toyota Land Cruiser.

This relentless touring—'white line fever' as it's called in the United States—paid off for the group in November 1993 when they gathered at the spacious Rooty Hill RSL for the 'People's Choice' Awards, a ceremony organised by *Australian Country Music* magazine. Due to a mix-up with the organisers, no table was reserved for them, despite their finalist nomination. So the four Chambers gathered in the back, figuring they'd at least stay for the show. They got a huge surprise, however, because voters from throughout the nation chose Dead Ringer Band as 'Best Duo/ Group', ahead of such stalwart acts as The Fargone Beauties, The McCormack Bros Band, The Kanes and Bullamakanka. That victory earned them mention in country music newspaper *Capital News*, with writer Jon Farkas noting: 'The band's win was well received by everyone present and is a good indication of the respect and credibility that they have built up since hitting the road to tour Australia about eighteen months ago.'

Diane: Winning the People's Choice Award was the biggest 'eye-opener' I had to realising that we had fans out there and that we were part of something that was happening, I thought we were just always a little band travelling around, playing our music and enjoying what we were doing. But when we were voted People's Choice for 1993, it was our first realisation that there was a public out there who saw us as professional entertainers. That gave us enormous encouragement and fulfilment within ourselves and a strong desire and determination to continue in music.

Though the group perhaps did not realise it at the time, *Red Desert Sky* can today be viewed as the pivotal recording of their career, for it marked the biggest step in the development of their unique sound. The album also brought them industry recognition beyond South Australia, earned them their first exposure in the national media, set the wheels in motion for even better recordings, solidly established both Nash and Kasey as extremely promising singer-songwriters and first presented their gloriously warm family harmonies. The enthusiastic reception the album received proved the validity of their musical vision so the CD also served as a stimulating mental catalyst for the family.

With this encouragement and an awareness of their steady musical improvement, the band moved into 1994 with more confidence in themselves and the music they were making. Now all they had to do was figure out how to survive.

7

Giant Steps

Dead Ringer Band's steady touring and their relocation to the New South Wales Central Coast were the group's major highlights in 1994. Their move placed them about ninety minutes north of Sydney, as opposed to being four hours south of Adelaide. The Beachport/Southend area had always been their touchstone, the place to which they had always returned after every one of their extended stints into the bush. The nomadic family was finally settling down now, about 1900 kilometres from Southend.

Bill: We moved up here because we were getting more work. When we hit the road, we nearly starved for a while, then we gradually got a little more work and a little more success and we realised that most of our work was coming from the east coast area. We got a little bit of an inkling of the music business part of career development; if we were going to be successful, we had to at least be seen to be part of the industry. So we figured we'd better move closer to Sydney. This was as close as we dared to get.

We drove into Avoca Beach one Sunday. We'd just done a gig the night before up at Newcastle. There was a sign in front of the hotel saying: 'Keith Urban and band on here tonight'.

Nash: We thought: 'Yeah, this place is happening. We're gonna live here, it's got a beach, got surf, you can fish here and Keith Urban plays at the pub.'

Kasey: Of course, no one good has played there since.

This northward move didn't stop them from touring and performing back in South Australia—in fact, in the winter of 1994, they had one of their most unusual onstage drop-in guests, an incident Nash vividly recalls.

Nash: We did the Maree Camel Cup, way out in outback South Australia. We were playing outdoors; it was very cold. Dad and Bryan De Gruchy, a friend of ours who'd just come up to stay the night, decided to get stuck into the port to warm themselves up. Halfway through the gig, Dad was more than warmed up. Since it was the Camel Cup, camels were around everywhere; this one walked up near the stage and Dad stuck the microphone out in front of him, and asked him to sing along. The camel went, 'rrrrrrahhhhhahhhhh' over the PA.

The band didn't release an album in 1994, recording only a couple of songs for special projects. Nash wrote the achingly sad 'Lonely Child' following a show done for the Barnardos Foundation in Melbourne, an organisation benefiting families in need. The song first appeared on the 1993 Gympie Muster compilation CD, then was released as a bonus track with the band's first single, issued by Massive Records in 1995.

Additionally, Dead Ringer Band also participated in the 'Bridge of Love', a 'We are the World'-type 'event' single written by Roger Corbett. This was a project designed to raise funds and increase awareness during the International Year of the Family. The single featured about twenty of the nation's top country artists, united in an effort to raise money and public awareness for the work of the Barnardos Foundation. According to a Jon Farkas article in *Capital News*, the Foundation works to 'take an active support role when Australian family life is shattered by death, poverty, illness, violence, child abuse, drug and/or alcohol dependence'.

They also found themselves part of a compilation album, *Nu-music Sampler, Series 10*, issued by Studio 52 in Melbourne, appearing on a CD which billed them as 'The Dead Ringers' and showcased Kasey singing the languid and sultry 'Ever Make Me Cry'. The song was sandwiched smack amidst eighteen hard rock and alternative bands, all thrashing away furiously. Though quite compelling, the band wasn't particularly keen on the result; 'Ever Make Me Cry' remains probably the most adventurous track they have recorded to date.

Kasey: I went to hear a band called Reggae On in Adelaide and I decided I wanted to write a reggae song. I was *so* influenced by everybody that was around me throughout my life. Now I look at myself and I think: 'I'm so not like that.' I like what I like and I don't care what anybody else likes. When I was growing up I was very easily influenced: I met Kym Warner and all of a sudden I just loved heavy metal music; I met Beccy and then it was Dolly Parton all the time. Then I went to see this reggae band and I decided I wanted to write a reggae song, so I wrote 'Ever Make Me Cry', but it didn't come out like a reggae song the way I wanted. The band tried to get it into my head that we're not a reggae band, but no, I wanted this as a reggae song. It came out a little bit differently than I thought it would.

Bill: I think that was inspired by Jackson Browne. We never ever wanted to be just a regular country band. Even though we admired Slim Dusty, we loved Hank Williams, we loved the Carter Family, we also liked Jackson Browne and Bob Dylan—people like that. I've always believed that music shouldn't be restricted, you should just go do what you feel. That was an attempt to do something totally different. I'm not sure if it completely worked, but it sort of reflected how we felt at the time. We'd been listening to a lot of Jackson Browne, with David Lindley on the slide guitar; his band's always been really hot and we admired them. Not that we could totally imitate them; it was simply another direction that we wanted to try. We didn't put it on an album because we realised afterwards that our fans would be slightly confused. I guess by then we were starting to understand that a band needs to have a direction. You don't want to confuse people too much.

'Ever Make Me Cry' marked another turning point for the group. All their recordings up to that point had been

Nash, Kasey and Bill, live at the Cat & Fiddle in Balmain,
Sydney, June 1995.

co-productions, the EP and *Red Desert Sky* with Eddie Sikorski in Adelaide, and the 'Ever Make Me Cry' track with Parris Macleod in Wyong. Despite employing expert help, none of the Chambers family felt that the sound they had in their minds when they walked into the studio was the sound that they had on tape once they walked out the door. As they prepared to make their second CD, they opted for a radical change in their production methods.

Bill: During the sessions for 'Ever Make Me Cry', we discovered— like a lot of musicians have—that the guy you're paying the money to produce doesn't always listen. We weren't happy with what was going on tape. He had his say, we had the impression that we were co-producing, but before long he started to take over and we realised that he was producing and we were just doing what we were told. So we paid him what we owed him, packed our gear and walked out. 'Ever Make Me Cry' and 'Gypsy Bound' were two songs that came from that session.

We were so disillusioned. We'd made an EP, then an album, had started our third record and were still unhappy with what was going down. We got together and decided the only way to make this work was to create our own album, in our own studio. But we didn't have any money—didn't have a cent. We got on the phone and started to call places that hire studio gear. We hired two ADAT machines, digital recording machines which we'd heard about, eight-track recorders—since we had two, that gave us sixteen tracks. We hired a mixer and some monitors and with the last bit of money we had we bought a $900 microphone, which is not much for a condensing mic. Years later, when we went to Nashville, we saw that they were using the same mic in [leading producer] Garth Fundis' studio, so we figured we must have made a good choice. It was a great mic and we still use it all the time: a Japanese Audio Technica 4335.

We got halfway through the album, which turned out to be *Home Fires*. Everyone that we spoke to said, 'You're crazy, you can't record an album by yourselves. You've got no experience, you don't know how to do it. All the albums that win awards are done by hotshot producers like Garth Porter or Mark Moffatt, people like that.' We were aware of both those guys: we had talked to them, but they were too expensive, we couldn't afford them.

Nash: When we set up the studio I didn't really have any idea whatsoever of what I was doing. I was just sick of paying 800 bucks a day for a studio and then have some idiot engineer tell me how we're supposed to sound when he's never heard us in his life and doesn't give a shit anyway because to him it's crap country music. So that's the main reason we got our studio: we couldn't find anyone else around to engineer. For the first twelve months that we had the studio, I was either in the studio or doing a gig. I didn't have a day off at all.

Bill: We were talking with Greg Shaw, Keith Urban's manager, and to MCA Publishing. They said the same thing, 'You're absolutely crazy, you can't record an album if you've never had any studio experience.' But we had this dream that we were going to make an album, and we didn't want a producer to come and tell us how to do it. We were very pig-headed and very naive, but it's amazing what can happen when you've got that combination. We battled with making the album for twelve months; it was trial and error. When Nash got the mixing desk, I knew very little about mixing desks, but I had to tell him what the faders and the EQ did, he didn't even know how they worked. I explained that much to him because I'd been doing some live mixing and that was the extent of my knowledge. We hired [multi-instrumentalist] Andrew Clermont one night and he showed us a little bit more. We got halfway through the album, then we ran out of money to hire the gear and we didn't know what to do.

My sister and brother-in-law, Julie and Terry Moran, lent us $27 000 to set up a studio. In fact, they didn't lend it to us, they gave it to us, 'cause we haven't paid them back yet. They didn't need convincing as they have always believed in us, and knew we were having a problem making the album. We weren't sure that we believed in ourselves! When they gave us this money, we thought, 'That's a big responsibility, we've got to come up with something good now.'

When we were six months into the album and Nash still barely knew how to do it all, we ran into Jeff McCormack, who lived in the same town and we got to talking to him. We said, 'Would you mind playing a bit of bass on the album?' We wanted a really good studio bass player, and he was the best that we knew. He came up to the studio and said, 'How come you're doing this like this and how come you're plugging this in there and how come you're mixing this like this?' Typical studio questions. We said, 'Well, I don't know, have you got some better ideas?'

He said, 'Well, why don't you try this, and why don't you try this mic there' and just a few little things. Within half an hour, we suddenly realised we had someone helpful who knew a heap more than we did. I asked, 'Are you actually an engineer?' He said, 'No, not really, I just mess with it a little, I'm just interested.' I said, 'What experience have you had?' He said, 'Well, Garth Porter gets me in to help him.' We realised we were talking to someone who actually did know what they were doing. Once Jeff was on board, he put Nash on the right track within a couple of sessions. Once he started to understand how the studio worked, Nash took to it like a duck to water, he loved it.

Within the next six months, we'd finished the album, which we titled *Home Fires*. The industry people were still saying we were crazy and it wasn't going to work and 'you guys have to to wake up to yourselves, you can't just do things your way. You've got to do it the tried and tested way.' But we didn't believe them—we were still too naive and pig-headed—so we finished the album and Laurie Dunn from Massive Records heard it, came and heard us perform live a couple of times, loved the band and put it out. We paid for the album; he released it. Within the next six months, we'd won an ARIA with *Home Fires*, the album that people said we couldn't make! Even though it had a few flaws, and we learned a lot from making it, I think we shocked the whole Australian country music industry and even a few guys in the rock world. And we proved that we could do it—you've just got to believe.

That really gave us the encouragement to keep going, to invest more money in the studio, and to go on to make some serious recordings after that.

'Family Man', written by Nash and Bill, gave a preview of their upcoming project when it was released in mid-1994 on the Gympie Muster compilation album. The song, touching in its simple sincerity and warmth, earned Dead Ringer Band a finalist nomination for a Golden Guitar at the 1995 Country Music Awards of Australia. This trip to Tamworth, their fourth, found them far removed from their humble beginnings as buskers: they performed seven shows at two of the city's highest profile venues, The Longyard and West Tamworth Leagues Club, then appeared at the traditional Australia Day outdoor concert at Bicentennial Park.

Family Man

Born under a southern sun
Never rest 'til the work was done
Times were hard in the town where I was born
Daddy built this two room shack
His working hands and his aching back
It's not much but it always felt like home

Chorus
He's a family man
From the heart of this land
It's a way of life for you and me
He'll always be a family man

I'd walk to school five miles away
As Daddy left for work each day
A job was hard to find in our hometown
We were always poor but we never cared
There was happiness in the times we shared
I'd give anything to be there again

Some people never understand
How this life and how this land
Is in my heart and it never fades away
It's a way of life and a family
With future plans and childhood dreams
These things they'll never take from me . . .

Nash and Bill Chambers ©*1995, Gibbon Music*

8

A Year of Redemption

By the time the Tamworth Festival rolled around in January 1995, things were looking good for the Chambers family. Dead Ringer Band were performing at all the 'right' venues at Tamworth and the group were finalists for their first Golden Guitar, in the Group/Duo of the Year category at the 23rd annual Toyota Country Music Awards of Australia.

Diane: We just don't expect to win. It's certainly a buzz to win, there's no doubt, but we never expect to do the winning. Even when things looked pretty good for us, it's a very political industry that we're caught up in and sometimes—or really quite often—the public's favourites are not necessarily those of the industry.

Kasey: Oh God, no, we didn't expect to win 'cause we've never really been industry people, we don't really have a whole lot to do with the industry. We just thought that industry people won those sort of things so we didn't expect for a minute that we would win it. And then we won. I had to make a speech and I have no idea what I said, but I know that it wasn't very good.

Dead Ringer Band also shared a Golden Guitar for singing in the award-winning Vocal Collaboration of the Year, the 'Bridge of Love' project.

All smiles with their first Golden Guitar, January 1995.

Their unexpected Group/Duo victory placed them in the Award winners' circle in January, 1995, along with Graeme Connors, Lee Kernaghan and Gina Jeffreys. Oddly, when they claimed the Group/Duo Golden Guitar, Dead Ringer Band had no record label, as their deal with Larrikin was a licensing arrangement covering only *Red Desert Sky* and their winning track, 'Family Man', had been issued on a compilation album, released as a charity effort through the Gympie Muster, the largest outdoor country music festival in Australia.

'Suddenly there was a lot of interest from record companies and publishing companies in our music. And instead of having to go out and hustle for gigs, they were coming to us,' Nash told country music journalist Sue Jarvis in an interview for *Total Country* magazine.

Nash: We decided to wait and see what happened, and a few of the major companies seemed to lose interest. For us, country music is a full-time, full-year job. We felt we needed a company that would support us all the time.

We decided to sign with Massive Records, partly because they were a fairly small company—we felt we could be involved in what they did and have a close relationship with them—and partly because Laurie Dunn was so enthusiastic. He also has very similar musical interests—for instance, he's a huge fan of Gram Parsons—and we reckoned we needed that personal level to our business relationship.

Bill amplified Nash's remarks in an interview with Stuart Coupe for *Country Music* magazine.

Bill: It's more of a personal set-up, which suits us. I guess we're a little bit more involved in the whole process with Massive whereas Larrikin is a very big company. I'm not complaining about that at all. We've had a good relationship there, but I think Massive will suit us better for the new album.

I love the personal contact we've got with Laurie Dunn at Massive. We like to do things ourselves, we've always been a little bit of 'to hell with the industry, we'll do it our way' sort of people. I'm not saying that's great—it doesn't work for everyone and maybe we're just a bit pig-headed in that way. But it seems to work for us, and I still reckon artists need to have control of their own career as much as possible.

Massive staffer and former Mildura radio presenter Kaye Crick brought Dead Ringer Band to Dunn's attention. She recalled those days.

Kaye Crick: The first time I saw Dead Ringer Band was in Mildura. I was working for 3HOT-FM and it was the same time they had released their EP. I was also working in the Sand Bar, the bar where they played, so I saw them perform and did an interview. I just fell in love with them straight away because they are just so upfront, honest people, really down-to-earth, and from there I suppose my love affair with Dead Ringer Band began, as it does with most people once they meet them. I didn't see them for quite some time. Then they came to Sydney, they played at the Town Hall, a post-Tamworth performance. Diane and Bill remembered me straight away, they came up and we spent all night chatting.

I had originally moved to Sydney to work in radio but by then I had started working for Massive. I was in charge of their country music division. As soon as I started there, I started telling Laurie Dunn, the Managing Director, about this band, how good they were. I think every day I must have told him how wonderful they were. Then we went up to Tamworth and they met Jann Browne [an American artist brought out by Massive for the festival]. She fell in love with them when she saw them perform. Kasey sung some of Jann's songs and they admired Jann, so then she was in Laurie's ear as well. From there they were signed to Massive. I think Laurie had no choice because he was being bombarded from all directions, especially by myself.

Dunn, well-spoken and in his mid-40s, had previously worked for Virgin Records in the United Kingdom before starting an independent label called Static. He then returned to Virgin to become Managing Director in Australia. He expanded the company's operations but was caught in the undertow following EMI's purchase of Virgin in 1992. He founded Massive Records, with EMI's backing, shortly thereafter.

Massive began by licensing in several highly regarded US country and folk albums from independent artists like Jann Browne, Kate Campbell, George Hamilton V, and Wylie and the Wild West Show. Dunn also engineered a deal to market the UK-based Ritz Records catalogue featuring the fabulously successful Irish crooner Daniel O'Donnell. Massive began to build a local roster, first obtaining the rights for the back catalogue and future work of rock icons Icehouse, headed by Iva Davies, then signing a strange array of acts such as Ian Stephen (whose 'Jesus Saves White Trash' remains a cult classic), and TV figure Cameron Daddo. Keith Glass, a singer-songwriter/journalist/promoter/radio presenter with one of the most impressive and eclectic résumés in all Australian roots music, came on board in a consulting role.

Massive tested the waters a bit by releasing a single prior to issuing *Home Fires* in October. The three-track single featured 'Australian Son', penned by the whole family, accompanied by Kasey's 'Guitar Talk' and 'Lonely Child'.

Once Massive and Dead Ringer Band joined up together, the four Chambers began working on a more day-to-day basis with Louise Stovin-Bradford, an energetic and charmingly direct

'Australian Son', the first single released from the Home Fires *album, logged several weeks atop Music Network's country singles chart in February 1996.*

woman with impressive experience in the rock/pop arena. Prior to arriving at Massive about the same time as Dead Ringer Band, Stovin-Bradford had five years' experience in music publishing (with APRA and Warner-Chappell) and five years in artist management, at firms headed by Rod Willis and Peter Rix. There she worked with such stars as Cold Chisel, Don Walker, Icehouse and Deni and Marcia Hines.

'She really took us under her wing', Diane remembers. 'Up until the split with Massive, she was functioning more in a management role than strictly as a label employee. She was a huge help to us in so many ways.'

'We wanted to use "Australian Son" as the single because it says a lot about who we are and what we're about. It kind of encapsulates that Australian attitude of standing firm and giving it a go. And it says a lot about the way we approach music: the do it yourself approach, getting in, boots and all,' Nash told journalist Sue Jarvis.

Perhaps to everyone's surprise, 'Australian Son'—remarkably, Dead Ringer Band's first actual single—shot straight to number 1 on the country airplay charts and stayed at the top for seven weeks in late 1995 and early 1996. This feat kept them in the public eye following the release of *Home Fires* in November.

Bill: I'd written 'Australian Son' for Slim Dusty and sent it to him. He rang me and said: 'It's a nice song and I think we can do something with it, but it needs changing, can you change it?' I said, 'I think I can.' So all four of us got together and we sat around the kitchen table. We haven't written many songs as a family but that night we sat down and started changing it, Kasey started singing it and we suddenly realised it was more of a Dead Ringer Band song than a Slim song, so we didn't send it back to him. We just changed it and kept it.

At this point, let's pause to reflect on what Bill, Diane, Nash and Kasey accomplished with this achievement. Their first single—the initial release created entirely by the band, a recording made in their homemade studio—went to the top of the charts, ahead of singles by such artists as Slim Dusty, Lee Kernaghan, Gina Jeffreys, Colin Buchanan, Keith Urban and Beccy Cole, winner of the prestigious Best New Talent Golden Guitar Award in 1994. Somehow, Dead Ringer Band and Massive Records, a tiny independent label, laid claim to the top single in the land, and for nearly two months fought off all the challenges issued by such industry Goliaths as Sony, ABC, EMI, rooArt and, for that matter, Larrikin—their previous recording home.

While such a feat was not unprecedented in the much freer environment of the Australian country industry, no US artist on an independent label has scored a number 1 hit with their first single since Jeannie C. Riley turned the trick with Tom T. Hall's classic tale of small-town hypocrisy, 'Harper Valley P.T.A.', way back in 1968.

Australian Son

He'll never walk away
He's just looking for a better day
Up and gone when the sun comes up
Hard times but he won't give up

He lives a simple way of life
Made a home for his kids and wife
Never asks for a helping hand
Lives his dreams across this land

Chorus
He's a true Australian son
In the heart of everyone
Won't ever walk away
An Australian son

No one could understand
What goes through the heart of a man
He's got his back up against the wall
He's on the edge but he won't fall

He's a true Australian son
In the heart of everyone
Won't ever walk away
An Australian son

Bill, Diane, Nash and Kasey Chambers © 1995, *Gibbon Music*

The *Home Fires* reviews were gratifying, to say the least. Bruce Elder, the often acerbic *Sydney Morning Herald* pop music critic, described it as a 'sharp, up-tempo, exciting and vibrant recording which effortlessly blends bluegrass, rockabilly, folk and rustic humor into a potent potpourri of country music'. Elder ended his review by stating, 'This is the best Australian country album this year.'

Keith Glass of the *Melbourne Herald-Sun*, with over thirty years' experience in numerous areas of the industry to his credit, seconded Elder's motion: 'Kasey Chambers just may be the best female singer in Australia and she is only 19 years old.' Glass described the album as 'an astounding leap from *Red Desert Sky*'.

Trade publication *Music Network* noted:

the band has escalated from buskers to Golden Guitar winners at Tamworth while ever improving their vibrant meld of country fills and feels with astute songs and vocal finesse. Star at the microphone is daughter Kasey, though brother Nash is no slouch. Meantime father Bill plays one mean guitar, adds harmonies and co-produces with Nash. Mother Diane plays bass and is business manager.

Thus 1995 became a year of vindication. It started with a Tamworth victory and ended with the *Home Fires* release and a number 1 single with 'Australian Son', two examples that showed an industry that considered them 'crazy' and as 'pig-headed' as they themselves felt they were, Dead Ringer Band might actually know what they were doing when it came to making music.

If touring alone were the yardstick used to judge success, few acts could boast of a dance card as full as this band's. Their itinerary for the year, with all bookings coordinated by Diane, listed 135 dates—even more than in 1994—and included aerial jaunts to festivals in Tasmania and on Norfolk Island. They journeyed to the other shows overland, making ten separate tours into Queensland, South Australia, Victoria and the ACT as well as racking up nearly ninety shows in their home state. Ranging from Cairns to Coober Pedy, from Melbourne to Sydney, they performed between eight and fifteen nights every single month, hard travelling in anyone's book. Tack another 55 000 or so kilometres on the odometer.

Importantly, 1995 was the year when the Chambers family first ventured 1500 kilometres across the Pacific, northeast from Sydney, to Norfolk Island to perform at the island's annual Country Music Festival. Though Dead Ringer Band approached their shows there initially with mixed feelings, once on the island they seemed to have found their spiritual home.

Kasey: To tell you the truth, I wasn't even really looking forward to going. It was just like another gig for me. I didn't know anything about Norfolk Island before I went there and it was like, 'Oh yeah, we're just going to Norfolk Island to do a gig.'

It's really hard to explain. Lots of people ask me about Norfolk, and it's just the people there. I've never met people like that in my life apart from where we come from, I'm sure it's probably like that in lots of other places as well but I've never had a place affect me like Norfolk did, apart from maybe the Nullarbor. And it's the absolute opposite to the Nullarbor. Norfolk is all hills and grass and water. Maybe it's because they are both really remote. The people there have a simple way of life, they're just so down to earth, they treat everybody equally, they treat everybody so well. It was an amazing time. That's the first time we ever met Darren Coggan and we became really good friends with him after that. He actually started playing with the band for a while— he was playing drums for us after that. He'd come on a few tours and sing a few songs and we became really, really good friends. Then he started his own career, he didn't want to be a drummer any more for Dead Ringer Band. We met on Norfolk and he went through that amazing time of realising what Norfolk Island was all about at the same time as we did.

In addition to beginning their still-enduring relationship with Darren, the Chambers also formed a lasting friendship with the Menghetti family, Norfolk residents who are now part of their family circle, as close as kinfolk.

Kasey: I remember a little girl came up to me and Mum and said, 'Can you sign my jeans?' Mum said, 'Will you get in trouble with your mum if we do that?' and she said, 'My mum just died.' We felt really awkward but she was fine. Then this guy came to us at a gig. He said, 'Look, I really love your music. Do you want to come back and have a coffee at our house. It's my little girl, the one whose jeans you signed.' We never usually do that, go back to somebody's house after a gig, but for some reason we really wanted to. It turned out to be the Menghettis' house. It was six months after their mum had died. I don't know why we had this connection, but we did, and from that moment on, they were just a huge part of our lives.

I didn't even meet Kurt [Kasey's future boyfriend] that

day, he wasn't there. He came up at the gig afterwards; he brought up his little brother, Jess, to ask for my autograph on Jess's hat because Jess was too shy. And we just created this bond with his family. That's one of our main connections with Norfolk, the Menghetti family . . . Kurt and I weren't even together for about a year. We were just friends. We even spent the first six months hardly even saying two words to each other, 'cause Kurt was the shyest guy in the whole world. I was really closer to his sisters, Dana and Gemma. Then Kurt and I became really, really good friends . . . We weren't together or anything like that, didn't even think of it 'cause Kurt's four years younger than me.

Diane: I remember the first time we were approached to go to Norfolk, we couldn't believe our luck, that someone actually asked us to go to such a prestigious place. We really, really felt instantly at home on that little island and with the people who were to become our lifetime friends. Maybe it was because we too are easy-going, simple, home-grown folk, whose values are more focused on quality of life and friendship, rather than quantity of life and friendship. Whatever it is, Norfolk seemed to take us into their hearts, and we took them into our hearts. I think it's a bond forever with us now.

9

Notice From Abroad

Riding the crest of the success of 'Australian Son' and the warm reception the media had given *Home Fires*, Dead Ringer Band were again nominated for the same Group/Duo honour they had surprisingly won in Tamworth the previous January. Most pundits predicted a repeat victory, but this was not to be. The award was won by The Wheel. Undaunted, Dead Ringer Band cheered from the audience as The Wheel accepted, not in the least dismayed. As Kasey remarked, 'Why shouldn't we be happy? Those guys are all close friends of ours. We're glad they won.' Indeed, Wheel members Rod and Jeff McCormack were both key contributors to *Home Fires*.

The title cut, 'Home Fires' (written by Darren Coggan), and 'Gypsy Bound' followed 'Australian Son' as single releases from *Home Fires*. Though neither enjoyed the chart success of that debut single, both songs received plenty of airplay and both further enhanced the critical reception of the band. Penned by Kasey, 'Gypsy Bound'—the album closer—is a spooky song of alienation. 'I wrote that down in a little place called Amphitheatre. We were playing a gig there and while they were having sound check, I just sat out in the car and wrote it. That song was about lots of living on the road.'

Gypsy Bound

This little town makes me restless
There ain't no reason to stay
Last night I went to sleep in a fairytale
But I woke up in the real world today

Everybody knows my name by now
They all know what I'm gonna do and say
I went to sleep in a fairytale
Woke up in the real world
I guess it's time for me to get away

Chorus
Tonight I must be gypsy bound
You'll never know where I'll be hangin' 'round
While this little town just stays the same
No one else will know my name
Tonight I must be gypsy bound

Kasey Chambers © 1995, Gibbon Music

Dead Ringer Band's touring dossier for 1996 was even more ambitious than their staggering 1995 workload. Diane oversaw 135 shows, marking the first year they racked up appearances in all seven states and the ACT. In addition to their usual full slate of appearances in New South Wales, Queensland, Victoria and South Australia, they travelled to Norfolk Island and Tasmania twice each, made their first trip to New Zealand, and played in Darby in Western Australia and Alice Springs in the Northern Territory.

After years of touring and a few hundred thousand kilometres of overland travel without serious incident, the family was reminded that danger lurked everywhere, not just out on the Nullarbor.

Bill: We were travelling the huge highway between Melbourne and Sydney when our car started to cough and lose power. I climbed out, then I screamed at everyone to move because I could see flames beginning to lick up from under the motor. We carried about ten expensive guitars and $50 000 worth of PA and amplification equipment in the trailer. We

130

had just enough time to unhitch it when the car exploded in a gigantic ball of flames. We lost our clothes, blankets, tapes, CDs and about $1000 in cash but I guess we were very lucky to escape with our lives. Life on the road has never been easy for us.

This was the time when the Chambers family made the biggest jump of their lives, in terms of both distance and audacity: they ventured 15 000 kilometres to Nashville and performed five times in 'Music City USA'.

The year also marked the beginning of the outside world's awareness of Dead Ringer Band, as well as my own discovery of the band. I had the honour of penning the first overseas review for *Home Fires*, noting in the June issue of *Country Music International* (UK) that the album was 'a refreshing experience for lovers of the real thing', and later describing Kasey's voice: 'Take a pinch of Dolly Parton, a smattering of Alison Krauss, a dash of Patty Loveless and a smidgen of Jann Browne and you've got the most exciting new country singer in years.'

Similarly enthusiastic reviews followed from other publications in England, the Netherlands, Scandinavia and the United States, with the CD garnering top marks and 'Spotlight Album' status from both of England's major country publications, *Country Music People* and *Country Music International*. Al Moir of *Country Music People* noted:

> They sound as good, even better, perhaps, than many American acts yet they manage to retain a certain Australian identity in what they do . . . Great songs, contemporary, yet never straying from the best traditions of country music, with excellent musicianship and a crisp, clean production.

The following comments from world music business bible *Billboard*, penned by Nashville Bureau Chief Chet Flippo, were even more impressive. He tagged *Home Fires* his 'Fave of the Week', describing it as 'a gem of pure, straight-ahead, timeless country. Kasey Chambers has a crystal bell of a voice with a million-dollar catch in it that will melt your heart.' That writeup, published in April, had an enormous impact on the local country industry, for no one there could remember *Billboard* ever taking note of home-grown Australian country artists at all, much less in such praiseworthy terms. At year's end, Flippo chose *Home Fires* as one of 1996's ten best albums. Despite the fact that *Home Fires* then had no distribution in Europe, the album wound up on year-end best lists published by magazines in Sweden, Switzerland, the Netherlands and England.

Reviews such as these resulted in a licence deal with London-based Demon Records for the release of *Home Fires* in Europe. Demon, founded in 1981 by Elvis Costello, his manager Jake Riviera, Andrew Lauder and others, was primarily active in the reissue market though the label occasionally picked up contemporary recordings. In this case, Pete Macklin at Demon liked what he heard enough to offer US$3000 as an advance for European rights for a five-year period.

Macklin's offer was made in late 1996, but *Home Fires* didn't become readily available in Europe until 28 July 1997, due to negotiating time, paperwork delays and shipping of the contracts, masters and artwork. This was twenty months after the album's initial release by Massive and, even though Demon lost lots of import sales during that period, the CD still sold 'reasonably well, between two and three thousand', according to Macklin.

Icons like Johnny Cash, Dolly Parton and Willie Nelson do quite well in Europe. Additionally, while a few fringe artists—all long-time UK touring veterans like Don Williams, Lyle Lovett, Steve Earle, Nanci Griffith and Emmylou Harris—sell reasonably well in Europe, almost all of the most popular artists currently ruling US country radio sell so poorly there that their records aren't even issued in England, much less on the continent. It is also extremely rare for a European label to license in a country album from Australia. *CD International* (Winter 1996/97), a semi-annual publication which listed available CDs in the world's five biggest markets—the United States, Japan, England, Germany and France—showed one Slim Dusty album, his fiftieth, in print only in the United Kingdom, one Tex Morton album in Germany and

Working in the studio with legendary producer Garth Fundis (shown here with his wife Anne) was a major highlight of Dead Ringer Band's first trip to Nashville, in late November 1996.

Dead Ringer Band's previous record, *Red Desert Sky*, on offer in both England and Germany. Virtually none of the other prominent Australian country artists had available recordings in these markets, which represented about 70 per cent of the world's music sales.

As the band toured relentlessly, by mid-1996 interest was building in Nashville as promotion of the album got underway. Garth Fundis, the very successful producer for Don Williams, Keith Whitley and Trisha Yearwood, was the first high-level Music City executive to become interested. Fundis headed the Nashville office of a new label, Almo Sounds. The label was begun by Herb Alpert and Jerry Moss, founders of A&M Records. Almo Sounds had achieved considerable early success by grabbing the North American rights to modern rock band Garbage through a deal negotiated with Australian label Mushroom's International Division in London.

By mid-1996, Almo Sounds' Los Angeles office had also released *Revival*, a critically acclaimed debut album by Gillian Welch. Garth's Nashville operation had signed several acts, including songwriter/artists Billy Yates and Paul Jefferson plus the duet team of Bekka Bramlett and Billy Burnette, both veterans of late-period Fleetwood Mac.

Early in May, Garth Fundis left the following message on my answerphone:

> John, it's Sunday about noon, Garth here. I've been listening to the CD all weekend and . . . You're right, this woman is pretty amazing. Anyway, let's talk on Monday . . . about what we do next. All right . . . But I'm really diggin' this. I appreciate having the opportunity to hear it. I'll talk to you Monday, buddy, take care.

His uncertainty regarding the next step was understandable when you consider the fact that no Nashville country label has ever picked up an album made by an overseas country artist for a foreign label. Nor had a Nashville label ever made a direct signing of a new artist without acquiring worldwide rights.

Fundis asked to hear more of Dead Ringer Band, so I taped selected tracks from *Red Desert Sky* and fed him background information about their itinerary, home studio, previous awards and singles chart activity. Pretty soon he asked for video footage but, as none was available, he decided to fund a modest 'shoot' at a future show to see what the band looked like onstage. He simply didn't have the time to fly to Australia since he was General Manger of Almo Sounds/Nashville, was producing Yearwood plus all the acts signed to the label and was owner of Sound Emporium, a two-room recording complex which was then, and still is, one of the town's leading studios.

Garth sent US$5000 to Laurie for the video, arrangements were made and a three-song live clip, shot by Mark Leonard, was created from a Dead Ringer Band show at The Cat & Fiddle Hotel in the inner-city Sydney suburb of Balmain. It was a one-camera shoot: the group sang each song three times to permit different camera angles for Leonard's crew. The resulting ten-minute video was an honest, no-frills document of the group onstage and it whetted Garth's appetite enough for him to take the next step.

He began negotiating with Laurie Dunn and, in September 1996, they began discussing general deal parameters.

At this point, Dead Ringer Band were plowing through their ambitious live appearance schedule. They returned to Norfolk Island for their second Country Festival in May, zipped over to New Zealand for eight days, scooped up a MO Award (based on live performances only) in mid-June for Best Country Group, filmed the clips for Almo Sounds in July and were in the midst of opening thirteen shows for Irish superstar Daniel O'Donnell in September when the author made his first visit, thanks to an air ticket supplied by Massive. The affable O'Donnell was making his first extended tour in Australia, hoping to stimulate sales of his albums, now on release in the market for the first time, due to the licensing deal with Massive. O'Donnell attracted packed houses of several thousand in such venues as Sydney's State Theatre and the Festival Theatre in Adelaide. But his audiences were virtually exclusively composed of the over-fifty-five crowd and it is doubtful the Ringers connected musically with many in attendance.

In mid-August, the nominations for the 10th Annual ARIA Awards were announced and the Chambers family were stunned to learn *Home Fires* were chosen as a finalist in the 'Best Country Release' category, along with albums by Graeme Connors, Lee Kernaghan, The Wheel and Tania Kernaghan, all issued on labels substantially bigger than Massive.

Kasey: I didn't even know anything about the ARIAs except they were the biggest awards you could win in Australia and there was just no hope. I just remember being nominated and thinking, 'Ah, good. At least we've got an excuse to go 'cause I didn't think I'd ever get to go to something like this.' And we did not think of anything to say, anybody to thank or anything, 'cause there was no, absolutely *no way* we were going to win that award. We didn't even talk about it; we didn't even say, 'So do you think we've got a chance?' We didn't even mention it—there was just no way that we were going to win it.

Kasey had reason to handicap their chances of winning as dismal. It had been almost a year since *Home Fires* was released, so the initial flurry of media excitement had long since abated. Connors had taken out seven Golden Guitars in the past two years, Lee Kernaghan had won this ARIA in 1993 and 1994, The Wheel had defeated Dead Ringer Band for the Group/Duo Golden Guitar at Tamworth in January and Tania Kernaghan, Lee's sister, was being touted by her and Lee's label, ABC, as the successor to Gina Jeffreys' crown as the top female country artist in the land.

'We went along to the ARIA night, but certainly didn't expect to win. We were the rank outsiders. It was exciting be be caught up in the whole ARIA whirl,' Diane told Philip Moore of *Australasian Post*. 'It was pretty scary being up against such a quality field,' she informed *Country Update*.

So imagine the jolt of electricity which surged through Bill, Diane, Nash and Kasey when they were announced as ARIA winners! 'Actually, it was amazing, and quite an honour to think people have viewed our album as the best in country music. We were really thrilled,' Diane commented.

Kasey: It was just so weird. I remember we didn't come down from cloud nine for a long time from that one. It's great on the night, but we've never been people that really take awards all that seriously—probably everyone says that. I love winning awards—who doesn't like winning them? But that one was extra exciting.

Diane: It's one of those fulfilments and rewards for the knocks and the hard times you get. Because the music business is no sweet, pretty, easy-going little industry to be caught up in. Winning an award like that is one of the rewards that keeps you inspired and challenges you to move on to the next stage in your musical growth.

Nash: We didn't think we had a hope in hell of winning the ARIA. I'm still not sure why we won it, but you learn to take awards when you get them because you don't generally get the choice as to when you want to win them.

Capital News carried the band's official statement in November, written by Diane and attributed to them all.

Dead Ringer Band with their 1996 ARIA Award, October.

We feel honored to have been nominated in the finals of the ARIAs along with The Wheel, Tania, Lee and Graeme and over the moon to have been judged the winners of the ARIA for 1996.

We would like to take this opportunity to sincerely thank everyone who has supported and believed in us over the years.

With the ARIA honour displayed proudly on the mantelpiece, the Chambers returned to intensive touring, spending the rest of October in New South Wales and making plans for their first-ever trip to Nashville in late November. The talks between Garth and Laurie at Massive seemed to be getting even more serious and, given that Bill and Diane had wanted to go to Nashville all their lives, the pending record deal seemed to offer a perfect opportunity. Again, Terry and Julie's faith and commitment to their growing success made it financially possible for the four Chambers, and the ever-present and irrepressible Worm, to fly to Tennessee and witness first-hand the inner workings of an industry they had long admired from afar.

Dead Ringer Band in a Nashville studio shoot, December 1996.

Diane: It was like really going to the big smoke, the big time, to head overseas to America and Nashville and investigate our music dream. I absolutely loved it, loved the people, didn't like the food so much—it was very different. We certainly met some beautiful, beautiful people and experienced some pretty amazing things musically.

It was one of the highlights of our lives for sure—just the thrill and the excitement of being somewhere that you never thought you would ever get to see. It was just an enormous adventure.

Kasey: Hey, I loved it. I had no idea what to expect, I didn't even know if it was a little town or a big city. When we got there, Nashville changed my whole perception of music and everything. I can even remember the actual point—the *moment*—that it did that.

The first night we were so tired we just went to sleep. The second night we didn't have anything on either, 'cause we had a couple days to recover from the flight. We looked in the paper to see if there was anything on. It was a Monday night, and there was Edwin McCain playing at the Exit/In. I had just seen him on Letterman, doing a duet with Darius Rucker, the main guy from Hootie and the Blowfish. That was the only name we were familiar with playing that night, so Nash, Worm and I went, the first thing we ever went to in Nashville, our first night out. We walked into this gig and there's a whole lot of young people there—it wasn't majorly packed, but there was a fairly good crowd. And then this guy came on stage, he was the support act. I'd never heard of him, don't even know if anybody introduced him or anything, he just walked on with his band. It was Matthew Ryan and I was in a trance for the rest of the set, until he walked off stage. It was just the most unbelievable thing I'd ever seen in my life. I just thought it was the best thing I ever heard, I'd never heard anybody telling stories quite in the way that Matthew does; musically it was one of the turning points of my life. Well, Nashville on the whole was a turning point for me musically. I know it was for Nash, too. I looked at music differently after that—I mean, I've seen great artists before, people that have really moved me. I saw Lucinda Williams on her tour with Rosanne Cash and Mary Chapin Carpenter. I'd seen Lucinda again on the 'Sweet Old World' tour and that moved me like nothing else. I saw Jann Browne—she was one of the most unbelievable artists I'd seen, I saw Steve Young, heaps of people, I don't know if it was the vibe of being in Nashville, or maybe it was also not knowing what to expect. I went to that gig to see someone else and I ended up being the number one Matthew Ryan fan.

Edwin McCain came on and he was very good, but we left halfway through the show. He was great but there was just *no way* that he was ever going to top Matthew Ryan. That was a real turning point for me. Listening to the words of his songs changed the way my songwriting went after that. His music made me look differently at songwriting. I went home that night and wrote 'Things Don't Come Easy'. I actually had half the song written at the gig and

I went home and finished it that night. I think that's one of the best songs I've written.

Nashville had a vibe, even after we came home from Nashville. Both times I've been there all I wanted to do for the next six weeks was write songs—it's so inspirational being there. It was at that point that I decided that song-writing was what I wanted to do as well as singing.

Nash: I've never been a huge country fan like Kasey and Dad. I love a lot of certain types of country music but I didn't like the generic stuff, this 'pop-country' that gets shoved out of Nashville these days. It was exciting to go to another country, but as far as going there for the musical side, I wasn't expecting to enjoy it all that much. But it sort of had the totally opposite effect on me. We were very fortunate because we were involved with Garth Fundis, one of the best country producers. We got to hang out with him, he's a great guy and really helpful.

On our third night in Nashville, Garth said, 'Garbage are in town with Smashing Pumpkins tonight. Would you like to come along?' We said we'd love to. Kasey, Worm and I got free tickets, went to the show and went backstage to meet them.' We thought this was pretty cool. Then Shirley Manson, the lead singer, asked, 'What are you doing?' We said, 'Nothing.' She said, 'Why don't you come out for dinner?' So we jumped in the limousine: we'd been in America for about two days and we were cruising around Nashville with Garbage, in a limousine! I remember we sat down for dinner and I had Butch Vig, who produced Smashing Pumpkins and Nirvana, on one side of me, Garth Fundis, who's produced Trisha Yearwood and Don Williams, on the other, then Tony Brown walked in—he's produced Lyle Lovett, Vince Gill, George Strait, just heaps of albums. He popped in just to say g'day to Butch. I figured 'yep, this is the place for me'.

Kasey: There's a vibe in that town that nowhere else has. Nash was restless after that—I think he has been ever since. After going to Nashville, producing-wise, it just opened his eyes.

I think that it was at that point he decided that producing
was his thing and that's what he wanted to do.

Nash: Watching Garth Brooks' engineer, Mark Miller, doing demos
and recording with Garth Fundis—which was only a few
days apart—they were very large turning points in my
recording career. I heard all these great-sounding records
coming out of Nashville and out of America and I thought,
'Great, I'll get the opportunity to learn the tricks of the trade
and how they do it.' Then after hanging out with Mark, who
is a great guy, and working with Garth's engineers, Dave
Sinko and Brad Hartmann, I learned it's just using your ears,
getting good sounds and using good equipment. I was
expecting to find all these really cool little tricks that they
do to make it sound like a million dollars but it wasn't that
at all. When I came back, I really tried to get my act
together, especially on the engineering side. There's really
no trick to it: it's getting off your ass, using your ears and
making sure it sounds good going on to tape. It's experimen-
tation and experience. It was cool just sitting there with
Mark Miller in Jack's Tracks, looking through the studio and
there's all these master tapes sitting there of Nanci Griffith
and Kathy Mattea, Emmylou Harris, Garth Brooks and all
the acts they had recorded there.

There was plenty for the various Chambers to do in addition to
hanging around studios, going to concerts and schmoozing with
the stars. In addition to spending a couple of days recording with
Garth Fundis and several of the city's top sidemen—Dave
Pomeroy, John Gardner and Russ Pahl—Dead Ringer Band
appeared on the evening news on the local ABC-TV affiliate and
made two appearances on Nashville's NBC network TV outlet, on
Terry Bulger's award-winning *Backroads* feature and at the
un-musician like time of 6 a.m. for *Good Morning Nashville*, engaging
world-renowned drummer Craig Krampf to keep time on the skins
for them on the latter date. Performance rights group BMI hosted

Douglas Corner invite to Nashville Showcase for Almo Sounds, 1996.

a special Nashville welcome reception in their honour, capped by a short acoustic set by Bill, Nash and Kasey. They were special surprise guests on Billy Block's weekly variety show, *Western Beat Roots Revival*, the city's home for edgy country, roots rock and Americana artists.

Lastly, with Gardner augmenting them on drums, they staged a full-blown 'showcase' for Almo Sounds and invited guests at local club, Douglas Corner, with Worm kicking off the show by blowing a sustained blast from a didgeridoo. Dead Ringer Band performed to a more than capacity crowd of well over 200 and earned a standing ovation after their hour-long set (25–35 minutes is standard for such events in Nashville). The Almo Sounds staff attended in full force, but for Kasey the most important guest was Phil Kaufman, aka 'The Road Mangler'—the effervescent road manager who had worked for a long line of music greats, beginning with The Rolling Stones, Joe Cocker, Frank Zappa, Gram Parsons and Etta James and, more recently, an extended stint with

The first photo session in Nashville, featuring Worm and his didgeridoo.

Emmylou Harris. Kaufman is notorious in rock circles as the man who kidnapped Parsons' body from the freight loading dock at Los Angeles airport, hauled it out to the desert in a borrowed hearse and set it ablaze. 'Gram and I had gotten very drunk at Clarence White's funeral and made a pact whereby the survivor would take the other guy's body out to Joshua Tree, have a few drinks and burn it,' he recalled in his lively autobiography, *Road Mangler Deluxe*.

Kasey: That night I was really thinking about the little stories I'd tell before songs and a lot of them mention towns in Australia and I was thinking, 'They're not going to get this.' I was really worried about what I was going to talk to these people about, if I was going to talk too fast and if anyone

Kasey and Bill at Douglas Corner Showcase, December 1996.

was going to understand what I was saying. But I was excited. Phil Kaufman was there. I was like 'Wow, Phil Kaufman is at our gig!' It was unreal. Worm was stoked!

The show got off to a wobbly start, the band members were visibly nervous and had only had time for one rehearsal with Gardner. During their third or fourth number, though, they hit their stride and sailed through the next forty-five minutes, growing more confident as each song gained a better crowd reaction. As at the BMI reception, they closed with their breathtaking version of the gospel chestnut, 'The Sweetest Gift'. The Ringers' performance, even better than on their track on *Red Desert Sky*, stopped the jaded 'Music City USA' audience in their tracks, as Ed Morris, one of the city's top journalists, noted in his *Nashville Scene* column a few weeks later:

> Listening to Australia's Dead Ringer Band at its Nashville debut was a lot like witnessing the Judds for the first time . . . simple acoustic instrumentation, Appalachian-blue vocal harmonies, earnest and eager-

to-please mannerisms . . . Just as Naomi and Wynonna had on their get-acquainted tour of Music Row in 1983, Dead Ringer Band brought listeners to tears with 'The Sweetest Gift', James B. Coats' tale of a mother's unflinching love for her 'erring but precious son'.

Chet Flippo, who had written the earlier rave in *Billboard*, checked in with his own take on their BMI show:

> One of the great privileges of working in this industry is the chance to see truly great performers and performances. One such moment came recently when fourteen-year-old LeAnn Rimes joined septuagenarian Eddy Arnold for a duet of 'Cattle Call' . . . I had a similar feeling about Australia's Dead Ringer Band when I saw it make its US debut for an industry crowd at BMI. The act's ethereal sound suggests a brand of country music that developed in a parallel universe. The members' obvious love for the genre and its traditions was evident.

Author and TV producer Bob Oermann, the most popular and enduring Nashville entertainment journalist, checked in with his comments for industry bi-weekly *Music Row*:

> They were just adorable. Dad Bill Chambers is a handsome lad in his early 40s who plays old timey dobro, mandolin and guitar. Mom Diane plays bass and never misses a note. Kids Nash and Kasey are even cuter. With their earrings, tattoos and hair they look like alternative rockers. But when they open their mouths, out come Gram Parsons and Dolly Parton, and the sweetest family harmony blend this side of Appalachia . . . 'it's Alison Krauss in the body of the Mavericks,' gasped *Country Weekly's* Clif Dunn.

Their successful Nashville introduction behind them, and with applause doubtless still ringing in their ears, Dead Ringer Band returned to their Avoca Beach home, thoughts of their upcoming record deal bouncing around their heads. The entire staff of Almo Sounds' Nashville office had attended and enjoyed the show, the label's General Manager, Paul Kremen, had flown in from Los Angeles and seemed pleased. Almo Sounds had wined and dined the band on several occasions, and had sent them fruit baskets and despatched flowers after their Douglas Corner performance.

Dead Ringer Band in Tasmania, 1996.

After being around Kasey for several hours, Shirley Manson of Garbage had told Kremen, 'That girl's a star.' So the Almo Sounds association seemed poised to proceed to the deal memo stage, when the artist's legal representatives and the label business affairs department work out the general parameters for a contract.

The Chambers had just three days at home before launching into their December bookings, beginning with a three-day swing in New South Wales and a week in Tasmania. Then there was another three-day jaunt in their home state before they closed the year back on Norfolk Island, a sojourn which saw them perform five shows and enjoy some well-earned rest.

10

Things Don't Come Easy

Everything looked rosy at the beginning of 1997 as Dead Ringer Band kicked off the year with a quick four-day foray to New Zealand and also worked on pre-production for their next, as yet untitled, album. A US record deal seemed imminent, they were touring steadily, their singles were getting solid airplay and charting well, the big to-do at Tamworth was approaching and they were again nominated for the Group/Duo award. With their ARIA win just three months earlier, most wags figured them as the favourite to unseat The Wheel and regain the title they had won in 1995.

On the live performance front, Diane assembled an outrageously ambitious touring schedule, outdoing even her Herculean efforts from 1995 and 1996. In 1997, Dead Ringer Band performed in New Zealand, recorded on Norfolk Island and again played in all seven Australian states, hitting Tasmania twice for good measure. The month before recording began, they performed eighteen shows in four states. By 31 December, another 130 shows were under their belts.

Between 1 August 1993 and New Year's Eve of 1997, Dead Ringer Band performed 597 engagements, the vast majority multiple-set appearances—a staggering average for that 1613-day stretch of one show every 2.7 days! That's eleven shows every month for fifty-three consecutive months! They travelled about 240 000 kilometres overland, around 95 000 kilometres more by air.

This year they planned to try out a new strategy for their Tamworth performances. Rather than multiple dates at the popular spots they had been playing for years—the atmospheric Longyard and the more modern, larger Wests Leagues Club, they felt they were ready to promote their own shows. This approach had both advantages and drawbacks. The Longyard and Wests Leagues Club had substantial built-in audiences and they charged no admission. Packed houses were a given at those venues. Low pay was, however, also a given. The clubs were only willing to pay a flat fee for the four-hour shows and a plethora of acts were eager for the exposure such high-profile slots guaranteed.

International artists and the top-level Australian acts usually performed at special, ticketed events, earning a large share of the gross revenues and pocketing a few thousand dollars per appearance, as opposed to earning a few hundred per date at established venues like Wests Leagues and The Longyard.

Dead Ringer Band could also present themselves in a concert setting during such a show, doing a couple of hour-long sets instead of grinding out four fifty-minute shows in a noisy nightclub. Lastly, by scheduling their performances during the latter half of the second weekend, the band could reduce the amount of time spent in Tamworth from ten or eleven days to four or five. Tamworth *per se* wasn't the problem, the lodging and food costs were the culprit. The glitter, glitz, excitement and emotional performances of Tamworth are one side of the coin. On the other is the hard truth that it costs hundreds of dollars per day to house and feed a band's eight-person entourage. In fact, most acts *lose* money during this ten-day extravaganza.

It's a pretty simple equation: costs are higher than those incurred during normal touring dates; however, pay, for all but the superstars, is lower. The Ringers were lucky since they only had to make about a 600 kilometre round trip to play the festival. Acts based in Queensland, Victoria, South Australia or the more remote areas of New South Wales faced journeys two, three, four or five times that distance. True, everyone makes some money on merchandise sales and there are indirect benefits in meeting and performing for their fans. It's unlikely, however, that many acts are able to sell enough CDs, caps and t-shirts to offset the shortfall. So, while the fans may believe the artists are making a

148

killing at Tamworth, the truth is that most of them are reaching into their own pocket to entertain them—in effect paying their audience to see them perform!

This year, the Ringers decided to do two shows at the Workmen's Club, hoping to raise revenues and lower costs. Though they did improve their balance sheet in 1997, they still didn't make a profit—in fact, Dead Ringer Band didn't actually make money at Tamworth until 1999, their ninth consecutive year there.

The 1997 Toyota Country Music Awards of Australia were a bit of a surprise to many, for ABC acts Lee Kernaghan, Graeme Connors and Tania Kernaghan swept to victory in six of the twelve categories while ABC stablemates Tina Martyn, Mark O'Shea and Lawrie Minson added one honour apiece. EMI's Slim Dusty took out an additional two, meaning that EMI—which distributed ABC—laid claim to eleven of the twelve awards. Alas, Dead Ringer Band went home empty-handed as The Wheel, on independent label rooArt, repeated their win as Vocal Group/Duo of the Year.

The awards were also lopsided from a publishing viewpoint: Warner Chappell writers were in on six awards, EMI won or shared three and Rondor, via Graeme Connors, snagged two. Minson was the only award winner not published by one of these three industry behemoths.

If this defeat bothered them, Dead Ringer Band didn't let it show. They just resumed their gruelling touring schedule. In addition to touching down in New Zealand, Tasmania and on Norfolk Island, they ranged from Darwin to Melbourne, and Cairns to Mandurah, just south of Perth.

The awards show disappointment wasn't the only kick in the teeth the group suffered during 1997's first quarter. Almo Sounds, their ardent recording suitor, got cold feet and, instead of proposing deal terms, decided to 'pass' on signing the group. In a 24 March letter, Director of Nashville Operations Garth Fundis put it this way:

> I wish I had better news to deliver but the fact is that Almo Sounds can't give the Dead Ringer Band the kind of commitment that they deserve at this time. I have never meant to string anybody along in this process and my interest in this project has been genuine from the

beginning. It will take more than just my interest here to do justice to the project, however. While many here at Almo Sounds recognise the talent and merit of this group, there is concern about where they fit into the scheme of things.

While they [the group] clearly feel comfortable with the idea that they are a country act, there is a concern that mainstream country radio is not going to respond to the group's efforts or appeal and from label General Manager Paul Kremen's point of view, there is not enough 'edge' to work this by way of [label distributor] Geffen's machinery to triple-A or Americana radio.

I certainly don't expect for you to agree with this analogy and you have shot holes in these theories before. Nonetheless, I don't feel that I alone can commit this company to breaking this act in America . . . To say that I am sorry for taking so long to get to this point would be a large understatement. I thoroughly enjoyed getting to know these people and do not regret our investment of time and money in these artists. You have been straight up with me and have done a wonderful job of representing the group . . . they are everything you described and more. I wish you and the group all the luck in the world and hope that we can keep the door open to further discussions down the road. Now is just not the right time for me . . .

The band's response to Almo Sounds' abrupt withdrawal is illustrative of their character. Diane's letter to Garth, sent on 1 April 1997, follows.

Hi Garth,

John has kept us informed of the Almo/Dead Ringer saga, and the closing chapter, which is upon us now. We would like to thank you, Paul Kremen and the staff at Almo—especially Juanita Duthie—for their time, friendship and interest over the past number of months. We sincerely thank you for your hospitality during our stay in Nashville, and that extends to Anne, Ben and little Emily also [Garth's wife and children]. Tell Emily I still have the lovely necklace she gave me. We have gained valuable experience through our association with you all, and with John's continued belief in us, we plan to continue our search for a US label.

We fly to Norfolk Island tomorrow to begin recording our new album. John is forwarding the A-DAT—thank you for that. We wish Almo continued success and look forward to possibly catching you all

again further down the track. Thank you again, Garth and Juanita—we certainly enjoyed getting to know you and spending time with everyone. Love,
Dead Ringer Band

In a 1999 interview, Diane was philosophical about the setback: 'Maybe it was meant to be that way. We were fairly shaken. We floundered for a little while, but we re-grounded ourselves again. Obviously we weren't meant to move on at that particular time of our life.'

Almo Sounds in Los Angeles shuttered their Nashville label less than a year later, so even this kick in the teeth was a blessing in disguise. Had Dead Ringer Band signed before the closing of the office, they would have been stuck in limbo, contracted to a defunct division of a record company.

This major setback reached the Chambers just as they were finalising preparations to record their second album for Massive. They had decided upon a seemingly radical course of action, but first they needed to sell Massive on their unusual plan.

Bill: By the time we did the next record, Massive had sold a reasonable amount of *Home Fires*, and Laurie Dunn obviously saw the potential and decided to put enough money up so that we could make what we felt was a good album with a reasonable budget. Then we knocked on his door one day and said, 'We don't want to make an expensive album, but what we want to do is make it on Norfolk Island.' He looked at us like, 'What do you want to do that for?' His assistant, Louise [Stovin-Bradford] was there and she's a very practical lady. I think they thought we'd lost the plot. Because the only way over there is to fly, you've got to fly all the equipment over. There wasn't a studio over there, there'd never been any recording done on Norfolk. But the year before, we'd met these people that had this empty house. Just a beautiful old building, made out of Norfolk Island Pine. It had lots of different rooms, it had a nice bit of carpet on the floor, it had wood everywhere, it just looked like a perfect studio.

Diane: The environment we'd discovered over there was too special to us to let go. We felt we could capture in our music what we were feeling in our hearts, and I believe we did that. Yeah, it was a big thing though, getting all our gear together and making sure we had everything, because we couldn't leave anything behind. We reset it all up in a little home-stead over there—it had been a restaurant; it's now a working restaurant again. It was vacant then, so we didn't have any hassles getting someone out. We changed things around a little bit, filled up some rooms with mattresses and rigged it up for recording.

There's ghost stories to that restaurant on Norfolk. As you can imagine, there's a lot of ghost stories on Norfolk because of its history; it's a very, unique, spiritual island. The first night we tried setting all the gear up we kept blowing the power, couldn't figure it out until in the end we were really starting to think it was a ghost, even though we didn't believe in ghosts. We were starting to think, 'Maybe there's someone here trying to tell us something', but we ended up getting things sorted out.

Norfolk's a very relaxing environment to work in, the surroundings are pleasant, the people are great. We were filled with love and care and the sheer beauty and atmos-phere of the island—everything about it is just so inspiring.

Nash: It was a strange period, during the making of the album. I'd actually given notice that I was leaving the band. I wanted to get more into the production and recording side, but there just weren't a lot of opportunities open to me here in Australia at that time. We'd been to Nashville and loved it over there; the general attitude towards recording and pro-ducers and stuff is quite different to here. I was going to leave the band, go to America and pursue my producing career. Then we finished the album and a few things started happening and I forgot about moving away then.

It would have been easy then to lose faith in the wake of the lost deal, to reckon that this little family band from Southend by way of the Nullarbor had got as far as they were likely to get in the rough-and-tumble show business world. Instead, Diane, Bill, Kasey and Nash shrugged it off, bowed their necks and crafted an even more accomplished record than *Home Fires*. While Bill and Nash had collaborated as producers for that album, this time Bill stepped back, making Nash the sole producer for this critical record.

Nash: It was a bit scary. Generally, it was just learning for myself, although Jeff and Rod McCormack—especially Jeff—were great as far as helping me along the way. *Home Fires* was the first project I'd ever recorded or produced and that won an ARIA—I don't know how! *Living in the Circle* was more progression and a step again, but I look back now and cringe, thinking how much better I should have and could have done. But it's all a learning process, I expect to keep producing for the rest of my life; I just hope that I keep getting better all the time.

Bill: We had the album finished on Norfolk, but we didn't have the title track. [ABC radio presenter] Richard Porteous had mailed me a song called 'Living on the Circle' the week before we left. It was a very rough demo: Richard had sung it into a little mic, just his guitar and voice. I listened to it on the last day we were on Norfolk; we'd virtually finished the album, but we didn't have the title track.

The last night we were there, we had a bit of a party, and a couple of drinks. I'd written the words out to this song. I'd gotten Nash and Kasey and Diane to listen to it before and they all said, 'Yeah, okay, I dunno', but nothing was done. I started singing around the kitchen table that night; they all got merry over a few beers, and Kasey started to sing it then. She said, 'That's a pretty catchy tune.' We changed one word, 'living *in* the circle' instead of 'living *on*'. That night we rang Richard and said, 'Richard, do you mind if we change this song to "living in the circle" instead of "on"?' He said that was fine and we said, 'Well we're starting to like it and we're going to record it right now.' So we put all the beers and the food down, raced over and recorded 'Living in the Circle'. Kasey had learned it about two hours before. We put it down real fresh, played it once or twice and kept it. I still think it's one of the best songs that we've ever recorded. It's a different kind of song, it's got a message, it's got harmony, it's catchy, it's simple. So 'Living in the Circle' became our title track.

The family packed the gear up, flew it home to Avoca, reassembled the equipment, worked a few more weeks on it at their Beach House Studio and the new album was ready. The CD was dedicated to the Menghetti family, their best friends on Norfolk Island. The booklet featured a striking painting by Kurt Menghetti—a watercolour which showed the sun setting into the sea, beyond a hillside dotted with Norfolk pines. Above the yellow orb and bands of coloured clouds, the inscription reads:

'As long as the sun sleeps
Memories are forever . . .'

The CD's kickoff single, the hard-driving 'Already Gone', had already enjoyed a great radio run upon *Living in the Circle*'s release in June, when the second single, 'Am I the Only One (Who's Ever Felt This Way)', stood at number 1 on the *Music Network* chart. Kasey wrote 'Already Gone' after getting her inspiration from her favourite TV show.

Kasey: I'm a big *Seinfeld* fan, major, major *Seinfeld* fan. There was a part in an episode where Kramer points to his head and says, 'Up here, I'm already gone.' They had a t-shirt printed up that says, 'In my mind I'm already gone.' I thought that was a really good name for a song so I wrote it—all credit to Kramer, I guess.

Bob Oermann, the sometimes savagely critical singles reviewer for Nashville's *Music Row* magazine (he once referred to a major label artist's latest release as 'the sound of a dinosaur stuck in the La Brea tar pits', had already voiced his opinion on the Dead

Ringer's new material. His biweekly column from 23 November 1996 reviewed 'Already Gone':

> She's one penetrating, powerful hillbilly singer. The band punches hard and fast with percussion, mandolin and electric guitar alternately piercing the mix. The song's got meat on its bones. This bunch could definitely go places.

In May, Oermann noted the release of Dead Ringer Band's follow-up, describing their take on Maria McKee's 'Am I the Only One' as: 'Penetrating Appalachian soul that hits like a flaming arrow into a haystack. If this is Australian country, point me to the Southern Cross and let's go for it.'

He wasn't the only one raving about the McKee cover. The track became Dead Ringer Band's most successful single to date, standing atop the *Music Network* charts for *twelve* weeks until it was finally knocked off by Tim McGraw and Faith Hill's huge US duet hit, 'It's Your Love'.

Kasey: Laurie gave it to us and it's the only song we haven't chosen ourselves to record on an album. On every other album, we just chose them between ourselves, we didn't listen to anybody else. And you know, I can't remember the last time we played that song without making a mistake. That is the least Dead Ringer song I reckon we've ever done; we just don't relax when we play it. I think it's a great song, but we've never ever felt comfortable playing it.

Bill: That was our most successful radio song, which is slightly ironic because we didn't write it and it's probably one of the most pop songs we've ever recorded. I still love it, but it's not particularly country. We've always loved Maria McKee's singing, particularly with Lone Justice; we loved the song, so we did it for the album.

Nashville producers Paul Worley and Blake Chancey also loved 'Am I the Only One' and they recorded a version in 1998 with a new act they were working with from Dallas: three dizzy blondes called The Dixie Chicks. Worley later told the author

Kasey and Diane flank Lucinda Williams during her 1994 tour.

that he liked the Dead Ringer track better than the one he himself had cut with the Chicks.

However, as good as those selections were, the biggest showstoppers on the album were two bittersweet new songs of Kasey's: 'Things Don't Come Easy,' the song she'd written after seeing Matthew Ryan in Nashville, and 'Just Like Yesterday (Song for Gram)', her tribute to Gram Parsons and the effect his music has had upon her.

Lucinda Williams said after hearing the album: 'I knew "Things Don't Come Easy" was a great song within the first four lines and I was crying before it was over.'

Kasey: Personally I think that is one of the best songs on that album. I've noticed some songs you get majorly attached to, 'The Captain' is one song I'm majorly attached to, and 'Things Don't Come Easy' is another. I think that was the most well-recorded song on the album, too; that got the vibe more than any of the other ones, I reckon. It's all true, it kind of best describes us.

Things Don't Come Easy

Hey Moses, part that sea I can't walk on water
My mother cared for me 'cos I'm her only daughter
And you think I'm tall
But that's the shoes upon my feet
Things don't come easy to me

Well the story of my life is mostly filled with questions
And I haven't lived it long enough to ask the best ones
And you think I'm clean
But I feel dirty underneath
Things don't come easy to me

Well I'm older now than yesterday
But my answers seem to get further away
And you think by now that I'd have all I ever need
But things don't come easy to me

When I was a child I lived on dreams and Jesus
My brother always said it don't take much to please us
And you think I'm strong
But that's a weakness that you see
Things don't come easy to me

I once lost my heart in spite of all my learning
But nothing plays a part in my life more than hurting
And I've hurt someone
But monkeys do just what they see
Things don't come easy to me

And I sit here now with nothing that I really need
Things don't come easy to me
They don't come easy
To me
They don't come easy
They don't come easy
To me

Kasey Chambers © 1997, Gibbon Music

157

Dead Ringer Band join Emmylou Harris backstage after her 1997 Sydney show at the State Theatre.

The album closer, 'Just Like Yesterday (Song for Gram)', paid homage to Parsons accurately and lovingly.

Kasey: Dad was a big Gram fan and brought me up on him. There's no one in the world that sounds like him and no one ever will. His music affected me differently than a lot of other artists—everybody affects you in a different way but generally I get the same sort of thing out of listening to Iris and Emmylou and all of those people. Every time I hear Gram it just makes me feel different than when I listen to other music that I like.

I wrote that song on the day that Townes Van Zandt died but I didn't know he had died then. You could change that song for Townes and it would mean the same thing for me because Townes had that sort of effect on me. The day

I found out he died, I got out a 45 of him singing 'Pancho and Lefty' and listened to it over and over again and just bawled my eyes out. I didn't even know the guy—imagine what it would be for the people who did?

It's such an *obvious* thing to say about Gram, 'cause everybody says it, but he was *so ahead* of his time, the sound that they were making for those songs and everything like, oh God, most of the bands today sound like that. I guess I thought about that song, about the lines, more than most other songs. Lots of times they just fall out, but that one I really thought about what I was saying and every line has got such a major meaning towards Gram—every single line. I guess the one that stands out mostly is 'thanks to you, my father understands me'—I mean me and Dad just . . . I guess musically are more the same.

Just Like Yesterday (Song for Gram)

Under labels of dirty sounds and heroes
There's your name written in stone
And I can hear the steel guitar is playin'
And it sounds like someone that I've known

I've no shoes upon my feet to stand on
But my feet feel concrete on the ground
Thanks to you my father understands me
Boy you sure know how to turn the world around

Chorus
Me, I'm from a small town
But I've been spending most my time away
But I still hear you every time the wind blows
And it sounds just like yesterday

There's no wall of steel wrapped around me
There's no hand that holds me when I fall
But all my years of hearing you remind me
That feeling bad is not the worst of all

159

Now sometimes you're the last thing I think of
'Cos I try not to think much anymore
And thanks to you I sometimes understand me
But I wonder what the understanding's for

Kasey Chambers © 1997, Gibbon Music

The June release of *Living in the Circle* again drew praise from key critics in Sydney and Melbourne, including Keith Glass' review in Melbourne's *Herald-Sun* on 29 June:

In daughter Kasey, the Chambers family has the best female country singer in Australia, no contest.

The family also has a great multi-instrumentalist in father Bill, while son Nash managed to record this album as well as handle bass, guitar and vocal duties . . . *Living in the Circle* is raw, but right, traditional yet progressive. The world should be their oyster. *Living in the Circle* is a pearl of an album.

Bruce Elder, of the *Sydney Morning Herald*, checked in the following day with even more fervent praise, beginning his remarks by stating:

This is, without dispute or argument, the best country music album ever recorded in Australia. The Dead Ringers are the only Australian band who have understood, in a profound and intelligent way, how the best of Australian and American country music can be blended to create something with a distinct Aussie sensibility and a level of American musical sophistication . . . Forget every other Aussie vocalist, male or female, Kasey Chambers has a voice to die for—a delicious mixture of huskiness, tenderness and country heartache. Her version of Townes Van Zandt's 'If I Needed You' puts her on a par with Iris DeMent or Lucinda Williams. Five stars.

Bob Oermann, on the case again, sent his praises from Nashville in his 8 July column:

Enchanting. This girl has the voice of a hillbilly superstar and the family backing band does everything exactly right. Simply eloquent. Somebody give these Aussies a US deal, then stand back and watch 'em charm the pants off the public.

160

Once again, their work attracted interest in Music City. Rick Blackburn, President of Atlantic Records, Nashville, absolutely adored the title cut and expressed an interest in discussing matters with the band. Blackburn was an industry veteran who had helmed CBS's Nashville office, overseeing the careers of such artists as Johnny Cash, George Jones, Tammy Wynette, Merle Haggard, Rosanne Cash, Ricky Skaggs and Rodney Crowell, among others. By 1997, he had been in charge of Atlantic's Nashville's office for the last eight years and was then enjoying success with John Michael Montgomery, Tracy Lawrence and Confederate Railroad.

Inasmuch as Massive was the issuing record label for *Living in the Circle*, discussions—like the prior talks with Almo Sounds— were conducted between the US label and Laurie Dunn. Blackburn proposed a deal where he would license the *Living in the Circle* album in the United States and also have rights in the rest of the world, excluding Australia and New Zealand. Massive would get a substantial advance for the album and a royalty rate on all sales. They would also be allowed to use all the Atlantic singles and videos in Australia and New Zealand without charge during the entire course of what could be a seven-album deal, if Atlantic exercised all their options to retain the group.

Matters proceeded further this time than they had with Almo Sounds. Blackburn, Atlantic's Business Affairs people in New York, the band, the author and Dunn had discussions and reviewed proposals over deal points during the next few months.

Meanwhile, the band played on, scooping up their second consecutive MO Award in June, receiving another reminder of their importance to the fans as a live act. They were headliners at the raucous Gympie Muster in August, darted over to Tasmania for a week in September and worked a week on the west coast of Australia, driving about a 2500 kilometre loop from Perth to Kalgoorlie, south to Esperance and Albany, then back to Mandurah.

Just before undertaking the transcontinental hop to Perth, Dead Ringer Band was again in attendance at the ARIA Awards. *Living in the Circle*, like *Home Fires*, was one of the five finalist nominees. As defending champions, some reckoned them the favourites in 1997 but the judges felt otherwise: Graeme Connors carried home the trophy for his *The Road Less Travelled* album, winner of two Golden Guitars back in January.

Alas, over in Nashville, the Ringers' bid for a contract with Atlantic had met rough seas. Though Rick Blackburn had been doggedly trying to engineer a deal with Massive for some four months, he was losing patience by October. According to him, Massive wanted too much in the way of royalties and they refused to consider any compromise position.

The situation between Massive and Dead Ringer Band had become strained. The band's legal status was complicated by the fact that, although they had agreed to a three-album deal with Massive, and a contract was prepared by the label, it was never signed. With the Atlantic offer on the table, Laurie was pushing them to sign a new agreement which would have tied them to Massive for all the albums covered by the Atlantic contract. Additionally, Massive was demanding to be cut into the potentially lucrative publishing revenue the band would receive should their recordings become popular in the United States and/or elsewhere in the world. Inasmuch as Massive had not, to that point, even established a publishing operation, the band was none too keen on entering into such an arrangement.

Though Dunn had always maintained Dead Ringer Band was like a family to him, and that he was 100 per cent for the Ringers landing a US deal—indeed, up to that point had done everything possible to help in that effort, now that a contract was on the table he was singing a different tune. According to Blackburn, Dunn continued to demand that he receive '40 per cent of worldwide gross' from Atlantic and that the band cut him into their publishing.

Dunn's efforts to control every aspect of the negotiations, to extend their recording deal with Massive and to share in their potential publishing revenues did not sit well with the fiercely independent Chambers family. On the one hand, they felt an obligation to Laurie and realised that Massive had been very beneficial to their career development. Initially, they expressed the desire to include Laurie and Massive as a part of the pending Atlantic deal. But on the other hand, they did not feel comfortable in signing their publishing interests over to Massive and were puzzled and frustrated by Dunn's continuing inflexibility in the negotiations.

During this period, the Chambers family looked for career guidance from Michael Browning, one of Australia's most successful rock managers. Browning had played a vital role in building AC/DC's career, especially their US breakthrough, and he had also been a key player in the team that had launched INXS, another globally successful Australian rock band. Everyone in the Dead Ringer camp felt the group needed help from someone with experience in creating overseas success and with practical knowledge of how to resolve knotty contractual issues.

Bill: He came to one of our gigs. He was an interesting guy, very helpful and quite enthusiastic. I don't know if he fully understood where we were coming from—I think that was one problem. We got involved with him for a while and he was helpful in trying to get us out of the Massive deal, talking to lawyers, all that sort of thing. I somehow fancied if he'd gotten our music, he'd still be involved . . . we got on well with him and we left on good terms . . .

In early December, Blackburn lost patience and formally withdrew the offer, suggesting that the group stay in touch with him and let him know when they were able to deal as free agents. Once again, Dead Ringer Band's US deal had gone sour, this time even closer to fruition than the Almo Sounds contract had been just seven months before. Losing two possible US record deals in less than a year would be enough to knock the pins from under anyone, and this latest setback was a hard blow for the band.

Diane: I don't think we did totally shake that one off; that was a pretty big knock and it was also at a time, emotionally, that we all floundered incredibly. Restlessness started to creep into our lives then. I don't think we ever really fought back strong enough after that one.

Years of constant touring and living together were taking their toll. The stresses of trying to keep a band, a family and a marriage together mounted and were exacerbated by the loss of the deal with Atlantic. The band's family unity, so long a given in their lives, was shattered when Bill moved out of the house. He began sharing accommodation with Audrey Auld, a Tasmanian-born singer he had met and befriended while producing her debut EP, *Audrey*, earlier in the year.

The year had begun full of promise with a pending US record deal, a fresh ARIA award in hand, a hot new single atop the charts and a hot new CD on the way. By November, the family unit was shaken and the Chambers' emotional state had all but disintegrated. As 1998 dawned, they still had no US deal, they'd lost the ARIA Award in October, relations between the band and Massive were strained, to say the least, and Bill and Diane, after twenty-seven years of marriage, had separated.

Bill related his feelings in a 1998 fax:

> Nash, Kasey and Diane are spending Xmas at Norfolk Island. So this is my first Xmas alone, ever. A little weird and sad but I could not have kept going the direction I was in the last twelve months. I almost had a nervous breakdown due to band pressure, touring and family upsets, then the added pressure of the Atlantic deal and our rough treatment from Laurie Dunn nearly sunk my ship for a while.

Bill elaborated on the situation in a 1999 interview:

Bill: I felt Massive let us down in a few different ways—we were a little disillusioned by then. We'd had three or four albums out and it hadn't happened, we hadn't made any money, our gigs were becoming hard work and we felt that no one understood us. By this time, too, the pressure of touring, the pressure of booking and all that sort of thing had started to take its toll on Diane and myself. We were arguing a lot and the kids could see all this. It was mainly over the pressure, not the music itself, but trying to run a band of this calibre when it was all in the family. We were in a band with our children, we all lived in the same house, every time the phone rang it was about music. We toured together.

164

If we ever went on a holiday, which was fairly rare, that was all together. We just spent too much time together.

We started to have problems with our record company—that turned into a minor war. We had to hire a lawyer to try to sort it all out with the record company's lawyer. By the time we finished all that business, which took a while, we'd run up a bill big enough that we had to sell our house at Southend, which Diane and I had owned. That created pressure. Our lives just turned into one big argument for about twelve months straight. We were just arguing the whole time, mainly over business. And we wanted to get away from Massive Records. We wanted to leave on good terms: we still liked Laurie as a person—still do—but we had one album to go.

11

Hopeville

Thus, as the first rays of light from 1998 fell on the Chambers family—first on Diane, Kasey and Nash on Norfolk, then on Bill, at Avoca Beach—all of them had to be wondering if the price of fame was worth the cost they were paying. For the first time in their lives, the family were not together for Christmas, turning what should have been a time of joy and celebration into the saddest holiday season any of them had faced.

Diane: It was definitely the toughest time of our lives and career. Our personal life was disintegrating all around us. The downfall just slowly continued. In fact, looking back, I don't know how we even coped, but people always find strength from somewhere. Overnight, Nash had to handle the music office work because I became emotional and distraught—it was his strength that helped us all get through. But there were still bigger and better things ahead and I think that's manifesting itself through Kasey.

The Australian country music industry is a small world. It wasn't long before news of the Ringers' problems spread beyond their Avoca Beach household. Gossip started to build via radio pro-

166

grams and the following item, which appeared on 3 January in the eccentric online publication, *Country Beat*:

Exclusive: Max Thorburn is the first to speak to the Dead Ringer Band.
The Dead Ringer Band will fold. They will perform one gig at Tamworth (but not at the Awards night because they were not asked) and then do a handful of gigs on a tour of Victoria with South Aussie artist Doug Ashdown.

'A number of things have happened,' Nash Chambers said. 'Mum and Dad have split but not for the reasons which have been rumoured.

'It's a combination of things,' he said. 'We have been touring for eight years now—it's been hard and we want to have a bit of a break.

'The last straw was when our American deal fell through. It wasn't us, it wasn't America, it was the Massive label in Australia. I phoned Rick Blackburn at Atlantic myself and he said that the label wouldn't even let us sign a deal like Massive wanted. We would have been stitched up for fifteen years. The Aussie label would have got all the money. It was greed . . . A lot of people are blaming Dad for the break-up but that's not the reason. We've been under a lot of strain, a lot of pressures and a marriage breakdown is just one of those things which happen—it's life.'

Nash did not deny that his father was romantically linked with singer Audrey Auld, who did a recording project at the Dead Ringer Studios last year.

'They are very good friends,' Nash said. 'The stories have got just a little out of hand.'

Indeed. It's unclear whether the stories began with the radio accounts or Thorburn's piece but, in Nash's mind, Max had turned what Nash had thought was a confidential, friendly conversation into an interview for publication. The Dead Ringer Band's 11 January press release, penned by Nash, attempted to set matters straight:

We wish news regarding our gigs would spread as quickly as the recent rumours regarding the Dead Ringer Band. Here is the *ONLY* official report.

The band has not split up. We are currently working on our new album, which will be released through Massive Records later in '98 and are also recording a song for the new Slim Dusty Tribute album for EMI.

Aside from these things we will not be touring for at least six months while we take a well-earned break that we have not had since 1992 . . .

. . . It is true that our proposed deal from Atlantic Records in Nashville will not proceed any further. It is also true that Bill and Diane have separated due to career, financial and personal pressures. This separation is the result of the pressures and *NOT* the cause . . .

. . . We do *NOT* appreciate private conversations being placed on the Internet, especially after they have been extremely exaggerated and quote us saying things that were never said.

We would like to thank those who have supported Dead Ringer Band over the years, it has been greatly appreciated and we hope you will continue to do so.

We are a little worn out but are all alive and well.

Regards,

Dead Ringer Band

That release either fanned the flames until they burned themselves out or extinguished them, or perhaps the industry moved on to other topics of gossip. In any case, the furore died down, leaving Dead Ringer Band to work on finishing the new album under the most trying of circumstances and to prepare for their Tamworth show.

The one bright spot shining through the haze was that the band was nominated for two awards in 1998. In addition to a finalist placing in the Group/Duo category (their fourth in a row), they were nominated for the first time for the prestigious Album of the Year honour, competing with Troy Cassar-Daley, Shanley Del, Anne Kirkpatrick and Beccy Cole. Additionally, their recording of 'Living in the Circle' was nominated for Song of the Year. Should 'Living in the Circle' be victorious, that award would go to the songwriter, Richard Porteous, but as the recording artists the Ringers could certainly share in the glory.

Before they headed north to Tamworth, however, there was an album to complete. As you can imagine, given the stresses and turmoil surrounding the family, that CD was not an easy one to record. The group decided to make an album of 'cover' songs, to create a CD of favourites, songs they had been playing for years, instead of writing new material, rehearsing it and adding a few covers, as they had done on *Red Desert Sky*, *Home Fires* and

Living in the Circle. Thus the fourth Dead Ringer CD, *Hopeville*, contained no new songs written by any of the Chambers.

Diane: Well, we weren't there emotionally to do that, were we? I guess it was the right type of album to close an era. We felt it needed a positive swing somewhere and that's why titled it *Hopeville.* And we all did need some hope back at that era. Our lives were really crumbling . . . I know we very much liked the title 'Tainted', referring to the influences of so so many people on our music, but we knew that that word, 'tainted', coupled with what was happening in our personal life would be misinterpreted.

Nash: *Hopeville* was sort of a strange album for us. We were a little bit frustrated with the country music scene here and the style of music we were doing. We had problems with our record label; we were sort of fed up. We'd been on the road for ten years, virtually without a break, mainly due to financial reasons: to just survive we just had to keep working. And when *Hopeville* came around, we wanted to do an album of all our favourite singer/songwriters.

Bill: *Hopeville* was made for two reasons. One was that we had to make another album to complete our contract with Massive. But the main reason, the true reason, was to pay tribute to some of the many singer/songwriters that we covered songs from over the years. Fans and radio people used to ask us who our influences were, so we thought, 'Let's do an album and show who our influences are', so we recorded a Jimmie Rodgers song, a Hank Williams song, a Nanci Griffith song, a Steve Earle song, a Townes Van Zandt song, a Rodney Crowell song, all our favourite people in the world. We didn't make *Hopeville* for radio, we didn't make it to sell a lot of albums, we made it for us. We wanted to say, 'These are the people who have influenced us', all these people have shaped our music and our lives.

Kasey: It was pretty inevitable what songs were going to go on it. We didn't really have any arguments about anything;

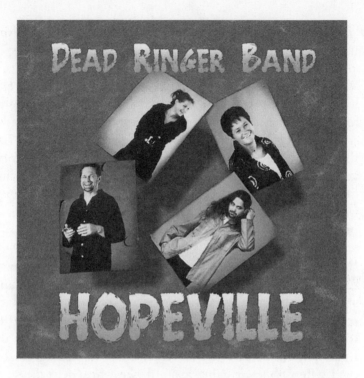

The long-delayed album, Hopeville, *released late 1998.*

without knowing it, we basically let the crowds choose all those songs. I think 'Speed of the Sound of Loneliness' is the best song Nash sings, and he likes singing it which means something, 'cause there aren't a lot of songs that he likes to sing. We get lots of requests for that song. I've always wanted to record 'I Wish it Would Rain', ever since I heard Jann Browne sing it—that was just unbelievable.

Nash: Mum and Kasey were out on Norfolk a lot of the time, so Dad and I recorded most of *Hopeville* in a totally different way to *Living in the Circle*, where we had plenty of time. *Hopeville* was done more like a standard album where you go in and do the band tracks and then build on it from there.

Bill: It didn't receive great reviews, but when I listen to it, I'm still proud of it. It's hard to make an album like that: it's not easy to make better versions of the best songs of all time.

We knew before we even started it that we were biting off something we maybe couldn't chew. How can you improve on an Emmylou Harris classic or a Steve Earle song, or a Rodney Crowell or Gram Parsons song? They're all classics. But it was our way of saying, 'These are the people who have influenced us' and the album still says what we wanted it to say. We're still very proud of *Hopeville*, even though some of the critics didn't quite get it. Some of the Australian critics thought we'd lost the plot totally because, unfortunately, some of our country music experts hadn't ever heard most of these artists, which is a bit of a worry in itself. These are the people that are the best in the business of writing songs and singing. In my opinion, if you're not familiar with Gram Parsons or Lucinda Williams or with Townes Van Zandt or Rodney Crowell, maybe you don't know much about country music.

Kasey: I just love 'Sometimes She Forgets'. I first heard it on the *Train a Comin'* album when I went to Gympie. I just sat in the car and listened to it and I thought it was the best album Steve Earle had ever made. It was just around the time when there was a lot of the Nashville crap coming out and I was at my wit's end about music and everything. It'd been a while since I bought an album where there'd been true country music on it. 'Sometimes She Forgets'—man, it was such a beautiful story, but the melody and everything was just unreal. I sat down and wrote 'The Hard Way' after that, after hearing that song.

I've been doing 'Something About What Happens When We Talk' for years and years. I've probably done more Lucinda songs in my set over the last ten years than any other artist. If somebody wanted a Lucinda Williams cover band, I could do a night just like that. Of course, it's a lot better live than it is on that album. It's one of those songs that I've never gotten sick of singing.

The album title was drawn from 'Hello Hopeville', a Michelle Shocked song whose lyrics about a vacation and a cruel world seemed particularly poignant to the shattered family group.

There was just one small problem. After hearing the record, Massive refused to release it, claiming that it was not up to 'industry standards' inasmuch as it contained no original material. This was an interesting position for Laurie Dunn to take, since covers records have a long, proud tradition in country and pop music, dating back to the 1950s and the birth of the album as an art form. Many country stars, even ones who write most of their own material, have at one time or another done a record of 100 per cent outside material—in fact, Dolly Parton, Reba McEntire and Dwight Yoakam had released covers records in the past year alone. Nevertheless, another legal struggle between the Chambers family and Massive Records now loomed.

This, then, was the background when Dead Ringer Band rolled into Tamworth, late in January. It was a particularly difficult time for Diane. Now that her and Bill's marital problems were public knowledge, she had to endure the sympathy of well-meaning friends everywhere she went, the wound to her heart reopened with each fresh encounter. She had to go onstage, performing with her head held high, beside her now-separated husband, in her roles as bass player and mum for the band, despite the heartbreak and pain raging inside her.

Somehow she and Dead Ringer Band found the inner strength to make it through their show at the RSL club and the additional pressure they felt when they noticed several high-ranking EMI executives in the audience. They also made it through their induction into the 'Hands of Fame' sidewalk of star hand prints ceremony, but they were all running on emotional fumes by the time of the Toyota Country Music Awards of Australia on Saturday night. In retrospect, it may have been a blessing that they didn't perform on the show that night.

This time, however, the fickle finger of fate pointed in their direction: they won back the Group/Duo of the Year trophy from The Wheel, repeating their 1995 victory. Troy Cassar-Daley was the big winner, taking home trophies for Male Vocalist, Video, Track and Album. Two former Australians now living in Nashville, Keith Urban and Sherrié Austin, won Golden Guitars, in the Instrumental and New Talent categories. Though Cassar-Daley's *True Believer* CD won over *Living in the Circle* in the Album of the Year category, Dead Ringer Band's title track was chosen APRA

Song of the Year. Writer Richard Porteous thus earned a Golden Guitar with the very first song he had ever had recorded by a major country artist, just as Bill Chambers had done six years before when Slim Dusty had recorded his 'Things are Not the Same on the Land'.

After Tamworth, Dead Ringer Band soldiered on through another month of contracted shows, then retreated—for the first time in their respective lives—to separate corners, each attempting to understand and absorb the changes to their emotional terrain as well as their business situation. They had not taken a vacation during the six years of hard touring since they had decided to make music their full-time career. And they had never in their lives been apart from each other for an extended period.

12
Retreats, Resolutions and Renewals

After completing their touring obligations, Bill, Diane, Nash and Kasey found themselves at loose ends for the first time in their lives. Each handled their unexpected vacation in a different way as they worked to cope with life as separate entities instead of a single band/family unit.

Diane: It was more than just a husband and wife splitting up. It affected all of us. I did a bit of a retreat to Norfolk where I felt comfortable. I was surrounded by people there who cared and loved and nurtured me in an incredibly special way. I owe so much to them for the part they played in helping me rebuild myself emotionally.

Kasey: We went to Africa a little while after Mum and Dad broke up. Mum really wanted to do something outrageous, something on her own. I was a bit worried about her going to Africa by herself. She was just talking about it, and I kind of felt as though I really needed to do something that wasn't centred around music for once in my life. I'd never been anywhere or done anything except music. So we saved up, it took us a while, and we picked out this safari that went from Zimbabwe to Kenya.

Diane: Kasey and I went to Africa at that particular time as we certainly needed something in our lives to give us some goals

Diane and Kasey atop Chaquenya in Zimbabwe, with guide Zonzo attending.

to strive for, to rebuild what we'd just lost. That was an amazing trip, an amazing experience. That trip was only made possible through the help of so many friends and family. But it brought, firstly, a challenge back into our lives, and it brought adventure and excitement. And it also brought compassion back in to our lives.

Kasey: Being over there and experiencing all of that was the most amazing experience. I remember ringing Dad when I first got to Africa. I just bawled and bawled, all I wanted to do was go home. I'd never been apart from Dad—a week here, a week there, but going to Africa is the longest time I've ever been apart from my family. I was with Mum but it was the longest time ever that we'd all been apart.

Diane: We did about seven weeks through six, seven countries on a big, old, rough truck. We did all our own cooking, pitched tents every night, Kasey and I stayed in a little two-person tent. We were with a group of fourteen plus the driver and the guide. The people came from all over: Scotland, England, Amsterdam, Germany, New Zealand, Australia. We've made lifelong friends with a few of them.

Kasey: I was just so homesick. I'd just never been apart from the family. Now the family was suddenly apart and it was really strange. I don't think we've been apart for very long since then either, two weeks here or something like that. Musically, I actually got a few songs out of that trip too, for my record and for the next Dead Ringer album.

Diane: It was quite an experience to see so many wild animals in their own habitat—animals that you only ever see in pictures or on telly—and to mix and mingle, hug and love kids and people, just the Africans in general, not just the kids: the mums and the dads and grannies. We actually went to school with the kids, we saw their lifestyle, their poverty, their hardships and their lack of materialism. But we also experienced their contented happiness despite their poverty. All of that was quite special.

It was good for Kasey and I. We've always been close, to do a trip together was very rewarding. Both her and Nash gave me enormous strength through all this. The love, the patience and care they've given to me is just heartwarming.

Kasey: Mum and Dad had just broken up. That had a big effect on me. It was a sad time. I was quite happy for them to be apart because they were happier then. Nash and I were mature enough to know that it's not all one big happy family all the time in this world. I just wanted Mum and Dad to be happy. I didn't care if that meant that the family wasn't the same kind of family any more. The bottom line is, if they're happier being apart, then I was all for them being apart. I think they are. I think Mum and Dad are kind of better people now than they were in the last couple years of their relationship. Mum is a stronger, more independent person than she's ever been. She's always been the mum of the family, now she's kind of a person on her own. We get along better now than we ever have. I reckon we're more like best friends than mother and daughter.

Bill: I think those six months really saved our relationship with each other. Diane and I are still not together, but we're friends again. We really abused that friendship for quite a few years, it was hanging on a very slender thread. In fact I wasn't getting on very well with Nash either. He's a man now. He's very confident, he knows what he's doing and when there are two men in the camp you're bound to have some problems. Nash and I were just fighting all the time. I was out of control, to be quite honest. I would jump down anyone's throat for no reason, at that stage. I was drinking, everywhere we went. I would get to a gig sometimes, and if the manager of the club said the wrong thing, I would jump down his throat. This is during that period when Diane and I were going through the worst times and the band was in the throes of—we talked about breaking up but we somehow knew we wouldn't. We wondered if we'd overdone it.

Diane: Well, we couldn't have kept the band going as in straight away. We had to have that break. All of us in our own different way had to deal with an enormous trauma in our lives because we had been so close as a family, a unit, everything.

Bill: Six months away from it changed my relationship with Nash. We suddenly started to get on really well, to talk about things like father and son, like old times. Kasey and I get on better now than we ever did and Diane and I do too. Diane and I are both very proud of her. Diane does the merchandise and helps out. Nash and I play in the band, so that's almost back to business. Things are really not that far from where they used to be.

During the Dead Ringers' down time, Bill worked on his side project, recording a few tracks as Luke & The Drifters, a group devoted to playing the music of Hank Williams and other 1950s country greats. He teamed with Audrey to record *Looking Back to See*, a charmingly retro CD of old-style country duets. The two also launched their 'Hillbilly Jam' in Sydney, a weekly show with a rotating cast of players and guest artists, all of whom wanted to perform 'real' country music, not the 1990s prefab Nashville variety.

Diane: The time off was very necessary. We had to do that. We'd all fallen apart, emotionally and musically, and for a while I thought that was the finish of it musically. But time away showed us that we could still continue with Dead Ringer, sort ourselves out on a personal level and we could still work on a professional level. And that's just what we did. I feel there's been a guiding hand seeing things we can't see. Somewhere along the line someone knew our path better than we did.

Maybe Nash and Kasey knew the path before their parents. After travelling about a bit with Worm, down to Adelaide and up to Cairns on an ill-fated expedition to work on a fishing boat, Nash settled in to do some serious thinking and planning.

Nash: Dad had moved out of the house here and Mum and Kasey were either on Norfolk most of the time or they did their African trip. So I was here on my own. I knew I was now doing the management and I also knew I wasn't very experienced in that area, so I spent three or four months reading books, talking to people and looking at what record companies were doing. I wanted to learn what labels were doing for their artists, analysing those relationships.

Kasey: A solo career is something I wanted to do. I didn't really know that it was going to be quite as serious as it is now, to be honest. I thought one day it would be, but I kind of thought that no matter what, Dead Ringer would always be the number one focus. I didn't really know people would take it quite as seriously as they have. That's fine with me, I probably don't take it as serious as everybody else, but that's okay, that's why I'm still having fun.

I'd saved up a lot of these songs during Dead Ringer time. I'd play them to Nash and Dad and they'd say, 'I think that's kind of better for your solo album, maybe you should save that one.' So I knew back then that I was going to. At one stage we considered bringing *Living in the Circle* out as a Kasey Chambers album. Nash had really restless feet and wanted to move to America. And we're like, 'What's going to happen to the band?' I was the one who said, 'I don't really want to do that.' I just wasn't really ready to be on my own. We'd recorded the album as Dead Ringer and I didn't want to do that. When I did my own album, I wanted to be different from Dead Ringer, otherwise I would have just brought out another Dead Ringer record.

Nash: We'd had offers from all the major labels here, they said to come and talk if we're looking for a deal for Kasey. EMI had expressed interest prior to that but definitely hadn't been pushy in any way. They just said, 'If you're ever looking for a deal, we're definitely keen to talk.' I pretty much didn't speak to anyone else. I worked out the deal we wanted, I went to EMI and just said, 'This is the sort of deal we want. This is the sort of artist Kasey is. We can talk to everyone else, but we don't want to, we want to be with you guys.' They felt the same. So we sat down and structured an agreement that worked for both of us.

EMI's interest in the band had begun with Leon Concannon and David Baxter, who had seen several Dead Ringer performances in addition to noticing them at awards shows and TV appearances. Concannon, in fact, had been excited ever since he saw them perform 'Already Gone' during the 1998 Toyota Country Music Awards of Australia show. The new EMI Managing Director, Tony Harlow, freshly in office from positions in sales/marketing and the international departments with the label in London, first saw the group at Gympie in August 1998 and was immediately enthralled by the music, look and attitude of this two-generational band.

Bill: I always believed Kasey would go solo. I think we all did. In fact, she's the only one that didn't—she was the last one to want to go solo. She always said, 'No, I love the band. I love what we do and I don't want to sing all night anyway.' Kasey's a little bit lazy, she's not all that driven, she loves to have fun. I don't think she'll ever grow up in some ways—she's a child in some ways. I remember Laurie Dunn used to describe her as 'nineteen going on twelve', and there's some truth to that. I'm saying that in the most sincere, heartfelt way: I love her. But she wants to have fun and that comes out in the music, in her singing. She doesn't take it as seriously as she should, but I'm glad she doesn't if you know what I mean. If Diane and I hadn't parted, I don't think Kasey would have gone on her own. I think the band would have just kept going if we could have tolerated the situation and each other. Kasey would have just stayed, 'cause she was reasonably happy just going along. But when everything changed overnight, that time apart made us realise that we all still love what we do, we all love each other and we want to do the best thing.

Nash came home from his holiday believing that it was time for Kasey to go on her own. She'd been writing a lot of songs—she wrote three or four while she was in Africa. I'd had enough time away from the band and my family to want to do more with it again. Suddenly, we started to realise what we had and I think that's come out in Kasey's album. Even though it's quite different to the Ringers' records, it's really an extension of what we'd been doing all along, Nash produced it, Kasey sang on it, I played on most of the tracks, and helped with the arrangements, so it was pretty much an extension of what was meant to happen, I guess.

Diane: During that time I'd never felt she was quite ready to step out. Over the years we'd had pressure from the industry and we fought against it. Being the mother, I felt she wasn't emotionally ready to take on a solo career and I believe I knew and loved my daughter more than they did to make that decision. Through Bill's and my split-up, she 'grew up', she matured and faced responsibilities that she hadn't before. I think that prepared her, stabilised her a lot for the next step.

When interest came in her going solo, I was a little sceptical for a start because I didn't want her making a move based on emotion. I wanted her to stabilise a bit from our split-up. You go through so many different emotions when you go through a trauma or a tragedy, and you can make wrong decisions in those situations, when emotions over-whelm reasoning. I was apprehensive when she first started talking about it because I felt she was still riding on emotion. I didn't know which, but she hadn't grounded.

But then, within six months, I could see stabilising in her and in Nash, and I felt, 'no, the timing is right.' Once I felt confident myself, as a mother, that they were able to be stable, to be grounded and that they could face all that was ahead of them, then I felt good about it. I wasn't interested in whether Joe Blow said she was ready, or Tom, Dick and Harry said she was ready, I had to know that she was ready in herself. From me as a mother, not from me as a manager or as a bass player or as a friend but as her mother. Once that happened and I felt it, then I thought that it was great for her to go solo.

It took a bit of evolving. When we were in Africa she was talking about it, but I knew then she was talking from emotion: I could feel it in her. She was grasping, clasping at something to replace what she'd lost. She wasn't ready then, in my mind. No, it just evolved itself over about six months.

Though they hadn't done a show since late February, the Ringers' near non-stop touring throughout 1997 and the first two months of 1998 was still fresh in the judges' minds when time came for the annual MO Awards in June. For the third consecutive year, Dead Ringer Band was chosen as Best Country Performer—Group/Duo. Though the award was warmly received by the group, it had to be a bittersweet victory as, at the time, they had no idea of their future—and indeed, were uncertain whether Dead Ringer Band would ever perform again.

Meanwhile, the logjam with Massive continued. Laurie still steadfastly refused to release *Hopeville*, leaving the band in a legal 'no man's land'. They couldn't sign with another label before they completed their obligation to Massive, and if Massive rejected the album entirely they would either have to make another record or sue the label to try to force the release of *Hopeville*. The irony of it all was that they had never actually signed the licensing contract Massive had presented back in 1995. They had hired a lawyer to examine it but, when he sent back a three-page letter detailing his concerns about numerous contractual proposals from Massive, and upon receiving his bill for just this simple procedure, the band realised it would take several thousand dollars (which they did not have) to try to effect the changes in the contract the lawyer felt was necessary. So they had just gone along, making their music and hoping everything would work out. By the time they realised that they probably ought to sign some sort of legally binding agreement, when the US interest started percolating, Massive began pressuring them to sign another contract, this one calling for even more albums over a much longer term.

So, even though they had not signed any agreement with Massive, they had been in business with them since the release of *Home Fires* in November of 1995. This meant they had given that contract their 'implied consent' and couldn't simply walk away. Now two-and-a-half years on, they were fenced in by the terms of an unsigned contract which had never been negotiated on behalf of the band. As anyone knows, if a person is selling something, as the Ringers were selling their services, the first offer is only a starting point for further negotiations during which each party attempts to obtain the best possible deal. But since the band had never formally responded by having a lawyer draft their initial requests for changes to the document, that original offer represented the only terms binding on either party. The pertinent clause relating to *Hopeville* read that an album was not deemed to be accepted until 'Massive provides written acceptance to the Artist that such master recordings are of a satisfactory technical and commercial standard'.

This was a debatable point. From a purely technical standpoint, *Hopeville* was probably a better record than *Living in the Circle* since Nash had learned considerably more about the recording process by then and had upgraded some of their recording equipment. Massive's main complaint was that, since the album contained no original material written by the band, it did not meet the above standard.

The songs themselves would certainly meet anyone's standards of being 'commercial'. Five of *Hopeville*'s twelve songs had reached a position of number 7 or higher on the US country charts during their original release or in subsequent cover versions. A sixth selection, 'TB Blues', a Jimmie Rodgers staple, predated trade magazine charts but is regarded as one of Rodgers' best numbers and is still in print today, over seventy years after 'the father of country music' first waxed the tune. Two additional selections on the album, John Prine's 'Speed of the Sound of Loneliness' and Townes Van Zandt's 'White Freightliner Blues', were charted singles by Kim Carnes and Jimmie Dale Gilmore respectively, though neither became big hits. The remaining four selections, Nanci Griffith's 'I Wish It Would Rain', Michelle Shocked's 'Hello Hopeville', Lucinda Williams' 'Something About What Happens When We Talk' and Gram Parsons' 'Return Of The Grievous Angel', would be rated as classic songs by any reasonably informed student of country or popular music history.

As for the 'commercial standard' phrase as it applies to albums of cover material, well who knows how commercial any album will be until it is actually in the record stores? Under this logic—refusing to release an album because it has no new songs by an artist who had previously recorded primarily original material, ABC-Paramount in the United States could have rejected

Ray Charles' *Modern Sounds in Country & Western Music*, an epochal 1962 album of country covers merged with big band arrangements. That LP became one of the most influential records in the history of country music and to this day, thirty-nine years later, is still the biggest selling album 'The Genius' has ever released.

While the Ringers probably had a stronger legal position on this issue, it would cost them thousands of dollars they did not have to do battle with their label. Massive was much better equipped to meet the financial obligations such a legal imbroglio entailed. And lastly, a legal fracas such as this could easily take months, even several years, to settle. Kasey could not embark on her solo career until this issue was resolved because the 1995 contract claimed a first option on any albums made by any group member.

In the beginning, the Ringers tried to play the game, engaging one of Sydney's top entertainment business lawyers, Randall Harper, to argue their case. However, after months of meetings with Harper and his subsequent contact with Massive's lawyer, they were still nowhere near a solution. By July, all Dead Ringer Band had from this effort was mounting legal bills. In fact, they eventually had to sell their family home in Southend to pay Harper the fees they owed him for his ultimately unsuccessful efforts on their behalf.

Desperate, Bill and Diane decided to meet personally with Laurie to try to negotiate a solution. They drove down from Avoca in mid-July to meet with him, at a time when their own emotional states regarding each other were turbulent, to say the least.

Bill: Diane and I talked our way out of the Massive thing. We were at our wits' end by then. I still remember the day we went there, we had a pretty heavy discussion all the way down. We'd spent a lot of money on lawyers, we sold our house, we tried lots of things and then we spent two hours one day talking to Laurie and we got further by doing that. We had to eat humble pie a little bit. Laurie just exasperated the lawyer, everywhere he turned, he simply wouldn't negotiate. So that's why we tried talking in the finish and that did it. But I think we'd be there still if we were hoping lawyers could fix it.

The price of their freedom was steep. In the agreement, signed by all parties on 30 July, Dead Ringer Band formally licensed *Home Fires, Living in the Circle* and *Hopeville* to Massive for five years, until the end of September 2003. Additionally, they were also required to license *Red Desert Sky* to Massive as soon as that album reverted back to the band when the existing licence with Larrikin (now Festival Records) expired later in 1998. Massive also had the right to release a 'Best Of' compilation album provided they paid the group a $20 000 advance. *Till Now: The Very Best of Dead Ringer Band*, an eighteen-track release, was issued by Massive in April 2000— though with little fanfare.

Finally, in October, Massive released *Hopeville*, some eight months after Nash had mixed and mastered the CD. Bruce Elder of the *Sydney Morning Herald* obviously disagreed with Massive's assertion that the album was not up to commercial standards, writing in his 26 October review:

> The result is fabulous. Kasey Chambers, all huskiness and sexuality, sings with great panache. [Bill] Chambers reaches back to the 1950s and sings 'TB Blues' like a true Okie and, with real imagination and intelligence, the band takes some of the great songs in the country ouvre and gives them all an original spin . . .

The year wasn't just one of legal wrangling and label bick-ering. On a professional level, it was the least active year in Dead Ringer Band's entire existence; they didn't resume touring until they made a ten-date swing through Queensland in October. Kasey, however, had a fresh, emotional rollercoaster to ride in April, although this trip was a pleasant one.

One of her major professional influences, Steve Earle, was booked to play at the 9th Annual East Coast Blues & Roots Festival, in Byron Bay on the New South Wales North Coast. Buddy Miller, another of her huge favourites, was also booked for a set in addition to his duties as Earle's lead guitarist/band leader. Buddy was accustomed to performing shows with his wife, Julie, herself an esteemed songwriter/artist and another of Kasey's

Nash, Buddy Miller, Kasey and Steve Earle at the East Coast
Blues & Roots Festival in Byron Bay, on the northern
New South Wales coast, 1998.

musical heroes. Julie, however, wasn't on this trip; it was a Steve Earle tour, and Buddy was scheduled to do just one show as a featured artist.

Buddy had heard the Dead Ringer Band CDs and asked whether Kasey would like to sing with him, in Julie's stead, at Byron Bay. Needless to say, that wasn't a hard decision to make. It turned out well for Buddy, too, as Kasey already knew all save one of the songs in the set list he emailed her. The show was a major success, as Kasey reported in a letter at the time:

> The gig with Buddy was the single best musical experience of my life. He is my new hero. It was just unbelievable. He is a great guy to work with and the most amazing singer and player. He was very well received, too. We had one rehearsal before the show in his motel room but he was very casual about the whole thing, which made me a little less nervous. Steve Earle came on and did a couple of songs too, which was a buzz for me but even better he stayed and listened to the whole set.

I sang 'The Dark Side of Life' (Lucinda) and Steve came up after the set and said, 'You did a great job and if you're free tomorrow night would you sing a duet with me at my gig?' I was blown away. We did his song 'Poison Lovers' and he also got me up on the last song, 'Johnny Come Lately' to end the show. It was a weekend I'll never forget . . . I'm off to write some songs. I just had the most inspirational weekend of my life so I'm sure there have to be few good songs come out of it . . . If you have Buddy's address could I have a copy 'cos I'd like to send him a *Thank you*.

Eighteen months later, in October 1999, she still recalled that performance vividly:

Kasey: I'd have to say that's probably the best set of music I reckon I've ever heard in my life. I've never heard that many good songs live in one set in my life. And to be an actual part of it, not just to be in the audience, but actually to be out there singing them was like *man*. I'd never met Steve Earle before and he walked on stage and sang in my microphone with me. I was like, wow, that was pretty amazing.

I remember when I first met him, I was in Buddy's motel room with Buddy and Brady and Kelly, the band, rehearsing the set. When I first got to the motel, we didn't know what room he was in but Buddy was singing and it was the *loudest* thing I'd ever heard. He's got the most powerful voice so we heard him from like way down the road, followed the sound up through the motel.

We went in and I remember the first thing Buddy said to me. I said, 'Do you have a piece of paper so I can just write out the order of the songs as we rehearse them' and he said, 'You're not having a list on stage. You can't have a piece of paper down there on stage,' and I go, 'That's okay, I won't then.' He just burst out laughing and he's like, 'You can have it if you want.' I wasn't really going to start yelling at him or anything, 'No, I will have a set list on stage' you know. This is Buddy Miller, man.

Then we're running through these songs, they're just great guys, all three of them and Steve walks in. We're in the middle of doing 'You're Running Wild', the Louvin

Brothers song, and I was like, 'That's Steve Earle.' I mean I've probably been a fan of Steve as long as any artist that I've listened to. I remember listening to Steve on the Nullarbor.

He'd just gone out to get food for Buddy and them. He hands out the food and Buddy introduces me to him. He hardly even says hello. He's got this package of chips, chicken chips, I remember, and he's offering everybody a chip and I was just waiting for him to come around to me, 'cause I wanted to be able to tell everyone that Steve Earle gave me a chicken chip. I was just, *'Please* come around and offer me a chip.' So he put them on the table in front of me and says, 'Help yourself to a chip.' And I didn't want one but I ate one anyway. I was like, 'This is Steve Earle's chip.' That was pretty exciting and then to have him ask me to sing with him was quite overwhelming really. I couldn't really comprehend that for a few days. But even though singing with Steve was amazing as far as, 'Hey, this is Steve Earle and I'm singing a duet with him', musically, I got more out of singing with Buddy that set than I nearly ever have in my life. It was really amazing to be part of that, to be singing harmonies that Lucinda and Julie had sung on the album.

We walked off stage at the end of the show and I said, 'Aren't you going to do "A Million Little Bombs", that's my favourite one.' And Buddy said, 'Oh, alright, let's go out and do it then.' So we went out and did it, just the two of us, after the show had finished. It was pretty amazing.

In addition to getting to see, sing and hang out with Miller and Earle, Kasey also got her first look at another of her musical touchstones in concert, Iris DeMent.

Kasey: I saw Iris do 'No Time to Cry' at the Blues Festival, which was absolutely stunning. I went in by myself. They only had one pass ready for us, it was right at the start of the festival and because I was the biggest Iris fan, I got the pass. I didn't know how good a singer she was, just on her own, until I heard her live. It was unbelievable. But there were about three or four songs that stood out at that show that were just incredible as well as 'No Time to Cry'. 'Easy's Getting Harder Every Day' is just the best song ever.

The ARIA Awards came around in mid-October. Sadly, Dead Ringer Band weren't invited this year. *Hopeville* had been issued far too late for judging consideration—in fact, it wasn't officially released until 5 October. The Chambers family—indeed, heaps of people in the industry—were thrilled to see Shanley Del receive the Best Country Release honour for her scintillating *Your Own Sweet Time* album, redeeming herself from a surprising Tamworth shutout at the Toyota Country Music Awards of Australia back in January, despite multiple finalist nominations.

Dead Ringer Band returned to the Beach House Studio for the first time in almost a full year to record a selection for EMI's *Not So Dusty* tribute CD to Slim Dusty. The concept was to honour the musical and cultural icon by creating an album of interpretations of Slim's classic songs. The commercial kicker was that not all the participating artists were from the country field. Dead Ringer Band were elated to be included, recording 'Saddle Boy', a song they had often sung in their Nullarbor days, as their contribution to a cast which featured Midnight Oil, Paul Kelly, The Screaming Jets, Mental as Anything, Karma County, Ross Wilson, Don Walker, Tom T. Hall and a host of Australian country superstars.

Once the Massive agreement was sorted and basic terms agreed to with EMI, Nash and Kasey began preparations for making her debut solo ablum. By early October, she had made guitar/vocal demos of the songs she intended to record. Unlike *Hopeville*—or, for that matter, any previous Dead Ringer album—Kasey's debut was to be completely composed of her own songs. This was a big step for someone who had never contributed more than four solely written songs to any one of the the group's albums. What's more, they again planned to return to Norlolk, as they had done for *Living in the Circle* two years earlier, transporting their studio 1500 kilometres over the southwest Pacific to the eight by five kilometre island of some 1600 folks that had assumed a special spiritual place in their souls.

13

A Return to Nashville

Kasey's first solo album, *The Captain*, began its journey to completion in October and November. After initial tracking on Norfolk, Nash and Kasey retreated back to Avoca for overdubs. This record featured some augmentation of the normal supporting cast for a Dead Ringer album—in addition to usual guest pickers Mick Albeck and the McCormack brothers, Mark Punch and Kevin Bennett added licks on a couple of tracks, and Bennett also sang background harmony on one tune. There were three more special guests Nash and Kasey wanted to contribute to her debut CD: Buddy Miller, Steve Earle and Julie Miller. However, getting those artists on tape meant a trip to Nashville.

In addition to the recording motive, there were other reasons for the younger generation Chambers to return to 'Music City'. It had been two years since their first visit and, even though the management had kept the media and industry well briefed on their career progress, it was a good idea to make the rounds in person as few of the label execs had met them on the first trip. They had stayed in touch with Rick Blackburn at Atlantic and several other label executives had expressed interest in hearing Kasey's solo material. Encouraged by this response, Nash had brought six 'rough mixes', nearly completed tracks from the forthcoming album, to present during the late November trip. A showcase spot was arranged at the legendary Bluebird Cafe, the city's most famous small club, at 6 p.m. on a Tuesday night, the ideal time for label personnel to stop in after work.

Nash, Kasey and Kurt, Nashville, 1998.

Though they had spent two weeks on their first trip to Nashville, their schedules this time only allowed eight full days in town, and three of those were holidays. Recording was the first priority, so on Sunday afternoon Nash and Kasey, with Kurt Menghetti in tow, strolled into Buddy and Julie Miller's in-house studio, Dogtown, located a few blocks off Music Row. By that evening Buddy had added guitar parts to 'Don't Talk Back', guitar and harmonies to 'These Pines' and harmony to 'The Hard Way', while Julie added her uniquely soulful voice to 'The Captain'.

Nash: With Kasey's album, Buddy Miller was sort of the only guy that we really wanted because we were looking for a particular style. We didn't want to go for hot licks, the best player in the world, although we think Buddy's one of them— maybe not from a purely technical standpoint, I suppose, but as a stylist and just being tasteful he's second to none.

Kasey: Obviously the first trip was the biggest because I'd never been to Nashville, but this one was probably even better musically. Recording with Buddy and Julie was a huge thing for me.

Julie wasn't there for the first half of the day. I had never met her at this stage, but I am her number one fan—no, her number two fan, Kurt is her number one fan. He was very excited and all, because we'd already met Buddy at this stage so we were over Buddy and ready to meet Julie.

We were just sitting around the studio, we'd done all the guitar overdubs. Then it was time to do the vocal on 'These Pines' and Buddy's saying, 'I'm warning you, this is going to take me a while. I'm shocking in the studio with vocals.' We're like, 'C'mon, you're Buddy Miller.' He says, 'You know it could take a while, so bear with me.' He went into the studio, I haven't even pressed red, he's just singing along to get a feel for the song. Hearing him singing along with my voice was the most unbelievable thing I'd ever heard, and I just burst into tears. I just don't think I'd ever had something do that to me. Not even the night I saw Matthew play, the night I saw Lucinda play. Tears just came to my eyes. And then Julie walked in and it was like: 'Man, that's Julie Miller!' It was amazing. It was the same with her, when she was singing along to 'The Captain', that's now my favourite part of the whole album, Julie's vocal on 'The Captain', there's just nothing like that, I reckon.

Alas, their other recording target, Steve Earle, proved elusive. Kasey had written a song, 'Unbreakable Heart', designed to be a duet with Earle, but he was in Dublin at the time. She left a tape with Buddy in the hope that Steve and he could synchronise times long enough to get his vocal on the track but alas, between Buddy's schedule (he was completing Emmylou Harris' live album, crafting his and Julie's next CDs and working the road as lead guitarist/band leader for both Earle and Harris) and Steve's touring and preparations to record a bluegrass album with Del McCoury, it never got done. Perhaps one day . . .

With the recording completed, Nash and Kasey spent the following five days meeting with representatives of six major labels (RCA, Atlantic, Warner Bros, Mercury, Sony and Lyric Street),

Kasey, modelling Gram Parsons' legendary Nudie jacket, with the author in 1998.

executives at six publishing companies and their Nashville attorney, and at a photo shoot with John Montgomery, the same man who had 'shot' Dead Ringer Band publicity photos on their previous visit in late 1996. Kasey got a major thrill by being photographed in Gram Parsons' famous Nudie jacket, the same one Parsons had worn for the cover of the Flying Burrito Brothers' 1969 *Gilded Palace of Sin* album. The white, western-cut jacket features embroidered drugs of various kinds, including marijuana leaves, silhouettes of naked women on the lapels and a large, rhinestone-bordered red cross on the back. In a bit of irony, Almo Sounds Records, one-time suitor for Dead Ringer Band, photographed that same jacket for the cover of their Gram Parsons tribute album, *Return of the Grievous Angel*, released in mid-1999. The jacket, property of the author's wife, Melanie Wells, is now on display at the new Country Music Hall of Fame in Nashville.

Making the rounds of labels and publishers showed Nashville that Nash and Kasey could 'talk the talk'. At the Tuesday performance it was up to them to prove they could also 'walk the walk' during her thirty-minute showcase. Since Kasey, Nash and backing guitarist Russ Pahl planned to perform as an acoustic trio, the author booked them into the Bluebird, with a capacity of eighty-five a much cozier, more intimate venue than Douglas Corner, site of their 1996 showcase. This appearance was an invitation-only affair, an unusual procedure in Nashville. Because there are numerous showcases in town in any given week, almost always between 5.30 and 6.30 p.m. from Tuesday to Thursday, most organisers of such events are delighted to admit just about any one who turns up, even if their showbiz credentials are less than stellar.

A lack of audience 'star power' certainly wasn't a problem at this show. Unlike the Douglas Corner showcase, when it seemed impolite to invite other labels as Almo Sounds was, in effect, sponsoring part of the Dead Ringer trip, this time invites went to all the major labels in town as well as to leading publishers and key media. Nine record companies sent representatives, including the Nashville bosses of Atlantic, Warner Bros, Asylum and Lyric Street (the Disney-owned label), setting what many media reps called a high-water mark for record label turnout for an unsigned artist performance. Plenty of high-level publishers and A&R execs peppered the audience as well, but it was Julie Miller's attendance that put Kasey 'over the moon' about the show, despite what she felt to be a slightly sub-par performance. The trio performed five songs from the upcoming album, then Nash and Russ left the stage so Kasey could finish the night solo, singing one of her most autobiographical songs, 'Southern Kind of Life'.

Southern Kind of Life

I grew up a long way from here
I slept with the lights on for fifteen years
And Sabbath kept me home on Friday nights
And Daddy sang me Rodgers
Just to make everything all alright

My town wasn't even on the map
You could pass right through it in twenty seconds flat
But the south was like the whole world to me
Wasn't easy to stay but it was harder to leave

Chorus
Yeah I was a south bound child
Yeah I had a small town life
But I turned out all right in the North
Living that Southern kind of life

Old friends and Bibles filled the house
No room for money and no money anyhow
Deprived was something we always heard
But to me and my brother it was just another word

I used to think the north was the end
'Cos people go there and
they don't come back again
But my father's father was a man of the sea
He lived the southern life just blocks
away from me

Kasey Chambers © 1999, Gibbon Music

Kasey: It wasn't the best I ever sang and played, but hey, I was doing a gig in the Bluebird Cafe, the same room where Garth Brooks was discovered! Like, who cares how I sang, as long as I can say that after the gig, I was happy. But that was pretty scary, playing to those people. I was really scared and nervous when I got up there, but I said to myself, 'Hey, I like what I do, if they don't like it, yaaah, their loss' kind of thing. I was telling myself, 'Forget about it, forget that they're really important people and just do the best you can.' As much as it's scary to play in front of people like that, I'm never, ever embarrassed about what I do. Sometimes I have a bad gig but I don't ever let it get to me. I'm so proud of the music that I do, more than anything else in the world. Sometimes I get people—even the record company—saying, 'when you do an interview with them, try not to mention country too much' and stuff like that, which is fair enough. They're trying to get to a new audience, but personally, I'll tell the whole world that I like country music. I love it, that's what I was saying to myself at the Bluebird.

I'm proud of the songs that I do and I know talent-wise I'm probably not the best singer in the whole world, or certainly not the best player in the world, but first I had to get into this head thing to do that gig, to play in front of all those people, and to know that no matter what happened that I would be proud that I played there. I wanted something to come out of it, but just doing the gig there was enough for me, it was like, 'Man, this is *the Bluebird!*'

Nash: It was great to play the Bluebird because it's such a famous venue. At the end of that trip, we stopped in LA; I had to go to the Troubadour just to say I'd been there because so much great music's come out of there over the years.

It was a totally different experience going back again because of the progression we'd been through in our careers in the period between the trips. You sort of view music in a different way: you're always learning, you're always doing different things. Although I think it was a lot more profitable trip as far as doing stuff, it wasn't half as much fun because the majority of it was interviews and meetings with labels. It was probably much more beneficial meeting those people than the first trip when the only label people were the Almo Sounds folks.

Yeah, it was a very, very exciting time, the first time. But then the second time was in some ways almost the opposite because we saw that Nashville hadn't changed. When we were over there the first time it was like there was no such thing as country music anymore. It looked like things might get better then because everyone seemed to be aware of that more over there, the first time. But going back it seemed like it had gotten worse. We were half expecting a few people, a few record labels, to be taking a few more chances. There are one or two there that are willing, but they've actually gotten more away from country music with people like Faith Hill and Shania Twain. Good luck to them. I think they create good music for a certain reason, but to get up and call that country music . . . What's called country music now is just miles away from what country music really is.

Miles away—15 000 kilometres southwest—was where Nash and Kasey were now headed, back to Sydney, then home and into the Beach House Studio to mix the four tracks containing Buddy and Julie's parts. Nash then could take *The Captain* in for mastering and submit it to EMI for approval and mid-1999 release.

By the end of 1998, the future looked much brighter than it did when the year had dawned. Diane and Bill, though still not completely comfortable with each other, seemed on the road to emotional recovery and they had not let their personal breakup disrupt their professional appearances with the band. The situation with Massive was resolved once and for all. Kasey was about to sign with EMI, a company much higher up the record label food chain—in fact, EMI has been Slim Dusty's label since 1946. They had a track on what was proving to be a high-profile release, the *Not So Dusty* tribute album. And, with *The Captain* 'in the can', Nash and Kasey felt they were ready to deliver a powerful artistic and commercial record to EMI.

To cap a year which saw their career momentum resume in October and increase significantly in the past three months, they were asked to perform on the 27th annual Toyota Country Music Awards of Australia, an honour they swiftly accepted. The band was again up for the Group/Duo Golden Guitar but, in a strange twist of fate, in addition to competing for the Award with Kevin Bennett's group, The Flood, The Crosby Sisters and The Wolverines, they were competing against themselves! The judges had chosen their 'Saddle Boy' track from EMI's Slim Dusty tribute as a finalist and also tabbed their spirited version of 'Hello Hope-ville', from their last album for Massive. (The entries are made by the releasing labels; both EMI and Massive had submitted Dead Ringer tracks.) Lastly, they were included in the cast of 'Various Artists' chosen as an Album of the Year finalist for the *Not So Dusty* CD and, should that album win, would also be entitled to share in the glory of that victory.

14

Strategies

Highlighted by record deals and major awards for both Dead Ringer Band and Kasey, 1999 was the most pivotal year yet for the Chambers family. 1998 had been their biggest trial by fire but, like tempered steel, they had emerged stronger from that year's turmoil. They began the last year of the 1990s in far better emotional shape than they were when 1998 began—and they had a new CD ready to spring on the world.

The group performed both 'Saddle Boy' and 'Hello Hopeville' at the January Awards show and picked up the Group/Duo honour for 'Saddle Boy', thus delivering EMI's only victory for their Slim Dusty tribute CD. Album of the Year honours and three additional Gold Guitars, one over Graeme Connors for his track on the *Not So Dusty* CD, went to Lee Kernaghan for his *Hat Town* album, a platinum seller. Exciting newcomer Adam Brand, originally from Western Australia, made his presence known by taking out three categories, for New Talent and Video of the Year and for co-writing 'Last Man Standing' with Clive Young, chosen as APRA Song of the Year for 1999.

Kasey officially launched her solo debut at Tamworth, performing at CMT International's Fan Fest, fronting a band which included dad Bill, bassist James Gillard, guitarist/backing vocalist Kevin Bennett and B.J. Barker, doing double duty drumming for both her and Dead Ringer. She previewed six songs from *The Captain* and was well received by the sold-out crowd at Town Hall. Additionally, although she hadn't actually signed a contract

Kasey signs with EMI in February 1999. Left to right: Leon Concannon, John Lomax III, Kasey, Nash, Bill and Tony Harlow.

yet, she was featured in EMI's ad in the Awards show program book, along with Slim, John Williamson and Felicity. Teaser posters for *The Captain* were up all over town, also identifying her as an EMI artist and advertising a May release for her CD.

Dead Ringer Band performed one show during Tamworth, again at the RSL Club. Kasey didn't make any additional appearances, save for a few impromptu songs on the 'Hillbilly Jam' which Bill and Audrey were running each afternoon at The Pub, a comfortable bar/restaurant/pokies and liquor establishment, founded by publicans Bevan and Joan Douglas and devoted to presenting songwriters and original music year-round. After Tamworth, the Ringers toured sporadically as everyone wanted the spotlight to shine solely on Kasey and *The Captain*.

Early in February she officially signed her recording deal with EMI during a festive Friday afternoon luncheon at Cannibal's, just down the road from the label's Cremorne offices. Company Managing Director Tony Harlow then assembled the combined

*Bill, Kasey and Nash entertaining the staff of EMI and Virgin,
February 1999.*

employees of EMI and Virgin to meet Kasey, Nash and Bill who
would then perform a short, acoustic set. It was significant that
Harlow included the Virgin staff as that label had no country acts
on its roster. This was a clear sign that EMI wanted Kasey's album
to be perceived as a mainstream release as opposed to a country
release. Harlow's plan was to present *The Captain* through both the
company's contemporary *and* country departments, a bold strategy
designed to expose Kasey's music to the broadest possible
audience.

After a bit of milling around, 'noshing' on snacks and chatting, a lull which gave everyone time to down a few libations,
the Chambers trio climbed on to a makeshift stage in the EMI
conference room and introduced themselves and *The Captain* to
the staffers of their new label home. At that time, it's doubtful
that more than 15 per cent of the EMI employees had ever seen
Dead Ringer Band. Polite applause greeted their first selection,
but when the trio wound into 'We're All Gonna Die Someday', a

curiously pleasant song about death, spiced by an instrumental snippet of the *Beverly Hillbillies* theme song, the seventy or so assembled in the conference room began warming to them in a hurry. The rock/pop workers in attendance realised that Kasey's voice, image and charm could—in fact, *should*—be marketed to mainstream music consumers.

We're All Gonna Die Someday

We're all gonna die someday lord
We're all gonna die someday
Mama's on pills daddy's over the hill
But we're all gonna die someday

Well it hurts down here on earth lord
It hurts down here on earth
It hurts down here, boys 'cos we're running out of beer
But we're all gonna die someday

Well all of my friends are stoned lord
All of my friends are stoned
Janie got stoned 'cos she couldn't get boned
But we're all gonna die someday

Well they can all kiss my ass lord
They can all kiss my ass
If they want to kiss my ass well they better do it fast
'Cos we're all gonna die someday

Kasey Chambers, Worm Werchon, Bill Chambers ©1999, Gibbon Music

Kasey: Worm, me and Dad were driving home from Canberra one night. We did a gig there, then Worm and I had to fly out to Norfolk the next morning, so we came back after the gig—we drove all night. We were just trying to keep Dad awake so we thought we'd write a song. You can very well pick out the Worm lines in it. The only other song he's ever written is 'Don't Go'. He doesn't know a thing about playing music or anything like that, only what he's learned from us over the years . . .

I didn't think for a minute that song would get on the

album, no way. But then we thought the album was looking a little bit down and depressing so we thought, well, we'd better add it. Then you [the author] wrote a description saying it was 'a happy uptempo song about death', so now whenever anybody asks me I say, 'Well that's the happy, uptempo song about death on the album.' 'Cause there's not many of those songs around.

EMI strove to position Kasey as a contemporary artist for solid business reasons. Because of the general media perception of country music being made by and for rural 'hicks', mainstream radio would rather be dragged slowly, cut and bleeding, through a sea of starving sharks than play a country record. Unlike the United States, where there are some 2100 radio stations (nearly 25 per cent of the total US radio universe) playing a dedicated country format, in Australia there is exactly *one* major market, full-time commercial country radio station 4AAA in Brisbane. Aside from 4AAA, the only airplay country releases receive are via John Nutting's ABC program, 'Saturday Night Country', and other syndicated shows such as 'The Outback Club', carried on over seventy stations. Country's only other radio exposure comes from dozens of low-powered community stations, some of which play a dedicated country format, many of which do not. The February 2000 cancellation of Nick Erby's 'Country Hoedown', which commenced in 1976 and was carried on twenty-seven stations, further reduced country's radio profile.

In the United States, *Billboard*'s two most important charts—the 'Hot 100' for singles and the *Billboard* 200 for albums—are liberally dotted with country releases. In Australia, it is extremely rare for a country artist to get enough radio play and generate sufficient sales to even place on these mainstream charts, much less ascend to the upper levels.

Because of this saturation of country radio air play, and considerable attention from other forms of mass media, in the United States it is not unusual for the biggest country artists to routinely go double, triple or quadruple platinum—sell two, three, four million units—or, in extreme cases like Garth Brooks, the

Dixie Chicks and Shania Twain, to sell over ten million CDs of their releases. With a population base one-fifteenth the size of the United States, sales of 70 000 copies earn platinum certification in Australia. But without mass market radio airplay, it is exceedingly difficult for Australian country artists to reach that level. That's the reason why American country singers like Twain, Brooks, LeAnn Rimes, Trisha Yearwood, Kenny Rogers and Reba McEntire are presented as mainstream artists: outside of the United States, the country market by itself is simply too small.

Historically, country music in the United States has accounted for between 8 and almost 20 per cent (in 1993 and 1994) of annual recorded music sales, which in 2000 surpassed US $14 billion. In Australia, country's market share is perhaps 5 per cent of a total sales of around A$960 million. Thus the big US country acts and all the homegrown country artists are slicing up a pie of about A$50 million (US$26 million)—about the same amount one triple platinum album by one US superstar would gross. Regardless of your feelings about country music, given the above economics, you've got to admire the audacity, the chutzpah, the sheer *balls* of the artists who have chosen this genre of the music business to provide their livelihood. (Trying to make it in Australia as a classical soloist, polka band or mariachi trio would be harder, but that's about it.)

After consultation with Nash and Kasey, EMI decided to kick off *The Captain*'s introduction by releasing a single and video of the lead track, 'Cry Like a Baby', a couple of months ahead of the 18 May release for the album. This proved a fortuitous choice, as the single reached number 1 for several weeks on the *Music Network* country chart, nudged into ARIA's mainstream chart for a week and the video climbed to number 1 on CMT's video chart.

Kasey: I wrote 'Cry Like a Baby' at the Continental Cafe in Melbourne, just before a live ABC radio taping. It was a Ringers gig and I just wrote it out the back. 'Cry Like a Baby' probably best describes me. It's not all good, but it's all true. It kind of says just what sort of person I am, and I knew, as soon as I'd written it, that it was going to be my first single. That's the first thing I really wanted to say on my own. I didn't really want 'The Captain' to be the first single 'cause it's a love song,

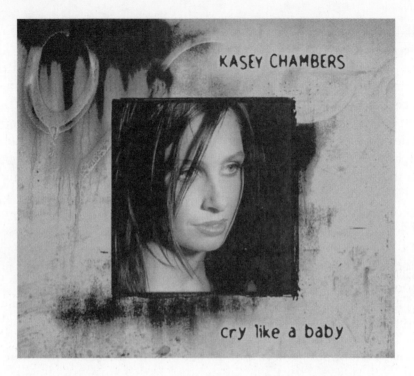

KASEY CHAMBERS

cry like a baby

'Cry Like A Baby', Kasey's debut single, briefly entered the pop chart, before going to #1 on the country chart and CMT's video chart.

I really don't write a whole lot of love songs. I write more songs about life, myself, stuff like that. Everybody writes about love. Lots of times when I'm down and depressed, when I write a lot of songs, it's usually not about love, it's usually about something else.

Cry Like a Baby

Well I never lived through the Great Depression
Sometimes I feel as though I did
And I don't have answers for every single question
But that's okay 'cos I'm just a kid

Well, I've seen pictures of my mother
When she looked exactly like me
And I've seen all my friends running for cover
Running from something they can't see

Chorus
And it's not easy to get a handle on my life
But I have tried it time and time again
But I still cry just like a baby
And I answer back to feel a little free
And I still fly even though I'm gonna fall
But I'm too far gone to let it get to me

Kasey Chambers © 1999, Gibbon Music

It's normal for a new artist to sign a record deal granting the label worldwide rights exclusivity but, at the urging of their advisers, Nash and Kasey chose to retain rights for her recordings in the United States and Canada, the two major North American territories which together account for about 39 per cent of the world market. EMI had rights throughout the rest of the world, including such major areas as Europe (32 per cent), Japan (17 per cent), the rest of Asia (3.5 per cent) and Australasia (2 per cent).

There were several reasons for Nash and Kasey to insist upon holding their rights for the United States and Canada. For one, it gave them the flexibility to 'shop' her recordings to any label active in the United States, the world's leading market, rather than just to labels belonging to the EMI family. Second, Kasey and her support team then felt that she should be presented as a country artist in the United States. The stylistic parameters for that genre are quite broad, encompassing everyone from Shania Twain and Garth Brooks' country-flavoured pop to Randy Travis and George Strait's traditional stylings. Additionally, country music has a long history of extraordinary female singer-songwriters, a branch of the music tree that had existed long before Lilith Fair came into being. In country music, that line began in 1960 with Loretta Lynn. The 'Coal Miner's Daughter' was joined in the late 1960s and throughout the 1970s by Dolly Parton and Tammy Wynette, who were then followed by Rosanne Cash in the 1980s and Mary Chapin Carpenter in the 1990s. With Chapin Carpenter's career in decline by 1999, there was a slot wide open for a 'true' singer-songwriter, a woman who actually wrote her own songs as opposed to the standard Nashville practice of pairing new artists in co-writing sessions with established tunesmiths.

Country was also overdue for new artist breakthroughs. The tremendous success of the effervescent, zaftig Dixie Chicks in 1998 and 1999 tended to mask the fact that Music Row hadn't launched any other multi-platinum-selling artists since 1996 when Deana Carter and LeAnn Rimes made their breakthroughs. The format itself was in dire straits. After peaking in 1993 with sales of over US$2 billion—smack on 7 per cent of the entire world recorded music sales for that year—country went into a six-year slide. Sales never again topped $2 billion, drifting downward slightly in 1994, plummeting the next year and continuing to drop annually, with 1999 clocking in another decline, some 4.5 per cent, while the overall US recorded music market rose just above 6 per cent to US$14 billion, dropping country's share below 10 per cent for the first time since the 1980s. Figures for 2000 brought little relief: overall sales rose slightly to US$14.3 billion, while country was off 0.2 per cent.

Country radio's listener population was also in a seven-year tumble, falling from a national audience share of 13.1 in 1993 to 8.9 in 2000, a 32 per cent drop which brought them below the 9.4 share they had had in 1989. Even more alarming was the fact that the number of full-time country stations, which had reached a high-water mark of 2613 in 1994, had fallen to 2105 by the end of 2000, leaving the format 14 per cent below the 2448 stations that were pumping out country music on 31 December 1989.

Another option would be to present Kasey as a mainstream artist in the United States and 'pitch' *The Captain* to label execs with the pop/rock labels based in Los Angeles and New York. The album's appeal was certainly within the stylistic parameters of that larger audience and, inasmuch as EMI was presenting Kasey as a mainstream artist in Australia, such a move would seem sensible. At heart, though, Kasey considered herself a country artist: she had grown up in a country environment and all her achievements to date were in the country field. Label brass on the East and West Coast would most likely bounce Kasey back to their Nashville division the second they realised her background. The Los Angeles and New York divisions of the major labels and their Nashville counterparts had for years operated under unwritten rules that in practice meant Nashville would channel all promising pop/rock artists to New York or Los Angeles while those two cities would stay away from initiating country, gospel and Christian projects, thus giving Music City a clear shot in those areas.

The chances of overcoming the above issues and successfully pitching Kasey in the two much bigger coastal cities would be vastly improved by forming an alliance with a management operation active in those two music centres. But this move would require time and money—items in short supply in Kasey's camp in early 1999.

At heart, Kasey is a songwriter-artist. Nashville's music industry, more than any other world music centre, is built around songs and writers as opposed to being constructed around artists, record companies, film or TV stars, as is the case elsewhere. There is a respect—almost a reverence—for songwriters here, a powerful and unique appeal which fosters a creative environment unlike anywhere else on earth.

Buying into this strategy of presenting Kasey Chambers as a country artist in America thus meant that she could only be shopped in Nashville. Therein lay another reason why all concerned wanted her to have the freedom to sign with any one of the approximately fifteen viable labels as opposed to being limited to the two EMI-owned imprints, Capitol and Virgin/Nashville. The easiest course of action would have been to approach these two labels, corporate cousins to EMI/Australia. However, all Kasey's advisers felt other companies presented Kasey with a better chance to break through in the crowded US country market.

Capitol Records, whose flagship artist was Garth Brooks, had run through three presidents in less than five years and was at the time overseen by Pat Quigley, a New York transplant with a career primarily in marketing. Before joining EMI in New York, Quigley had made his mark as a sales whiz through phenomenal successes hawking Lange skis and Rolling Rock beer. (EMI relieved Quigley of his duties in December 2000.)

Unfortunately, Capitol had devolved during the decade into being a label whose roster was completely dominated by Brooks.

Virgin/Nashville, a 1998 startup operation, was led by respected producer Scott Hendricks, until 1997 the head of Capitol/Nashville. Brooks had played the major role in ousting Hendricks, claiming that the label had done a rotten job of selling

Fresh Horses, due to its sales of a paltry six million. (Brooks had also forced Hendricks' predecessor, Jimmy Bowen, to walk the plank, in 1995.) Hendricks was generally well regarded about town, despite his abrupt forced departure from Capitol.

Unfortunately, startup operations and reactivations of long-dormant imprints had not done very well in Nashville of late. Rising Tide, Decca, A&M, Patriot, Liberty, Polydor and Career Records were all begun, or reawakened, then shuttered during the 1990s, so many industry wags felt that too much risk was involved in these types of label situations. Nevertheless, as a courtesy to EMI/Australia, *The Captain* was pitched to Hendricks, who politely passed on pursuing her for Virgin. (In February 2001, EMI pulled the plug on Virgin/Nashville, shortly after year-end figures showed the company's entire roster had sold less than 140 000 units.)

Undaunted, management circulated fully mixed and mastered copies of *The Captain* to a dozen other Music City label heads in early January, well before the release of the CD in Australia. After two false starts, the search for an American recording deal for Dead Ringer Band—this time in the guise of a Kasey Chambers album—continued.

15

All Hail The Captain

Meanwhile, back in Australia, Kasey had started headlining a few shows on her own in addition to continuing as lead vocalist at Dead Ringer Band's appearances. In the beginning, she enlisted Bill and Nash for her band, along with B.J. Barker, Dead Ringer Band's drummer, a mate who went back to their Southend days. Seasoned muso Chris Haig, who had worked with Tommy Emmanuel and other luminaries, came on board for a while, on bass, but was soon replaced by Jeff McCormack and James Gillard, both of whom played on *The Captain*. Nash soon moved offstage to supervise the live sound mix. Another Central Coast pal, Mick Albeck, signed on to play fiddle, guitar and mandolin. Thus, by early 2000, Kasey's band consisted of four musicians who had all played key roles in the recording of *The Captain*. The album was scheduled for its official launch on 17 May, with the formal kickoff planned for The Basement, one of Sydney's premier live-music venues.

By early June, 'Cry Like a Baby' had reached number 1 on the *Music Network* country chart, a feat duplicated by the video's performance on the CMT clip list on 4 August. Because of the excellent groundwork by EMI's publicity department and the fast start for the single, the media's appetite was clearly whetted when advance CDs were shipped early in May. EMI's Track by Track information sheet from her press kit closes with Kasey's summation of *The Captain* and her hopes for the album:

The Captain, Kasey's initial solo album, released in Australia in May 1999.

I'd like to convert some people with this record. I think it has the potential to prove that country music has a lot more depth and soul than what they've been force-fed over the last decade. Country music has gotten so far away from what I consider it to be that it disturbs me. This record is an attempt to bring it back to its roots but still sound modern.

While this statement, like Kasey herself, is earnest, honest and insightful, it leaves no doubt that she unequivocally considers herself as belonging to the country genre. Meanwhile, EMI had been furiously working for months to convince the media that Kasey should be considered as a mainstream artist.

The ensuing response to *The Captain* was overwhelmingly positive. Bruce Elder from the *Sydney Morning Herald* was first out of the box with a 12 May review that left no doubt where he stood regarding the CD:

Now, if Australia really wants to succeed in the dubious world that is American country music, at least we have a real contender. Kasey Chambers, the female lead vocalist with Dead Ringer Band, is the most talented and complete country performer this country has produced. She is a great songwriter. She has a voice which is both highly original and which is characterised by so much 'soul' that everything she sings is soaked with deeply felt passion and caring . . . And, like all great contemporary country performers, she can join the dots in that remarkable daisy chain that starts with Jimmie Rodgers, Bill Monroe and Hank Williams, and moves through the likes of Gram Parsons and Emmylou Harris to find its great contemporary voice in people such as Guy Clark, Lucinda Williams, Steve Earle, Lyle Lovett, Townes Van Zandt and Buddy Miller (who performs on her new album) . . . Chambers has produced an album which reaches deep into American roots country traditions—plenty of bluegrass, country folk balladeering, white gospel and Steve Earle-style country rock. But, and here's the daring, she has cleverly written lyrics which are quintessentially Australian . . . If there is any justice in the world, those who care about great country music (and understand it), will recognise that this is about as good as country gets.

Kathy McCabe of the *Sunday Telegraph* was next to check in with her take on *The Captain*, published on 16 May:

> Kasey Chambers looks more punk than Dolly Parton and her unabashed antics have already shaken up the country music establishment. The 22-year-old singer-songwriter has posed nude for a 1997 *Not Only Black+White* magazine spread, dressed like a Spice Girl at Tamworth and proudly wears a nose ring. With her debut solo album, Kasey is scoring lots of attention for a voice which some say is country music's answer to international pop balladeer Jewel.

Elder fired an additional salvo the following day, noting:

> If quality of voice is one of country music's pre-eminent qualifications, then Kasey Chambers is on a one-way ride to immortality. That huskiness, that little catch of pain and sorrow—here is a voice to bring the masses to tears . . . This is an album of such richness and honesty that it deserves to be hugely successful.

Keith Glass weighed in with his thoughts in Melbourne's *Herald-Sun* of 30 May:

> Kasey Chambers displays her hillbilly roots so openly on this remarkable album that the wider world, familiar with more mainstream sounds, might be daunted and never tune into Australia's greatest young female talent . . . I pray the blinkered local tastemakers can see past their prejudices and realise this will be hard to beat as the Australian album of the year.

By 1 July, over two dozen reviews—all save one of them highly favourable—had poured in, from publications as distant as Perth and the Gold Coast, from magazines as disparate as *Rolling Stone* ('piercing honesty and emotional clarity of her heavy-hearted country-rock'), *revolver* ('casual richness and pure, unadulterated charm'), *Juice*, ('Truly gifted songsmith . . . a powerful debut'), *Drum* ('One of the most startling record releases of the year'), *Rip It Up*, *Impress*, *Capital News* and *Rhythms*.

Such acclaim from the country media, and even from long-time supporters like mainstream writers Elder and Glass, were not surprising, but glowing reviews from rock/pop trend spotters *Rolling Stone* and *Juice*, and praise in the pages of relentlessly hip street weeklies like *Drum* and *Revolver* were unprecedented for an artist from the country field. Justified or not, country artists— particularly Australian ones—were usually the objects of ridicule, if their names ever appeared in the pages of such cutting-edge chroniclers of pop culture.

Rhythms gained the honour of becoming the first non-country publication to feature her on its cover, with editor Vin Maskell noting: 'The Captain has catapulted the lightly-built, exuberant woman into the heady world of rave reviews and big corporate dollars pushing her as The Next Big Thing.' *Rhythms* also quoted Steve Earle's reaction to Kasey after seeing and performing with her at Byron Bay: 'Kasey Chambers, man, is probably the best female hillbilly singer I've heard in a long, long time.'

In Maskell's article, the 'Next Big Thing' had a few raves of her own, laughing uproariously at the one bad review *The Captain* had received, from Brisbane, which began with: 'If you thought Shania Twain was bad . . .' 'I stuck it on my wall, it looks great,' Kasey bubbled and, airing her thoughts on Nashville's recent recording output: 'It's full of belts, hats and buckles, that's what a lot of people think country music is . . . What's coming out of Nashville makes me puke.'

Needless to say, management chose not to widely distribute that particular article around Music City. The critics' reaction there was extremely promising, with Bob Oermann delivering the first salvo in two separate raves in the 9 April issue of *Music Row*, first in the introduction to his singles column as follows:

> I have spoken fondly about Australia's Dead Ringer Band and its lead vocalist Kasey Chambers before in these pages. Kasey's debut solo effort as a singer-songwriter, *The Captain*, is heading for stores worldwide via EMI-Virgin. To date, she has no US deal. She looks like an alternative act, but sings like an Appalachian waif. Her brother/producer/sideman Nash Chambers is an earringed, tattooed handsome scamp. Folks, these kids are connecting the dots between Jewel and Dolly Parton. Isn't there anyone left in this town with vision enough to sign them?

Oermann's singles review of 'Cry Like a Baby' in that same issue was even more blunt:

We don't deserve someone this good. Kasey is just too real, rootsy, hillbilly and downright cool for contemporary Nashville. 'I'm not much like my generation,' she sings, 'their music only hurts my ears.' You said it, sister.

However, the Nashville label execs' reaction to *The Captain* was, in most cases, disappointing. The consensus among label A&R veterans and company presidents can be summarised as 'love her voice, like the songs, sounds like a demo. Doubt radio would play it. She needs to move here and co-write, get a producer, hire some A-Team studio cats.' In other words, Kasey should become part of the local process, play the game the way they say she ought to play it.

Never mind the fact that this was an egregious example of business trying to dictate art. Forget about the fact that to play the game their way, Kasey would have to move 15 000 kilometres from home and forsake her Australian career shortly after the release of her debut album. No, focus instead on the fact that these industry veterans refused to accept *The Captain* as a completed work, releasable as is. They didn't seem to care that this same CD was scheduled for release in Australia, was set for later issue in Europe and that Kasey wasn't going to stop in her tracks and make an album just for them, the way they thought she should do it.

For sheer audacity, the most ambitious scheme was hatched by one of the city's most prominent producer/publisher/label executives. He proposed that Kasey move to Nashville in July to co-write with 'his writers' and participate in a multi-artist showcase once a week 'with my other developing artists'. Then he'd produce sides on her, then try to set up a joint venture with one of the major labels. While it was flattering to see one of Nashville's largest big shots so interested in her, Kasey and Nash politely declined, wanting to present *The Captain* as Kasey's first US release instead.

Rick Blackburn at Atlantic, so eager to sign Dead Ringer Band just over a year before, was now saying he preferred Nash and Kasey as a duet more than he liked her as a solo artist. Blackburn was also seriously considering retirement at the time, so Atlantic didn't look like a promising port-of-call anymore. (Blackburn did retire in mid-1999.)

MCA's roster was top-heavy with female artists: Reba McEntire, Trisha Yearwood, Lee Ann Womack and Allison Moorer were just four examples. Their A&R department let it be known that they weren't going to sign a female singer any time soon. (In fact the label didn't sign another female artist until April 2001.)

Bob Saporiti, then Warner Bros President, absolutely loved Kasey's record but told her and Nash face-to-face he wasn't going to sign another act for at least a year. He felt he had to focus entirely on the artists already on the label, that he had an 'emotional commitment' to those artists. Strange language to hear from a label boss, but in character for Saporiti, one of the most compassionate, 'artist friendly' label heads Nashville has ever had. (Saporiti, whose motto is 'global peace through country music', took early retirement in March 2001 during cutbacks, mandated by AOL's now-finalised purchase of Time-Warner.)

Sony, who operated four labels, including Monument— home to the Dixie Chicks—passed after taking a very close look, even getting Nash and Kasey to stop off at their office to play a few songs as an acoustic duo. Alas, they decided that Kasey's music was different and wouldn't be instantly acceptable to country radio—virtually the only conduit for major media exposure, and hence record sales, available to country artists in the United States.

Luke Lewis at Mercury, home to Shania Twain, raved about Kasey, met with her and Nash, referred to her as 'a superstar', but was unable to sign anyone for most of the year because Universal had bought PolyGram, Mercury's parent company. This resulted in a signing 'freeze' while the newly merged company restructured its operations. (French corporation Virendi purchased the newly combined labels in 2000, bringing further changes there.)

The rest of the labels fell into the 'sounds like a demo, bring her to town and we'll make a record school', none, however, was thoughtful enough to offer any assistance for such a relocation. Nor, it seems, did anyone pause to wonder why Kasey would want to dump her budding Australian career and come 15 000 kilometres to make a record just like all the other records that weren't selling. This arrogant attitude might have been somewhat defensible in 1993 and 1994, when country music and Nashville were rolling in tall clover, when labels were popping new artists through to stardom every few months, but in the midst of a six-year sales nosedive, it made no sense whatsoever.

If 'shopping' for a record deal can be likened to fishing, then, after six weeks, all Kasey had to show for *The Captain* was one nibble and plenty of encouraging words. Dead Ringer Band had at least managed two fully fledged bites, even if they hadn't been able to land the Almo Sounds or Atlantic deals.

But suddenly, late in February, Asylum Records took the bait, in the person of label President Evelyn Shriver. Appointed to head Asylum less than a year prior, Shriver, whose background was in corporate, then show business public relations, had no experience even working at a label, much less running one. She was also the only woman helming a major record company in Nashville. At first the town's 'good old boys' privately snickered at her chances for success. Before the smirks were off their faces, Shriver had engineered a comeback record for George Jones, landed the long-awaited Linda Ronstadt/Emmylou Harris/Dolly Parton *Trio II* record and released *Western Wall*, 1999's atmospheric Harris–Ronstadt collaboration. Those Asylum artists garnered five finalist Grammy nominations in January 2000, more than any label in town save DreamWorks, who raked in six for their Asleep at the Wheel tribute to Bob Wills, *Ride With Bob*. Monument (Dixie Chicks) and Mercury (Shania Twain) were the only other labels with multiple finalist nominations. Later, Jones and the Trio both won awards at the 23 February 2000 ceremony. Those two victories put Asylum in a four-way tie for most Nashville label wins as Shania, the Chicks and the Wills' tribute CD also won twice.

Shriver felt Kasey could 'connect the dots between Dolly Parton and all the female angst singers' and was certain she could get extensive print and TV exposure for *The Captain*, then work the CD to the country, Adult-Alternative and Americana radio formats. She felt, as did management, that 2000 would offer a unique opportunity to 'break' an Australian artist to stardom and, since former Aussies Keith Urban and Sherrié Austin weren't really playing up their 'down under' background, Kasey could wrap herself in her Australian heritage and, as the Sydney Olympics approached, ride what was sure to be a growing wave of American interest in all things from the Great South Land.

Shriver outlined the initial strategy back in July 1999.

> We'll put a single and video out in February, then we can fly her through San Francisco, she can do the Gavin Radio Seminar there, pick up a few dates. I can probably get Willie, or Merle or George to put her on some shows, then she can do the Country Radio Seminar here, do some media and we'll officially launch the album at South by Southwest in mid-March.

This was a perfectly logical plan. Shriver's casual mention of getting Kasey slots on shows with Nelson, Haggard and Jones was no idle boast: all three country legends had been her PR clients for years before she took the Asylum job in 1998. Deal memos started moving from Ken Kraus, Kasey's Nashville lawyer, to Asylum parent company Elektra's Business Affairs department and, in due course, matters progressed to the contract negotiation stage. The legal discussions took a few months as the negotiations involved three parties: Kasey, Asylum/Nashville and EMI in Australia, licensor of the master recordings Asylum wished to license for the United States and Canada. Brett Oaten, Kasey's lawyer in Sydney, examined Elektra's proposal, as did Louis Calleja, EMI's Head of Business Affairs. There were, however, no major stumbling blocks or 'deal killers' and by August all involved felt matters were ready to move to the final stage: signing the formal execution copies of the contract, which the Elektra Business Affairs department would prepare within a matter of days. The deal, it seemed, was a certainty. It looked like time to pour the champagne and quaff a few glasses, amid copious toasts.

Well, not quite. Momentous events in Burbank, California, at the very top of the Time-Warner corporate structure, kept the corks in the bottles of bubbly. Bob Daly and Terry Simels, the two gentlemen who ran both the film and music divisions of the sprawling Time-Warner entertainment empire, suddenly resigned their positions on 15 July, more than five months before their contracts were due to expire.

Vacancies at the top of a recording business empire don't stay open long and by 16 August Roger Ames was appointed to the position of Chairman and CEO, Warner Music Group. Ames had been heading up Warner's European operation from his London headquarters and had previously been in charge of the recorded music and publishing divisions of PolyGram Music Group before that company had been swallowed by Universal at the end of 1998. Unfortunately for Kasey, Ames—or possibly someone else in the corporation—immediately froze all pending recording deals in Nashville until the new management team had a chance to examine every aspect of the company's operations.

Thus Kasey's contract—by year's end nearly five months after the completion of all negotiations—remained in the Elektra Business Affairs department as 1999 rolled over into 2000. Furthermore, Music City rumours positing a restructuring of the Warner Music Group began circulating.

In view of the above, Kasey's management had begun to sniff around town, hoping to develop another port of call in case restructuring wound up torpedoing their pending deal. The end of the year is traditionally a bad time to 'shop' an artist and the end of 1999, six years into a sales slump, was even worse. There was mild interest from a few places but by the time 2000 ticked over, no one except Asylum had offered a deal.

It was obvious that the original schedule calling for Kasey to come to the United States in February wasn't workable, so management decided to forgo the US market temporarily and focus instead on Europe, where the indefatigable Tony Harlow had aroused interest from high-ranking executives at both EMI and Virgin Records.

Virgin/UK executive Glenn Middleworth flew to Australia to see Kasey in performance and later met with her, Nash and Gary Rabin, who had joined Kasey's management team late in November.

Rabin is a hard-driving Sydney-based industry veteran whose background is in the rock arena, with groups such as the Screaming Jets, Daddy Cool and Mondo Rock. He also represents Ross Wilson and suggested that Nash produce a half-dozen sides of Ross's most recent songs. The original concept was that Rabin would have responsibility for Kasey in Australia and New Zealand (while I continued to look after her—and Dead Ringer Band— outside those territories).

The second single off The Captain, *'Don't Talk Back', which showcased another new look for Kasey.*

While all these activities were going on behind the scenes, Dead Ringer Band picked up their fourth consecutive MO Award, despite touring far less in the past year than they had in any year of their existence. Kasey's second single and video, 'Don't Talk Back', was released in August, with three bonus tracks—covers of 'Better Be Home Soon' by Crowded House, 'Another Lonely Day' by Ben Harper and 'Dam' by Nashville's Matthew Ryan.

Kasey: 'Don't Talk Back' was written in Africa. It's just about living on the road, saying how the road is better than a partner, 'cause it doesn't talk back. This song was written in pieces along our journey. It's about how I feel really free and secure when I'm on the road. I guess that relates to living on the Nullarbor and travelling around Australia when I was young.

Trade publication *Music Network* reviewed the single on release and did a fine job of describing her appeal:

Kasey has certainly started off her solo career on the right foot. 'Cry Like a Baby' made its presence felt on both the country and the Australian mainstream charts and critical acclaim has been endless. 'Don't Talk Back' is another step forward in a career that is slowly and subtly infiltrating the masses. It has enough of a quirky, pop element next to her country roots to again appease both audiences. Again, her appeal lies in her amazing voice which is innocent and childlike, but sexy, mature and incredibly fresh in its sound at the same time. Her knack of being able to write extremely well-crafted country/pop that really sticks in your mind after a few listens is impeccable. Check out her great version of Crowded House's 'Better Be Home Soon' as a bonus track!

Don't Talk Back
Well it's half my heart and a little bit of soul
That makes me feel I've gotta ride this road
I wouldn't change it if I could
Just me and this road you
know we got an understanding

It won't leave me at home and I am
Too tired to do just what I should
And last night I asked if I could
Take comfort in the rosewood
The road said nothing at all

Chorus
'Cos it don't talk back unless the wind blows hard
I drive it all night with the wheel of my car
It won't leave me running for the door
And if the paint's still wet I can just slow down
And it all goes away on the other side of town
And nothing is that easy anymore

Well the hurt won't leave with the sight of white line
But it eases up my pain for a while
The only habit that I keep
And miles take time but the time is mine
And always running suits me fine

I'll catch my breath when I sleep
And after all that I've done
I'm not half what I hoped that I'd become
There's still a long way to go

Kasey Chambers ©1999, Gibbon Music

Kasey and Nash weren't slowing down to read reviews. They were, as you can probably guess, on the road. Kasey did two Dead Ringer Band dates and nine solo shows in the second half of July and did thirteen shows in August, five as support for Chris Isaak's tour. She ended the month on the main stage at the Gympie Muster.

Her and EMI's hard work paid off in September when the finalist nominees for the October ARIA Awards were announced. Kasey was one of the final five for Best Country Release, the award Dead Ringer Band had won in 1996. That was no surprise, given *The Captain*'s excellent media reception, radio airplay and first three months' sales. The surprise came when she learned she was also named a finalist in the Best Female Artist category, vying for that honour with Natalie Imbruglia, Kylie Minogue, Suze DeMarchi and Lisa Miller. It was unprecedented for a country artist to gain a finalist ARIA nomination in any of the most prestigious, overall categories.

As soon as 'Don't Talk Back' began to fade, in late October, EMI issued a video and single of 'This Flower', an acoustic, bluegrass-flavoured track, as a country-only release.

On the surface, 'This Flower' seems to be a simple, straightforward love song, but there's a deeper current beneath, as there is in so much of Kasey's work. The Track by Track information supplied by EMI reveals part of the story: 'This was written for a woman who I'd never met but who nonetheless had a huge impact on my life. The flower in the song is actually referring to a flower I gave to someone to place on her grave back on Norfolk Island.'

She supplied further detail in an October 1999 interview:

Kasey: 'This Flower' was written for Sue, Kurt's mum. I wrote it because one time Kurt came over to visit me and when he went back on the plane he brought me ten roses 'cause we'd been together for ten months. He gave me the roses at the airport. I took out one of the roses and said, 'Can you take this back and give it to your mum for me? Go and put it on her grave,' and I didn't really think all that much of it then. He went home and put it on her grave, then after the flower died, he took it home and pressed it and kept it.

I was in Esperance, Western Australia doing a gig and I really felt like writing a song but I didn't know what to write about so I rang up Kurt but he wasn't there. I was talking to Kurt's dad, Jap, and I said, 'What can I write a song about? I've got no idea but I'm really in the mood for writing a song.' He said, 'I thought that was really sweet how you gave Kurt that flower, why don't you write a song about that?' So the pressure was on then because I thought, 'Oh shit, now he's going to be expecting this song' and that's a pretty major subject to write a song about. Most people just think it's a love song.

This Flower
Well this flower is my soul
But it's not half of what I owe
I should give you every rose that ever grew
But take this one here for a start
And you can keep it in your heart
I have everything I need because of you

Well if my life was long enough
To pack up everything I own
I would do just that and give it all to you
But it's impossible to pay
All the things you gave away
So this flower I give will have to do

All the flowers growing wild
For ten thousand lonely miles
It's not near enough to give you what I should
But I will owe you for a while
Maybe longer than my time
I would give you all the world if I could
Kasey Chambers ©1999, Gibbon Music

Kasey and the road continued their close relationship until early October when she and Nash took a scheduled pause to film the clip for 'This Flower' and attend the ARIA Awards. In addition to her double nomination, Dead Ringer Band could share in a victory due to their participation in the *Not So Dusty* tribute project as that CD was also a finalist for Best Country Album, along with *The Captain* and releases by Adam Brand, Tania Kernaghan and Kedron Taylor. The punters reckoned Kasey the favourite, even though Brand's self-titled debut album had been in the market months longer, was certified gold (sales of 35 000) and had captured three awards earlier in the year at Tamworth. Some thought the *Not So Dusty* disc would win due to the sheer starpower of the cast of participating artists and the status of Slim, the living icon of Australian country music.

Vigorous applause greeted the announcement of *The Captain's* selection as the winner of the country category. Thus Kasey won an ARIA to go with Dead Ringer Band's victory three years earlier. With her dark hair braided, and dressed in her usual quirky, yet stylish elegance, she looked nothing like what the public might perceive as a country singer. She gave a brief thank-you-filled acceptance speech with far more poise and dignity than most of the rock and alternative acts, all of whom seemed to be more concerned with maintaining their mid-1990s US grunge band attitude than in showing the slightest sign of gratitude for their victory.

The Best Female Artist trophy went to Natalie Imbruglia, who, after all, had sold millions of albums worldwide, including over two million in the tough US market. But merely by being nominated as a finalist in this category, Kasey had brought honour to EMI, to Australian country music, to Nash, who produced the record, and to herself.

Kasey: Yeah, it's great. I was excited and I didn't expect it. I think I felt like I kind of had a chance as much as anybody in it, but still . . . You never really think, 'Yeah, I'm going to get it.' It's an *ARIA*—it's great. It's great to be recognised for your music and everything . . .

Winning that ARIA the other night meant a lot to me 'cause the main reason I wanted to win was as a kind of reward

Kasey after winning the 1999 ARIA Award.

for all the hard work that EMI's put into me. Because for people at EMI, it does make a difference. They can get more interviews for me and sell more albums now. But for me, personally, it doesn't mean everything. I'm not sure I won because my album's the best—it's not always about that. I was kind of more happy to win for EMI than I even really was for myself. It's great to win awards—I mean, you'd be stupid to say it doesn't mean something to you 'cause it does. It's pretty encouraging to get an ARIA, but awards are for your career, not always for your music. EMI has more to do with my career than I do. I have more to do with the music.

Although *The Captain* was clearly a Kasey Chambers solo album, the credit for its success should also spread beyond her and EMI to Nash, who produced the CD, as well as to Bill, who played guitar, lap steel or dobro on ten of the twelve cuts, and to Diane, who quietly kept on being the behind-the-scenes person who handled the office routine and continued to be the emotional anchor for Dead Ringer Band as well as for Kasey.

In addition to producing *The Captain*, Nash, at twenty-six, was also managing Kasey and Dead Ringer Band in Australia, overseeing the live sound for both acts and supervising all music publishing activities. Additionally, he was producing singer-songwriter Brent Parlane, signed to the publishing company, and a few additional artists, giving him an extremely full plate by anyone's measure.

EMI recognised the Dead Ringer Band as a free-standing entity by signing them to a separate recording contract late in November. Kasey was not about to let go of her family band. Besides, all concerned felt she could record as a part of the band in addition to her solo work, like Neil Young, Willie Nelson and Phil Collins—artists who have established solo careers and who have also claimed success in a group setting.

There is a sort of intangible yet strong psychic balance to Dead Ringer Band that, to my knowledge is unique among groups. There are two 'grown-ups' and two 'kids', one of each sex in each of the two generations. On one side of the spectrum are Bill and Kasey, the dreamers and chief musical creators. The more pragmatic Diane and Nash balance out the equation by being the two members who actually turn those dreams into reality, Nash in the studio and Diane in virtually all their other affairs. She oversees the details: booking, scheduling, correspondence, preparing their fan club newsletters and merchandising, right down to making sure everyone is fed (Nash and Kasey lived at home up until mid-2000, the better to be close to the studio). When Diane and Bill split up, back in 1997, this harmony was upset and it was no wonder the band decided to take time off. Though Diane contributes the least to the group from a musical standpoint—she plays bass on the road but rarely on the recordings—she provides the emotional glue that keeps them together. A mother, even a show business one, is still a mother!

Diane: There's more to life than musical achievement. We've had to make a pretty big sacrifice to reach where Kasey and Nash are today. They've certainly had to experience some hard times in life and learn there's more to life than just the big times.

   If you're not content and happy within yourself, what's the point of the whole heap more, striving for something that's only going to make you more lonely and sad and disillusioned? So you've got to have inner peace.

Kasey also seems to be taking success in her stride.

Kasey: Music wasn't part of something I chose to do, it was just automatically something that was a part of my everyday life. There wasn't a point where I decided that I wanted to do music, it just kind of happened. It's been as much a part of my life as my family. I know if I can just play music forever, I'll be pretty happy doing that. And I'm still going to play music and write songs, no matter what, whether I get any bigger than I do now or everything completely flops for me . . . I just want to be able to play music. And I know I can—even if I'm playing to ten people, I know I can still do it.

More touring followed the ARIA win with one highlight from this period being her sharing the bill at Hootenanny, an Erskineville Festival, with legendary singer-songwriter Paul Kelly. After seeing Kasey at that show, Kelly invited her to come down to The Basement to sing a song or two with him during his sold-out three-night run there in November. Kelly, previously known as a

Onstage, 1999.

rock/pop artist, had just released a bluegrass-flavoured album, *Smoke*, cut with the gifted Melbourne ensemble Uncle Bill, composed of Gerry Hale, Adam Gare, Peter Somerville and Stuart Speed. That album raced up to number 2 on the country charts, just behind Shania Twain's *Come On Over*, a rather more fustian offering which had gone platinum fifteen times over by 1999's end. Kasey felt right at home in the Kelly/Uncle Bill milieu, amid mandolins, fiddles, dobros and acoustic guitars—a sound much like the music she had grown up listening to and hearing her parents perform. That association seemed to click so well that before month's end plans were made for Kasey and her band to open for Kelly the week before Tamworth, as he took his acoustic show to Western Australia. During that swing, she and Kelly recorded two duets on an off day in Perth, one of her songs, 'I Still Pray' and 'Heartbreak, Heartmend', which Kelly had written. Nash produced both cuts with backing provided by Uncle Bill.

Tamworth rolled around in January and this time the four Chambers were a lot more mentally together. They had survived a rough-and-tumble year which had seen Dead Ringer Band take their first extended vacation—from music and each other—in their seven year history. It was the first time that the four Chambers had ever gone their separate ways for any extended period of time in their entire existence as a family unit. The 1999 holidays again found them scattered: Diane and Kasey recharged themselves back on Norfolk, Nash went to New Zealand to be with his girlfriend, singer Camille Te Nahu, and Bill had done spot shows around Sydney, with Audrey and as a sideman in various ensembles when she was in Tasmania with her family.

Kasey and Dead Ringer Band each slated one Tamworth show, again at the RSL club. The country music establishment had recognised the brilliance of *The Captain* just as mainstream and even rock critics had. The Toyota Country Music Awards of Australia judges had made her a finalist nominee for four awards: Album, Song, Female Vocalist and Video of the Year. Additionally, Kasey had accepted a performance slot for the Awards show. Dad Bill Chambers added another finalist nomination to the family's credit when his duet album with Audrey, *Looking Back to See*, was selected in the Group/Duo category that Dead Ringer Band had won for three of the past five years.

What's more, the album Kasey, Nash and Bill had crafted showed early signs of becoming a lasting influence on youthful, upcoming female artists. Eight months after the release of *The Captain*, it seemed every aspiring young girl performing at Tamworth was singing Kasey's songs. In one afternoon alone, the author saw six budding starlets aged ten to fifteen using their turn in the spotlight to sing either 'Cry Like a Baby', 'Don't Talk Back' or the title cut, with one newcomer even having a go at 'We're All Gonna Die Someday'!

Over on Peel Street a family group, Strict-Lee-Us, was drawing large crowds singing exclusively Dead Ringer Band and Kasey Chambers songs, each of the four Lee children—Rachel, Jarod, Faith and Savannah—under the age of twelve. Parents Steve and Tracey Lee led the group, which in January 2000 was in the midst of a year-long tour travelling throughout Australia.

Kasey's posters were up all over town, *The Captain* was displayed in all the retail shops, her album sales were trending upward and the tour dates with Paul Kelly were generating her mainstream music media coverage. It seemed there was a feeling in the air early on in Tamworth that she would do well on Awards night.

Everyone's hopes for this success were jolted just a week before the Awards presentation by a controversial and fiery Bruce Elder piece in the *Sydney Morning Herald*. The extensive feature derided Tamworth in general and attacked the CMAA establishment specifically, accusing the latter of discouraging diversity by setting up restrictive, though unwritten, rules that encouraged performers who clung to the 1940s and 1950s bush ballad tradition first popularised by Slim Dusty, Buddy Williams and Tex Morton. According to Elder, this decision had diminished interest in Australian country music during a period when the form was booming in North America.

> at a time when . . . a whole new world of fans could have been created, a small club of friends decided, probably unconsciously, to back a narrow, bucolic, nationalistic style of music that has little or no appeal outside rural areas. Given that more than 80 per cent of Australians live in cities, and Australians have been exposed to American country music for most of this century, this was a pretty dumb thing to do.

Elder quoted Kasey and Bill extensively in the article, casting them as stubborn outsiders, forsaken by the establishment, despite the excellence of their American-influenced music. The quotes used from Kasey didn't dispute Elder's charges, instead appearing to buttress his main thesis with remarks like the following:

> I don't think it'll ever change. I think a lot of the problem with the Australian country scene is that people think that something is only an Australian song if it has got Goondiwindi in it or something like that, unless you mention that it's not a true blue Australian song . . . I was brought up on Slim Dusty and Slim Dusty was brought up on stuff like Jimmie Rodgers and the Carter Family. He had his American influences as well. If you listen to my album, I was mostly brought up on American country music but I've lived my whole life in Australia, travelling around Australia, and that's what every one of my songs is about. They're about my life. Because I don't mention Goondiwindi, they (the Tamworth taste makers) think I'm copying the Americans. That's just silly.

Never the shrinking violet, Bill's own assessment of the situation was also quoted:

> I don't think they (the taste makers) care what people like. It's about patting each other on the back and making sure they all feel important. I think that 'mediocre' has come to dominate. You listen to a lot of the Australian albums and they are just not good enough. They are not produced properly. They are not played properly. They are not sung properly.

Though he had been extremely supportive and enthusiastic over the recordings for Dead Ringer Band and Kasey, this wasn't the first time Elder had placed the Chambers family into the middle of what was increasingly being seen by some as a personal vendetta against Tamworth and the CMAA. He had inserted jabs into numerous previous features about Dead Ringer Band, saying in 1997, 'the Tamworth taste makers (now that is a real oxymoron)' and going even further in 1998, referring to the establishment as . . . 'the "style Nazis" in Tamworth'.

Though it is doubtless true that some members of the country establishment prefer the music of Dusty, Williams, Lee Kernaghan and Gina Jeffreys to that of Dead Ringer Band, the fact remains that the family group's music won or shared five Gold Guitars awarded by the CMAA between 1995 and 1999, indicating that the judges, all appointed by the CMAA establishment, clearly recognised the band's merit and innovation.

As for the CMAA's dogged determination to embrace the traditional style of country music, well the US CMA had done exactly the same thing right up until the late 1980s and early 1990s when a fresh, new crop of artists like Garth Brooks, Clint Black, Trisha Yearwood, Alan Jackson, Vince Gill and Patty Loveless started gaining major radio air play at the expense of the form's longtime superstars such as Willie Nelson, Dolly Parton, Merle Haggard, Tammy Wynette, Ronnie Milsap, George Jones, Emmylou Harris, Conway Twitty, even icon Johnny Cash.

This was the background as 4500 fans gathered at the cavernous Tamworth Regional Entertainment Centre for the 28th annual Country Music Awards of Australia show on Saturday night. Though Kasey had backtracked a bit by telling Tamworth's

Northern Daily Leader, in an interview published on the Friday, that her remarks to Elder were taken out of context, there was a hint of paranoia in the air. The larger question of whether the CMAA judges would back tradition or embrace innovation overshadowed the usual curiosity of who would win each individual award. Suddenly, instead of being simply an artist with four finalist nominations, Kasey had become a 'poster girl' for progress and a polarising point in the industry.

Hopes sagged somewhat when 'The Captain' fell to Troy Cassar-Daley, Colin Buchanan and Garth Porter's composition, 'They Don't Make 'Em Like That Anymore' for the APRA Song of the Year trophy. This was not a particularly controversial choice: 'They Don't Make 'Em Like That Anymore' had been a very successful release. Cassar-Daley's vocal style, incidentally, owes far more to traditional American 'hard-country' singing pioneered by Floyd Tillman, Lefty Frizzell and Merle Haggard than to the Australian 'bush ballad' form.

Then Kasey's video of 'Cry Like a Baby' lost out to Ted Egan's clip of 'The Drover's Boy'. Egan, who began recording in 1969, lives in the remote Northern Territory and is strongly identified with both the outback and traditional Australian music. He was developing his song 'The Drover's Boy' into a feature film, but the clip itself had received scant, if any, exposure on CMT.

What happened next may well be remembered as a turning point in the development of Australian country music: Kasey took out not only the Female Vocalist, but also Album of the Year Golden Guitar with *The Captain*. Here's part of Iain Shedden's account from the 31 January *Australian*:

> There was a breath of fresh air for country music fans when rising talent Kasey Chambers was named Female Artist of the Year [sic] and her debut album *The Captain* was awarded country album of the year on Saturday night.
>
> Her awards were significant in that the 23-year-old songwriter's style sits somewhere left of the Nashville-related sound that permeates the local scene.
>
> 'It's people like Kasey Chambers who are going to open people's eyes to the fact that country has come a long way and is not sitting back in the 1960s,' said Meryl Gross, chief executive of the CMAA.

Local country music, despite large sales in the regional areas and claims by the CMAA that 3 million Australians prefer country music to any other kind, has long suffered from a serious image problem in the cities.

Chambers, with her pierced lip, grungy hair and songs more influenced by old country stars such as Hank Williams and modern American roots performer Lucinda Williams, may be about to change all that . . .

The major city dailies gave the Country Music Awards of Australia surprising—even unprecedented—coverage: within three days of her multiple victories, five separate stories ran in the *Herald*, *Australian* and *Daily Telegraph* in Sydney alone. All the pieces featured Kasey more prominently than John Williamson, who had taken home three Golden Guitars, for Bush Ballad, Heritage Song and Best Selling Album. Most of these reports were 'hooked' around the theme of 'rebel wins at Tamworth', mentioning Kasey's hair, clothes and new chin stud (a gift from Worm) more than her imaginative music.

Ray Chesterton chipped in the same day in the Sydney *Daily Telegraph*:

The new pin-up girl of Australian country music, Kasey Chambers, is something else again.

There are few, if any, Australian award-winning female country singers with a stud in their chin . . .

. . . Chambers, 23, is part of a growing new wave of young talent that has swept over Australian country music. Her win confirms that judges at Tamworth have the experience to recognise major musical shifts while maintaining links with tradition.

Kasey capped her magic night by uncharacteristically staying all evening at the official CMAA post-Awards party at the Long-yard, helping those in attendance quaff what Chesterton reported was '42 kegs of beer'. Then, at 3 a.m., with cabs in short supply, she and various friends *walked* back to her small room at the Acacia Motel some three kilometres away. You don't need a limo when you're walking on air!

The CMAA wins and Kasey's October ARIA also lifted

Nash's profile as a producer. He also helmed 'Rollin' Along', the Sparnetts CMAA-winning entry for Best Group/Duo, ironically nudging out, among others, Bill and Audrey's *Looking Back to See*. Nash produced two albums which together earned an ARIA and three Gold Guitars, thus crafting more award-winning releases than perennial CMAA Producer of the Year, Garth Porter, victorious every year between 1993 and 1999.

National mainstream magazines followed with their own take on Kasey's unusual success story; suddenly all the months of EMI's groundwork with contemporary media began to pay off.

The video for Kasey's title cut from *The Captain* was released in mid-February and was embraced immediately, gaining 'Pick Hit' status and going into heavy rotation on CMT's 16 February chart. The exciting news came the next day: both Channel V and MTV/ Australia began airing the clip, the first time Kasey had gained exposure on contemporary video outlets.

'The Captain' was the track that EMI and Kasey had felt all along had the best chance of 'crossing over' and gaining exposure for her in the much bigger mainstream radio world. The haunting, mysterious song featured guitar work from both Mark Punch and Bill, as well as Julie Miller's celestial vocal harmonies. Kasey's comments in the CD insert noted Miller's contribution to the track: 'If angels could sing, they would sound like Julie Miller.' As with all of Kasey's songs, there's a lot more involved in the story behind the song than is apparent from a casual scan of its lyrics.

Kasey: I said to Kurt, 'You know I'm going to marry you and Worm's going to marry Dana.' We used to talk about it all the time, just joke about it. I sat down and wrote this song on Norfolk for Kurt. This was the song that I was going to sing to him on our wedding day. And we weren't even together at this stage, but we had this kind of bond thing. So I wrote 'The Captain' then, but I didn't play it to him, I went away and then I taped it for him and sent it back. We got together after that, so that song kind of got us together.

The Captain

Well I don't have as many friends because
I'm not as pretty as I was
I've kicked myself at times because I've lied
So I will have to learn to stand my ground
I'll tell 'em I won't be around
I'll move on over to your town and hide

And you be the Captain
And I'll be no one
And you can carry me away if you want to
And you can lay low
Just like your father and if
I tread upon your feet you just say so
'Cos you're The Captain, I am no one
I tend to feel as though I owe one to you

Well I have handed all my efforts in
I searched here for my second wind
Is there somewhere here to let me in, I asked
So I slammed the doors they slammed at me
I found the place I'm meant to be
I figured out my destiny at last

Did I forget to thank you for the ride?
I hadn't tried, I need to run away and hide

Kasey Chambers © 1999, *Gibbon Music*

Sales increased dramatically in the wake of Kasey's Tamworth victories, the broader video exposure for the new single and the increased print media attention. *The Captain* had sold 22 000 copies prior to the January Awards, an average of 628 per week since its 17 May issue. By 11 February, two weeks afterwards, sales for *The Captain* stood at 30 000, indicating that the album had shifted 4000 copies each of those two weeks. This performance brought *The Captain* up first to number 38, then on to number 16 in the mid-February ARIA charts of the nation's best-selling albums.

At this accelerated sales pace, *The Captain* seemed set to gain 'gold' certification (sales of 35 000) in another week to ten days. Instead, strong sales early the next week pushed the CD over the coveted mark on Wednesday, 16 February, sending an electrifying jolt of energy and excitement through the EMI staff, the Chambers camp and her management team in Australia and the United States.

By 1 May, she had climbed as high as number 11 on the ARIA chart and logged an amazing ten consecutive weeks on their Top 20, an unprecedented feat for an Australian country artist. Indeed, it is rare for *any* Australian country artist to break into the top half of the ARIA best-selling list, an achievement Dead Ringer Band had never accomplished.

The same week Kasey moved to number 11 on the main ARIA chart, she also, for the first time, pushed into the number 1 slot on ARIA's country chart, knocking Shania Twain from the summit where her *Come on Over* album had been parked for over six months!

The next day, the US Country Music Association called to notify Kasey she was one of four artists chosen to perform at a special International Show at Fan Fair, the American version of Tamworth, before a crowd of up to 20 000 people.

Simultaneously, (EMI-owned) Virgin Records in the United Kingdom firmed up the release schedule for *The Captain*'s issue there, slating it for early June so Kasey could proceed on to the United States after the album launch in England. This was a very positive development and another sign that EMI felt Kasey's appeal stretched beyond the country field, for Virgin was known primarily for alternative, rock and dance releases. The company had not released an Australian country record in eight years and had not even licensed in any albums originating with Virgin/Nashville!

If *Red Desert Sky* were a fairytale, it would now be time to relate the final, biggest good news, to tie the last loose ends neatly together and end with 'and they all lived happily ever after'. But this is a book about the real lives of four people in the music industry; despite Kasey's meteoric career surges, the fully negotiated Asylum contract remained pending, over eight months after all parties had reached agreement.

Time-Warner had seen major changes in their corporate landscape in the first months since Roger Ames had been appointed. America Online (AOL), the world's biggest Internet service provider, purchased Time-Warner in December, a business move said to be worth about US$130 billion. Before the dust had settled, Time-Warner announced in January they had bought EMI, a deal valued at about US$13 billion. Deals of this magnitude obviously take precedence over all else and so, as of mid-May, Ames and his top executives had not addressed the restructuring of Time-Warner's extensive Nashville music empire.

Gossip mongers in Nashville abhor a vacuum, so industry sources soon began speculating that Evelyn would be fired and Asylum shuttered. Others posited Asylum surviving but only after drastic staff cuts. Also, Ames and his staff also had not announced who would be overseeing the Time-Warner labels as well as the two EMI imprints, Capitol and Virgin, which would become part of their Nashville stable when the merger was finalised. The obvious candidate, Jim Ed Norman, who had headed Nashville's Warner Bros operation since the mid-1980s, was, so the rumour went, planning to retire. Finding a boss for the merged entities became a moot point when the European Union let Time-Warner and EMI officials know it would not approve their planned merger.

The year 2000 had started with Kasey winning double honours at Tamworth, then touring to increasing crowds and seeing her album sales attain gold certification. She was a double finalist for APRA's most-played song honours, being short-listed in both the overall field as well as in the country section. As April turned to May, she prepared for her first trip to Europe, a primarily promotional tour planned around Virgin's release of *The Captain* in the UK, Sweden and Norway.

Unfortunately, the unresolved US/Canada recording deal, encompassing a territory representing almost 40 per cent of global record sales, hung like a dark cloud over all Kasey's extraordinary achievements. The trip she planned for Fan Fair and her performance at the international show in June now loomed larger than ever: surely the Asylum deal could be resolved during that visit.

16
Around the World ... Twice

Though Kasey and Nash had already made two trips to Nashville and Dead Ringer Band had performed throughout Australia, ventured to Norfolk Island several times and journeyed to New Zealand, the family's late 2000 and early 2001 touring program encompassed a much vaster, near global scale of touring. Kasey's itinerary during the ten-and-a-half months beginning in May 2000 included two around-the-world forays, three additional trips to the United States, quick visits to Norway, Sweden and Scotland, numerous Australian dates, two full-fledged United States tours and one American 'mini-tour', all of which totalled over 230 000 kilometres. That's an average of 730 kilometres per day for 315 days!

It is said that the longest journey begins with a single step and on 15 May, Kasey, Bill, Worm and fiddler/guitarist Mick Albeck took a long first step—travelling from Darwin to London to debut *The Captain* in Europe. Tony Harlow and Gary Rabin had reached an agreement with Paul Conroy, Managing Director of Virgin Records in England, to release *The Captain* there. Virgin had become a part of the EMI empire in 1992 when it was purchased from founder Richard Branson for £560 million, an acquisition which added world-renowned artists the Rolling Stones and Janet Jackson to the EMI stable. It was felt that Virgin would be a better European home for Kasey than parent company EMI, partly due to the expertise and reputation of Conroy and partly because a project such as Kasey's could be lost easily at the far larger EMI label. Working together, Rabin, Conroy and

Virgin's Glenn Middleworth decided to launch Kasey to country music audiences first, then take her to the broader mainstream market. This approach varied from EMI's method in Australia, which was to bring Kasey to country and mainstream audiences simultaneously.

Conroy introduced *The Captain* via a pair of showcases at Virgin's spacious headquarters, transforming a large conference room into a concert venue for Kasey, Bill and Mick to deliver stripped-down, acoustic versions of *The Captain* to the company, selected media and various other dignitaries. It was an event that was extremely well received by the 200 in attendance. In fact, BBC Radio announcer Johnie Walker was so taken with Kasey that he rang up Bryan Ferry's manager to suggest Kasey be given an opening slot on some of Ferry's 'Stately Mansions' shows in July, outdoor events staged on the grounds of various large estates.

Virgin was also pleased with Kasey's performance and the audience's overwhelmingly enthusiastic reaction. They decided to commission a remix of 'Cry Like A Baby'. This move, it was felt, would make her music more accessible to contemporary radio, accustomed more to dance music, teen bands and angst-ridden male rock groups.

Over the next three weeks, Kasey did numerous interviews with national, regional and local press and the acoustic trio performed at various radio stations, at showcases for Virgin in Stockholm and Oslo and as the opening act for Steve Forbert at Dingwall's, a venerable London club. As in Australia, the early media response was encouraging. David Quantick, of the influential mainstream music magazine Q, assigned Kasey's CD a four-star rating in a rave review:

> *The Captain* is, frankly, an astonishing debut album. Songs such as 'You Got The Car' and 'Cry Like A Baby' are mature and rocking, and sound like a lifetime's experience rammed into the mouth of youth . . . this is the work of a new world pop star in the making.

The country press rhapsodised about the album, Kasey's personality and the live show. In an album review and a report of Kasey's Swedish showcase for *Country Music International*, reviewer Hugh Gregory raved over her show at Torsgatan 1, concluding that 'she could have played all night and no one would have minded, Kasey Chambers is that good.'

Kasey fondly recalled that show and her Norwegian debut, telling journalist Mick Daley:

> The first night in Stockholm it was dead silent and really scary. I've never played to a crowd that has been this silent y'know. You could hear all my mistakes. And after every song they would clap for so long, which is great, 'cause I had time to tune my guitar . . . When we played in Oslo it was exactly the same and we got three encores both nights. I've never even gotten two encores in Australia in my life, but they just wouldn't let us go.

Over in Nashville, Kasey's situation remained unresolved. Asylum survived as a free-standing label under the aegis of Evelyn Shriver, though the new corporate regime had decreed Evelyn dismiss about three quarters of her staff. In addition to the signing freeze, Asylum was not allowed to begin new recording, a circumstance which prevented them from taking George Jones into the studio for the follow-up to his Grammy-winning comeback, *Cold Hard Truth*. While Evelyn remained steadfast in her desire to sign Kasey and release *The Captain* in the United States, she had not received a green light from Warner Bros' Nashville head Jim Ed Norman or from Roger Ames, the overall boss of Warner Music in New York. To further complicate matters, Evelyn and Susan Nadler were both in the last year of their initial Asylum contract and neither knew the corporation's plans for them after April 2001.

Nevertheless, in early June Kasey embarked on an ambitious schedule in Nashville, beginning with a star-studded writers' night show at the Bluebird Cafe, the same cosy venue where she, Nash and local guitarist Russ Pahl had showcased on 1 December 1998. If Kasey was nervous at that first performance, just imagine how she felt this time—she was slated to swap songs with not only Lucinda Williams, one of her biggest influences, but also Joy Lynn White, a well-known and highly regarded artist with three releases to date, and host Cindy Bullens, who had first made her mark as an electric-guitar playing rocker back in the late 1970s and was now touring to promote her critically acclaimed CD, *Somewhere Between Heaven and Earth*.

These performances were done 'Writers in a Row' style, with the four women and a supporting musician for each lined up across the stage. Each performed one song per 'round'. Kasey immediately followed Lucinda Williams and, though Kasey was a little shaky on her first round, the packed house greeted 'Cry Like A Baby' with enthusiastic applause. Emboldened, she sailed through the additional four rounds with growing confidence, stealing the hearts of the packed house.

The next day Kasey, Bill, Mick and Worm were re-united with their rhythm section: drummer B.J. Barker and bassist Jeff McCormack. This Nashville trip, Kasey's third, had been built around her selection as one of just four acts chosen to perform at a special international showcase during Nashville's Fan Fair. She was picked for the show along with fellow Aussies Troy Cassar-Daley and Jane Saunders and UK singer-songwriter Adam Couldwell. Indeed, she was named first choice by each member of the seven-person committee of leading industry professionals.

Described by long-time country author/TV producer Robert K. Oermann as a 'crazed fiesta of the proletariat', Fan Fair is an event completely unique in popular music. The week-long country music festival, staged in Nashville annually since 1972, brings thousands of the world's most rabid country fans to Music City every June. There they pay homage to their favourite stars. The artists also spend several hours paying homage to their fans by signing autographs and posing for photos with them, activities centred in booths located in five nearby buildings on the state fairgrounds. The artists perform on two massive stages erected on an adjacent racetrack during a series of concerts hosted by the various record labels. By the time the last guitar chords fade into the humid June night, well over 100 artists have entertained the fervent crowds.

Kasey gained an unusual opportunity to perform twice on the big fairground stage. Her first showing was at the kickoff concert for Fan Fair 2000, joining a bill that included Bryan White, Chad Brock and Chalee Tennison. Kasey sang four songs with her full band and closed with 'We're All Gonna Die Someday', getting a major surprise when some members of the audience joined in to sing the chorus!

Holding her own with Lucinda Williams at the Bluebird Cafe and, the next day, doing the same on the Fan Fair stage in front of 10 000 people were impressive feats for a new artist on her way home to Australia after three weeks in Europe. With a full head of steam, Kasey and the boys sailed through a Tower Records in-store performance and a featured slot on Billy Block's 'Western Beat' show at the Exit/In on Tuesday. It was Billy's show that, in November 1996, presented the first public performance of Dead Ringer Band on US soil. The 2000 appearance was enlivened considerably when Lucinda Williams joined Kasey onstage for a riveting, rocking version of Lu's song, 'Changed The Locks'.

In addition to presenting Kasey to the public, the Nashville shows gave Warner Bros executives and the few remaining Asylum staffers several chances to see her onstage. Before this trip, only four company execs had actually seen Kasey perform. The label had, in fact, advanced thousands of dollars in expense funds for this trip and, while the Execution Copy of her contract was yet to be presented, it seemed unlikely that Warner Bros would bring Kasey to Nashville to say they couldn't do the deal that had been pending now for ten months.

Still, the biggest hurdle remained: a 15 June showcase performance for the record company at Douglas Corner, just a few hours after the international show at Fan Fair. This would be their last opportunity to play for the entire company, including Nashville President Jim Ed Norman, who had heard plenty about Kasey by this time. Even though the label seemed ready to finalise the deal, if Warner's didn't like what they saw at Douglas Corner they could still write off the expenses and say goodbye.

The beginning of the day did not bode well. Fan Fair's international show was a bust. It followed Audium Records' presentation of fan favourites Ricky Van Shelton, The Kentucky Headhunters and country music Hall-of-Famer Loretta Lynn. A crowd of about 10 000 was on hand, but as soon as Loretta closed the show, all but a few hundred departed, presenting Kasey, Troy, Jane and Adam with a crowd smaller than they were used to entertaining at home.

Each performer was allowed fifteen minutes onstage so, undeterred, Kasey and crew gave it their best before hustling over to Douglas Corner, where their real US fate would be determined before an audience of about 200. After two lost deals and a quest that began over fifty months before, the chips were really down: if Kasey, Bill, Mick, Jeff and B.J. delivered onstage, Warner's would move forward with the release of *The Captain* in the US and launch a new chapter in the Chambers family saga.

As the crowd filed in for the 6 p.m. show Gary and I noticed that all the key Warner execs from Nashville were in attendance as well as several from corporate headquarters in Burbank, California. We knew they'd all listened to *The Captain* and clearly enjoyed the CD; now, however, was when the rubber really met the road. Kasey and the band had to prove they could deliver in a live setting—record companies usually won't sign artists lacking a reasonable amount of onstage experience. (Though that rule has slackened in the past several years as labels sign increasing numbers of teenage and pre-teen singers.)

Kasey and the band put on a fine show, exhibiting more than enough talent and star power to make the label feel excited about moving forward. Though Kasey was 'a little croaky' during the show—she had stayed out late the night before watching Hank Williams III perform—it was clear that she was extraordinarily talented and very gracious onstage. The label also realised that Kasey's band had chops aplenty, that the licks they recorded on *The Captain* were not the result of overdubbing and 'patching in' but of skills equal to the top level of the Nashville 'cats'. All talk of assembling a separate US-based band for Kasey's subsequent touring instantly evaporated.

Their final performance on this trip, a guest appearance on the Grand Ole Opry, meant a lot emotionally to Kasey but was the fulfilment of a lifelong dream for Bill. Begun in 1925, the Opry is the world's longest continually broadcast non-news radio program and the main reason the country music business settled in Nashville when the recording industry surged after World War II. WSM radio pumped the show out with 50 000 watts of clear channel power. There were far fewer broadcast outlets back then so that blowtorch of a signal was received thousands of kilometres away. Indeed, the Opry has letters from listeners in

Europe, from country lovers who hear it above the Arctic Circle, in northern Canada, from far south in the Caribbean and South America, across the Rocky Mountains, in California and as far west as Hawaii. WSM broadcasts the Grand Ole Opry live every Saturday night in a variety show format, each fifteen minute segment hosted by a long-time Opry member who presents three or four artists, each of whom delivers one or two songs.

Even though it is far less important to an artist's career today than it was in its salad days from the 1930s to the 1960s, performing on the Opry is still a dream cherished by thousands upon thousands of artists. Few of those hopefuls ever make it to the Opry stage and, indeed, it would probably only take the fingers of two hands to count the Australians who have earned this enviable honour.

On the way back home, Kasey and Gary stopped off to visit a few folks at the Warner Bros offices in Burbank where they picked up—at long last—the Execution Copy of the contract. Now all that remained was for EMI and Kasey's lawyer to vet it.

Back home, Kasey had barely enough time—less than a month in fact—to play a few Australian shows. She also learned that she had been chosen for a Mo Award as Best Country Touring Artist, the first time she had won that honour as a solo performer. Then she and her hardy bandmates again set forth on what was to be a second trip around the world. This time they began by flying to England for a series of club shows, book-ended by two 'Stately Mansions' dates with Bryan Ferry. One of the club dates, at London's famed Borderline, showed clear signs that her reputation was spreading in England—a large crowd lined up long before the doors opened at the downtown London venue, a club that has hosted virtually all the greats of the rock, folk, blues and country worlds.

Then Kasey started receiving media attention in the mainstream press. An Adam Sweeting 4 July profile in *The Guardian*, inexplicably titled 'Daughter of a Preacher Man', marked her first major exposure beyond music-specific publications in Europe.

With her Goth-like eye makeup, studs in her nose and lower lip and a ring through her right ear, Chambers isn't much like anyone you'd associate with country music of any era. Then again, her life bears little resemblance to anything you've ever heard before either. While other Australian kids were raised on teen soaps and the Minogue sisters, Chambers was leading a nomadic lifestyle hunting foxes on the Nullarbor Plain.

. . . Consequently, while it's still a debut solo album by a young artist, *The Captain* exudes a maturity and self-awareness you'd expect from somebody ten years older, comfortably spanning bluegrass, hillbilly music and crunchy country rock.

All was not champagne and roses, however. Virgin's idea for a remix failed to meet Kasey and Nash's approval. Bear in mind, a remixer begins by stripping everything but the vocal from a track, then rebuilding the cut by adding new instrumentation and/or electronic effects. As Nash and Kasey are extremely meticulous about their recordings, one can only imagine the pair's reaction to hearing the sensitive memoir 'Cry Like A Baby' re-arranged to sound like a pulsing and throbbing dance-pop selection. So, without the tool that Virgin felt necessary to secure radio play, and unable to expose Kasey beyond the very limited country market, Virgin's enthusiasm waned.

The band returned home, flying east over Europe and Asia, while Kasey and Nash followed the setting sun so they could meet with Evelyn and the Asylum folks, pay their respects to the Warner Bros staff and enjoy a low key trip to Nashville, the first time they had come to Music City without a scheduled performance. There, they learned of Nash's selection by the CMAA membership as their Producer of the Year, the first honour which spotlighted him for his impressive recording achievements. His selection earned Nash a crown that had been held by Garth Porter for the last seven consecutive years, and it was a victory which marked another major triumph over the establishment for the maverick Chambers family.

Kasey recorded over seventy liners for Asylum's use in radio promotion ('Hi, I'm Kasey Chambers and you're listening to . . .'), Nash met with several publishers and, with the advance copies of the album set to go to US media in August, the pair got to spend

a night hitting local hotspots to enjoy some of Nashville's exceptional non-country artists strutting their stuff in the city's small
clubs. Kasey later told journalist Daniel Durchholz:

> All of the music that we get in Australia from Nashville is the mainstream
> country stuff. I kind of thought that's what Nashville was all about. But
> then I got there and realised there was this little underground thing
> going on that no one really hears about in Australia. There's just the
> best singer-songwriters in the world out playing in these little bars . . .
> I had no idea.

Now Warner/Nashville's task was to fire up the rest of the
label, to get them to be as enthusiastic about Kasey as they
themselves had become once they saw her show. Fortunately, EMI
had made an electronic press kit (EPK) a few months earlier—the
short film was a fine introduction, showing Kasey in live performance and interview settings, accepting awards and discussing her
unusual history. Warner's Janice Azrak, Senior Vice-President for
Artist Development, felt this was the perfect way to add another
dimension to Kasey. The EPK gave her fellow employees a close
look at this Australian whom all had heard of but few had seen.

Nash and Kasey arrived home on 31 July and twelve days later
they again returned to the USA for a quick series of shows and
press interviews to help set the stage for the album's planned
18 September issue. The label felt the best way to promote *The
Captain* was at a prestigious conference, the *Gavin* AAA/Americana
Summit, an annual gathering in Boulder, Colorado, a lovely
college town 1800 metres up the eastern edge of the Rocky
Mountains.

The Summit attracts only a few hundred radio programmers,
label staffers, radio promotion specialists, artists and media but
most of the key figures in AAA (Adult Album Alternative) and
Americana radio attend. A good showing at the Summit would
definitely start a 'buzz' with plenty of influential taste-makers in

those fields and hopefully pave the way for early acceptance of Kasey's album.

But Kasey was feeling a bit under the weather when she reached Boulder on 16 August. Was it any wonder? In fourteen weeks, she had ventured around the world twice, made one additional round trip from Sydney to LA and racked up thousands of kilometres of internal travel in Europe, the United States and Australia. She had journeyed at least 115 000 kilometres in 104 days, averaging over 1000 kilometres of travel every day for nearly three-and-a-half consecutive months! In addition, she and the band had to battle Boulder's altitude. All had spent their lives at or near sea level—now they were at 1800 metres, a circumstance that required some acclimatisation. There was a day of rest built into the schedule but Kasey would have to take the stage for her Summit performance before her body had time to completely recover.

The Summit showcases are held in two adjacent venues— historic small club Tulagi's and the much larger Fox Theatre, a converted cinema which earned its greatest fame as the primary launching pad for the Dave Matthews Band. Kasey was slated to play at Tulagi's while, next door, better known acts such as Joan Osborne, David Gray, Johnny Lang, Patty Griffin, old pal Matthew Ryan, Joe Jackson and Aimee Mann were booked. In theory the Tulagi's shows were supposed to happen during set changes at the Fox so concertgoers could bop back and forth and see every act to play both venues. In reality, sound checks for multiple bands took far too long. Thus sets overlapped and once seated in the Fox, people stayed.

We all knew we had a late start in promoting Kasey as advance copies of the album had barely reached the media by Convention time. Jon Grimson, the AAA/Americana radio specialist hired to gain airplay for *The Captain*, had been working less than a month. Evelyn had enacted several plans to spread awareness of Kasey and *The Captain* among the 450-odd delegates. She placed a full-page ad on the first page of *Gavin's* Convention insert, featuring Lucinda Williams' quote about Kasey being her 'favourite new artist'. Kasey's EPK was looped into the hotel's closed-circuit TV network. Asylum placed three huge posters in strategic spots throughout the official Summit hotel.

Despite our efforts, just over 100 people came by Tulagi's to see Kasey onstage. The scheduling was partly to blame: late sound checking meant Kasey's show did not begin until after Johnny Lang kicked off at the Fox. But the real culprit was too little lead time to arouse people's curiosity in this exotic import. The irony of this was cutting: *The Captain* had been in release for fifteen months in Australia and three months in England. Her contract, still unsigned, had now been fully negotiated for just over a year. Numerous US print media critics had received advance copies of the album in the form of the EMI release, the Virgin European CD or via Asylum. But this advance guard held off reviewing *The Captain* until it was in release so, while she may have been a secret to radio and the general public, Kasey was well known to print media taste-makers and was a hot item on several Internet music newsgroups. All of us, frankly, had hoped to entice more people to Tulagi's.

Kasey's health was even worse after the show. Four dates remained, including a critically important Warner Bros showcase at the Roxy, one of Los Angeles' best-known and most enduring clubs. At the Roxy, Kasey would be performing before dozens of the top Warner Bros executives from the company's film and music headquarters, Los Angeles' top media and other assorted music business dignitaries. If she and the band impressed this crowd, 'blew them away' as they say in the trade, it would almost certainly mean the label would support *The Captain* fully and make a long-term commitment to establishing Kasey in the US market.

Kasey, Bill and Mick had to fly from Boulder to San Jose, California then drive a hundred miles Saturday evening for a live morning show in Santa Cruz. All of us wondered how well Kasey would be able to perform. This was clearly the low point in the second half of 2000.

Maybe it is always darkest before the dawn. Kasey made a quick recovery and, on Sunday, she sang well on John Sandidge's morning show, 'Please Stand By', a Sunday staple on KPIG radio. She serenaded folks for half an hour and created a demand for the band which led to Santa Cruz shows on the next two tours, the second of which, in mid-March 2001, sold out the day tickets went on offer.

In an ideal world every act signed with a major label would receive a concerted effort for months, even years, from all divisions of the company. In such a situation, the label would work extremely hard at 'artist development' in the hope that they could build a 'career' artist, one who would become an established star and sell for decades. Today's reality is that new artists usually get a very short window of opportunity to demonstrate success, and the only indicator most labels deem important is the cash register. Record companies have dozens of acts to promote, too few employees to work them and too few hours in the day to devote to artist development. Thus, today's attitude is more, 'Develop fast or we'll find another artist.'

Kasey's album, as good as it was, wasn't a 'slam dunk' for radio. The production was sparse and the overall feel was one of mysterious melancholy, while the country music in fashion was heavily produced, up- or mid-tempo tunes with positive messages and happy endings. (Pundits derisively term this 'Hallmark Card Country' or 'suburban western'.) Though they were outstanding technical creations, most of these frothy concoctions lacked the 'heart' and 'soul' that had been essential to country music since its beginnings. Everyone admired the craft in such tunes but many worried that they were being written not from deep inside the writer but straight from the wallet. Lots of artists had abandoned the trappings of country music altogether and, with the help of skilled producers, fashioned outright pop records: Shania Twain, Faith Hill, Lonestar and Leann Rimes are prime examples.

Kasey's music didn't fit easily into this 'modern country' format and it would be hard to gain airplay on rock, pop or urban stations. The US radio market is highly regimented, with categories for numerous styles of music, each with reporting stations and a trade chart. On first listen *The Captain* fits best into the Americana/AAA formats, but these formats were not supported by enough powerful stations to drive sales into the 100 000 plus realm necessary for Warner Bros to recoup their substantial signing, recording, radio promotion, tour support and marketing expenses. The label felt Kasey needed to move from the

Americana/AAA format into pop and Top 40, arenas dominated by densely produced up-tempo, positive fare or rap artists.

However, the Warner Bros label family, including Atlantic, Asylum, Reprise, Elektra and Sire, has had a long and glorious history of finding, nurturing and developing enduring, often unconventional, artists who weren't initial sales smashes but who went on to sell records consistently for over twenty years—including such treasures as Aretha Franklin, Neil Young, Joni Mitchell, Prince, Madonna, Jimi Hendrix, the Grateful Dead, the Doors, John Prine, Talking Heads and Queen. Asylum Records, founded in 1970 by David Geffen, initially as an outlet to present the records of distinctive new songwriter-artist Jackson Browne, went on to help propel Linda Ronstadt and Joni Mitchell to mainstream success and to develop the most commercially successful country rock band ever, the Eagles.

If Kasey did not have contemporary trends on her side when she took the Roxy stage she did have lots of history in her corner. If she and the band impressed this crowd they could count on getting solid support for the US release of *The Captain*; if they stumbled . . . well, they could expect lip service and little more.

In such situations it's good to recruit a few allies and friends so the audience is 'salted' with a few wildly enthusiastic boosters. Kasey's team augmented the label's official list with some long-time media pals, kindred-soul artists like Jann Brownie, Katy Moffat and Patty Booker, and personal friends. I asked Lucinda Williams if she knew anyone in the area who might want to come, expecting a few names and addresses. Instead, a few days later, I received a *ten*-page list of contacts she'd made during her days of living in Los Angeles! Evelyn wrote a personal note to accompany the invitation to each one of the sixty-three people on Lucinda's list. Meanwhile, the Warner Bros publicity staff busied themselves getting the word out.

The Roxy sound check went smoothly on the night and we all assembled next door to the club at the Rainbow Room, a restaurant/bar whose fame as a haven for rock'n'rollers and other musical allnighters almost matched that of the Roxy. The darkness settled over us as we dined amid the splendour of LA's Sunset Strip—all of us knew tonight's show was certainly the most important US performance Kasey, Bill and the band had faced so far.

Simply and succinctly, Kasey and the band *soared* in front of a full house of over 400 of LA's most important musical movers and shakers. The sixteen songs in the hour-plus set included an equal mixture of covers and selections from *The Captain*. In addition to her usual rapid fire version of 'If I Could' (a Tim Carroll song popularised by John Prine), their two-song 'Fred Eaglesmith suite', and homages to Lucinda Williams ('Changed The Locks') and Matthew Ryan ('Guilty'), Kasey delighted the crowd by singing Woody Guthrie's tale of Depression-era poverty, 'Do Re Mi', and then she encored with a spine-tingling take on one of Warner artist Iris DeMent's most powerful compositions, 'No Time To Cry'. 'No Time To Cry' is not the type of song a performer would ordinarily use for an encore—it's a sad, slow, stately ballad that takes about five minutes to quietly build to a sombre payoff. Yet Kasey and the band held the crowd spellbound, well nigh breathless, for the duration of DeMent's masterwork. This, remember, was an audience mainly composed of veteran clubgoers and the most jaded, cynical industry figures this side of New York City. They had never seen Kasey Chambers before they sat down at 8 p.m. Yet when Kasey sang 'No Time To Cry', the Roxy quieted like a cathedral during a preacher's prayer.

Belinda Coward of the online magazine *Blunt Review* summarised the night:

> I ended up holding my water until Ms Chambers was finished serenading the stunned Roxy crowd with some of the most impressive songs written and sung. All this in a voice that would make even Emmylou Harris jealous . . .
>
> This 24-year-old sensation had the jaded LA music crowd on its feet not once, but twice. This is so rare an occurrence, I thought we might be breaking a city ordinance by giving Kasey a standing ovation . . .

In the eyes of Warner Bros that extraordinary performance elevated Kasey from two dimensions to a full-fledged three. Many in the Burbank headquarters had fallen in love with Kasey's look, attitude and sound from her CD, her EPK and the video clips.

Several staffers had said there was more excitement in the building over an artist they hadn't yet seen than at any time since Sire had launched k.d. Lang's career in 1987. Thus, there was a lot of anticipation in the room that night. Then Kasey, Bill, B.J., Mick and Richard came out and sounded even better than the album, proving to all at the Roxy that they could expertly deliver the goods in a live setting.

Everyone took a deep breath and prepared for the remaining two shows on this brief but high-profile tour. They had a short set at a small LA club, The Mint, before concluding with a showcase for a regional Warner Music Group sales conference at the Ritz-Carlton hotel in Pasadena. This show presented another set of challenges. It's always hard to get a good sound in the boxy, high-ceilinged confines of a hotel ballroom. There was no way to 'salt' this crowd with friends as it was a private Warner function. The sales reps had already been in meetings and presentations for three full days—Kasey's performance was the last key event of the convention. And this audience of Warner sales reps covered all music spectrums—there was no guarantee that all of them would appreciate Kasey's nuanced, quietly compelling songs and delivery.

But Kasey, Bill, B.J., Mick and Richard delivered a solid performance that kept the crowd in their seats and earned them a legitimate standing ovation at the end of their thirty minutes onstage. Thus in two nights they had captivated, first, most of Warner Bros and the Los Angeles media and, then, the much more hard-boiled sales reps, the ones out in the field actually selling the music to retailers.

Mission accomplished, everyone headed for home. Now it was up to the record company to finalise all the necessary preparations for the release of The Captain in America. Another of the Chambers family dreams was now on the verge of becoming reality.

17

The Captain in America

The performances at the Roxy and Ritz-Carlton really started the Warner Bros motors running; now they knew why their co-workers in Nashville were so excited. In the wake of those stunning shows, Chris Palmer, who coordinated projects between Warner Bros' Burbank and Nashville offices, quickly moved the album release from 18 September to 10 October. This would permit more time to set up the record with media, radio and retail accounts. It was also clear that Kasey, Bill and the band could deliver the goods in concert, so live performances became a major ingredient in Kasey's introduction to US audiences. Warner's envisioned a three to four week tour beginning in October, just two months away.

The wheels were already in motion for *The Captain* on radio. The album was shipped to over 100 AAA/Americana stations in August, following the Summit. The Americana outlets quickly embraced it: the full CD and 'emphasis' track, 'Cry Like A Baby', entered the weekly charts published by the *Gavin Report* magazine at number 24 and number 16 respectively, each the highest entry for 15 September. Both moved into the Top 10 within two weeks: *The Captain* reached number 5 on 12 October, the week the CD initially hit retail racks.

Soon everyone was smiling from reading numerous reviews, much like EMI had enjoyed upon *The Captain*'s original May 1999 release. Though not every review was a rave, all of them—and there were literally hundreds—were highly favourable:

The opening track immediately earns her a place on singer-songwriter Olympus with John Prine and Iris DeMent. Indeed, hers is the most impressive debut in the folk country field since DeMent's in 1992. (Randy Lewis, *Los Angeles Times*, 9 October)

. . . a moving, upbeat, well-crafted set of songs that refreshingly articulates the experience of being alive . . . Chambers' voice has a Williams-like quality to it. That could mean Victoria's wispiness, Lucinda's gutsiness, or even Hank's plain-spokenness. (Craig Havighurst, *The Tennessean*, 9 October)

Chambers' first effort is reductive and traditional, a masterpiece of country minimalism. In rock singer-songwriter terms, we're talking Richard (Television) Lloyd-reductive, Lou Reed-traditional, Leonard Cohen-minimal . . . As a country vocalist, Kasey Chambers parks herself just outside the Hillbilly Lament Trailer Park on Emmylou Lane. (Sam Slovick, *BIGWORDS.com*, 10 October)

An important new artist with something to say . . . When she sings, you believe. There are no contrivances here. She's an artist with a vision, not a marketing plan. (Mario Tarradell, *Dallas Morning News*, 15 October)

The Captain is as simple as a diamond and sparkles as brightly . . . If she can write songs this plangent and melodic for her first album, it is awesome to imagine the artist she may become. (Arion Berger, *Washington Post*, 18 October)

The year's best Americana album may well be the US debut of 24-year-old Aussie newcomer Kasey Chambers. Chambers' voice shimmers like polished silver, and her song writing reveals a youthful wisdom. (Richard Skanse, *US Weekly*, 23 October)

The dean of US rock critics, Robert Christgau, delivered his verdict in the 24 October issue of New York City's *Village Voice*, saying of Kasey's voice:

. . . its blurred drawl is deep country like Iris DeMent, its little-girl timbre evokes Dolly Parton and whispers Lolita. It's utterly arresting and as soon as it warbles, 'I never lived through the great Depression/ Sometimes I feel as though I did', you want to kiss her.

Thus, everything seemed to be going perfectly. Radio and the press were embracing *The Captain*, Bobby Cudd was setting up the next tour and retail orders were encouraging. Then a black cloud suddenly appeared: on 13 October the *Gavin Report* announced that it was dropping their Americana, jazz and several other charts and switching to monthly publication. The label's plan to establish Kasey in the Americana field, ease her onto AAA radio and move from there to mainstream play, was seriously affected. Kasey needed the exposure success a published chart brings to more easily cross over to a new format. Everyone had worked to hit number 1 on the Americana chart and, by reaching Top 5 in just six weeks, there was every reason to believe she would reach that goal no later than early November. Now, with the album finally in shops, Kasey's main supporting radio format was abandoned by the very magazine that had launched and nurtured it for five years.

Meanwhile, Kasey and her hard-working band were keeping the home folks happy with a series of shows throughout prime Dead Ringer Band territory in South Australia and Victoria. *The Captain* continued to sell well even though it was now entering its 16th month of release. Indeed, it remained in the Top 5 of the CMAA chart and even bumped back up to the top slot several times.

The ARIA Awards nominations were announced in September and Kasey was again a Best Female Artist finalist. The single of 'The Captain' was announced as a finalist choice for Record of the Year, a real surprise. A year ago she had won the Best Country Release ARIA with sales of *The Captain* no more than 15 000; now the album had passed 100 000 and was expected to reach double platinum before her second CD was released in mid-2001. These two nominations honoured Nash and Bill, as producer and guitarist, as well as harmony vocalist Julie Miller, guest guitarist Mark Punch, B.J. and Jeff. Kasey's four finalist nominations in the two years also gave Nash a claim on four—and there were few producers in any genre who could boast as many in 1999 and 2000.

This time the pundits reckoned Kasey a dark horse in the Best Female Artist category, a darker one still for the Record of the Year honour. Nineteen-year-old phenomenon Vanessa Amorosi, with 215 000 in sales, had six finalist nominations, including Best Female Artist. She and other finalists Kylie Minogue and Christine Anu had enjoyed high-profile spots at the Sydney Olympics closing ceremony just a few weeks previous.

'My vibe is I've got no chance this year to take home an award, but it will be fun,' Kasey told Dino Scatena of the *Daily Telegraph*. Elsewhere she assessed her chances as 'zero' and was clearly more excited about singing a duet with Paul Kelly at the ARIA show, her first performance at the glittering ceremony.

The Record of the Year prize went to Madison Avenue, for their dance/pop hit, 'Don't Call Me Baby'. Kasey and Paul performed a fine version of 'I Still Pray', earning a thunderous ovation. Then the 400 judges' decision for Best Female Artist was announced . . . *Kasey Chambers!*

'I never thought this would happen,' she told the *Courier-Mail*. 'I don't even know what I'm thinking right now. It's really weird. It's fantastic.' She commented to Zena Connell, 'People like me don't win awards like this. I'm just this little kid from the Nullarbor Plain and now I'm holding an ARIA. It's really weird.'

Later she advanced a new theory to Marcus Casey of the *Daily Telegraph*: 'There must have been some mistake. Someone must have been tampering with the awards backstage I reckon. So whoever it was I want to find them and thank them.' Deeper in the interview she exhibited even more of her endearing humility: 'I have been just really lucky. I was stoked I won last night but it doesn't make me the best female artist in Australia [laughs]. But that's OK with me. I know I'm not a better singer than Christine Anu, but it's pretty flattering.'

Even if she'd wanted to bask in this newfound glory, Kasey had scant time to do so. Her first large scale US tour, a three-week coast-to-coast journey, was set to begin on 31 October in Los

Angeles. She'd fly from Sydney on the 29th, just five days after her ARIA triumph. With the album finally in the US market and scintillating reviews pouring in, Evelyn and Warner's wanted her and the band performing before as many people as possible.

Diane Chambers and Camille Te Nahu augmented the normal travelling squad of the band—Diane would sell Kasey T-shirts, sweatshirts and caps while Camille would reprise her role as backup singer on 'The Captain' and add other vocal harmonies when necessary. Greg Wilkinson, an experienced tour manager they had met in Boulder, was hired to handle advance logistics.

Initially travelling in two vans, they drove from Los Angeles to Santa Cruz and on to San Francisco before flying to Nashville. A huge tour bus met them at the airport. All the travellers walked up and down, marvelling at the bunks on the side, the shower, plush couches, toilet, small kitchen and extensive video equipment. After years of cramped travelling in small vans or cars, they would now be rolling in luxury.

They cruised overland to the eastern part of the US to tape the syndicated radio programs 'Mountain Stage' and 'World Cafe', made a quick swing into Philadelphia, then headed to New York City for their official introductory Manhattan showcase, set for popular nightspot, The Fez. Next they flew to Austin for two shows, taped 'Austin City Limits', flew back to the east coast for three more club dates, appeared on 'Late Night With David Letterman' and then closed the tour on 21 November at the heralded Chicago listening room, Schuba's Tavern.

Despite the loss of the Americana chart, Evelyn kept Jon Grimson on as a consultant to continue to work those stations. After all, they didn't stop playing Americana records just because a magazine in San Francisco stopped publishing a chart. Also, no one expected *The Captain* to be a record with a 'quick burn' (one which bores listeners after just a few weeks). Jon kept right on calling and the stations kept right on playing Kasey's CD. Six months later, in mid-April, Kasey was still in the Americana Top 10 on the new chart which *Album Network* magazine began publishing in mid-March.

In mid-October Evelyn added another dimension to the promotional push by hiring Jeff Walker's company, AristoMedia, to service and promote the film clip of 'Cry Like A Baby' to US video outlets. Walker, an Australian, moved to Nashville over twenty years ago and had established the first video promotion company in Music City. Aristomedia's first report, dated 13 November, showed Kasey's clip on just 20 per cent of the available outlets. The 5 January report detailed video play on 59 per cent of outlets, including twenty-three of the thirty-one possible shows in the southern United States. Though the novelty and heyday of video clips have passed, they continue to be a vital element for promoting a new artist. 'Cry Like A Baby' was aired quickly by both CMT and Great American Country, the two national country video networks. VH–1 and MTV initially rejected it as 'too twangy' and 'cool, but just too country for our alt leaning format'. To their credit, however, Warner Bros and AristoMedia refused to take 'no' for an answer. By April, because of her continued great press, high profile TV spots and US touring, both networks agreed to reconsider.

By this time, Warner's was circulating the clip for the title cut, a surreal film noir-ish take on 'The Captain', shot in black and white. The striking, mysterious video looked nothing like a country clip and, indeed, had first brought Kasey mainstream exposure back home.

For the four Chambers though, the highlight of this tour was their first trip to Austin, widely touted as 'the live music capital of the world' and the one-time home stomping grounds of many of their favourite artists: Lucinda Williams, Townes Van Zandt, Buddy and Julie Miller among them. Evelyn's persistence and Kasey's growing media profile landed the booking on 'Austin City Limits', a superb public TV program now in its 26th year of presenting great artists in concert before a live audience. The show had become known as a program which spotted and pre-sented important artists from many musical genres at the onset of their careers. There are usually two artists per show: at the 12 November taping, Kasey was paired with one of her musical heroes: Steve Earle.

'Austin City Limits' is syndicated nationally and produced simply but the result is stunning: superb musicians doing what they do best with no intrusion from a host, no pausing for commercials, no flashy graphics or effects—just artists at work. Each artist performs about forty-five minutes before a live audience of 400. Dolly Parton, Phish, Jewel, Robert Cray, Lynyid, Joan Osborne, Wilco and Willie Nelson all performed during the 2000–01 season, illustrating the eclectic good taste of the program. According to Associate Producer Susan Carlson, Kasey and the band were the first Australian artists ever featured as headliners on 'Austin City Limits'. Kasey expressed her opinion of the show at an interview immediately following the taping:

> We don't get 'Austin City Limits' in Australia but I've heard about it a lot over the years. And I've also seen a few shows when I've come to America. All my favourite artists are playing on there.

The night before the taping they performed a free show for radio station KGSR at the famed Continental Club, Austin's best known and most enduring small venue. The Continental holds a couple hundred but the audience quickly overflowed onto the sidewalk. People stood outside in the chill air, viewing the show through the window while hoping someone inside would leave. It didn't happen.

What a way to start out in Texas, the state with the richest and most diverse music heritage in the US! This was their first show in Austin, they were performing on the same stage that a virtual 'who's who' of the best-known regional artists had called home; and they were entertaining a packed house—many sang along. Additionally, the KGSR-sponsored show gave everyone a glimpse of the interest that steady airplay on a major radio station could generate. Aside from KGSR, who considered her a 'core artist' (like Lucinda Williams, Steve Earle, Lyle Lovett, Emmylou Harris and Buddy Miller), most of her radio play came from specialist shows in major markets or on low-powered stations with limited audiences, similar to community radio in Australia.

Like 'Austin City Limits', 'Late Night with David Letterman' also prides itself on being ahead of the 'cutting edge'; hence their booking of Kasey only six weeks after the US release of *The Captain*. Though she was on camera for just one song, Kasey's selection for the show sent a strong message to the US media that she was a new artist on the fast track.

They spent the next day trying to fly from New York to Chicago, normally about an hour-and-a-half hop. Unfortunately, midwestern snowstorms forced an unscheduled landing in Cleveland. There they spent most of the day, sitting patiently in chilled planes or the bustling terminal, arriving in icy Chicago only two hours before their show at Schuba's.

Alas, after fourteen shows in twenty-one days, dozens of in-person and phone interviews, 'meet and greets' at almost every show, plus internal travelling of over 15 000 kilometres, Kasey's voice departed mid-set at Schuba's, in Chicago. She'd let the crowd know she wasn't at her best early on in the set and had faltered a couple of times thereafter but gamely ploughed on before stopping, saying she simply couldn't subject those assembled to her croakiness any longer. By then she was talking in practically a whisper and it was obvious that her voice was shot.

It was a nasty end to a tour wholly successful to that point. But Kasey, Nash, Bill, Diane, Worm, Camille, B.J., James and Jeff could look back on successful debuts in New York City, Austin, San Francisco and Philadelphia, two high-profile TV and three key radio appearances, increased airplay and heaps of favourable press clippings. As they flew back home, they could also see evidence of their hard work reflected in the increased US sales for *The Captain*: figures for the end of November showed an over 110 per cent gain above end-of-October totals. SoundScan® showed the album had documented sales of over 7000 copies and was trending upwards. While this total was far below the level normally necessary for a country or pop artist to sustain major label interest, Warner Bros' zeal was unflagging—quite simply Kasey, the album and the band had charmed the pants off them.

Then again, that level of sales in just six weeks was quite satisfying for a new artist working with only Americana/AAA airplay, especially one from Australia completely new to US audiences. Warner's believed that once they could get major radio play, sales would follow.

18
Racing Forward, Looking Back

Back home, Kasey and the band performed in Melbourne and Sydney then dug in at the studio to create the tracks which would become her second album. Once again Nash was producing, but this time instead of packing and moving to Norfolk Island they began at Mangrove Studios, a first-rate facility just down the road in Gosford. Thus, they created the basic tracks for the *Barricades & Brickwalls* album within easy commuting distance from their homes.

Just when it seemed everything in the US was running smoothly, another possible disaster appeared. Evelyn and Susan announced their departure from Asylum, effectively ending the label. After meeting with Jim Ed to discuss their future, the pair decided to leave and try to start another label, hopefully with George Jones and Jamie O'Hara as their kickoff artists. Due to the overwhelmingly receptive response Kasey had earned from all corners, the label decided to officially transfer her from the Asylum roster in Nashville to parent company Warner Bros. This wasn't as much of a change as it might seem for, once Asylum determined to avoid country radio, it made more sense to shift Kasey to their Burbank headquarters anyway. Her radio promotion, marketing and publicity activities had already moved there.

While Kasey enjoyed a short rest, Nash spent December and January at Mangrove, Bill again onboard as the core instrumentalist. Diane continued to organise the merchandising and oversee Kasey's newly launched fan club, run on a day-to-day basis by

Carol Paltridge, long-time operator of the Dead Ringer Band's fan club.

Before long it was Tamworth time again and Kasey was nominated for two Golden Guitars at the 2001 Toyota Country Music Awards of Australia: Best Video for 'The Captain' and Best Collaboration for 'Matilda No More' (cut with Slim Dusty). Kasey also accepted slots as a presenter and a performer. She booked one public show, at the West Leagues Club, since her drawing power now far outdistanced the capacity of the RSL club where she had performed the last two years. Dead Ringer Band opted not to schedule a date, to keep the focus on Kasey. This had to feel strange for them since the four Chambers had performed at every Festival since making their humble start as buskers in 1992.

The pressure was off Kasey in 2001, unlike a year ago, when she was amid a print media firestorm. This year she would come to the Awards as the gracious 2000 winner, ready to pass on her Album and Female Vocalist of the Year crowns. Since Slim Dusty was riding into town on the heels of the double platinum success of his 100th album, *Looking Forward, Looking Back*, most figured he would be the night's big winner.

This was not to be. While Slim took home awards for Bush Ballad, Video and Best Selling Album, Adam Brand was the big winner, as he had been two years ago. Brand's *Good Friends* CD earned him Album and Best Male Vocalist titles, while his Graeme Connors co-write, 'Good Things In Life', tallied for APRA Song of the Year. Kasey's close friend for many years, Beccy Cole, followed her as Female Vocalist of the Year and another friend, Darren Coggan, shared the Vocal Collaboration Award with Beccy, Adam Harvey and Felicity.

There were three other Chambers connections in the finalist ranks at the 2001 Awards, all, alas, non-winning efforts. Bill played and/or sang harmony on six tracks of Audrey Auld's CD, *The Fallen*, a finalist nominee for Best New Artist and Female Vocalist of the Year. Nash contributed acoustic guitar on one cut, 'Black Cloud', engineered that track and two others. And the track 'Two Pot Screamer', which Nash produced for The Sparnetts, landed that band a nomination in the Vocal Duo/Group category. Thus, the Chambers were involved in five finalist nominations, further cementing their positions at the top of the Australian country world.

In the United States, the airing of Kasey's 'Austin City Limits' show with Steve Earle helped her sales crest 2000 copies the first time for the week ending 21 January. This propelled her to a ranking of number 49 on Billboard's country album chart and was the highest entry there that week. She joined Australian expatriates Keith Urban and Jamie O'Neal on the chart, marking the first time in history three Australian artists were simultaneously on that list.

February brought Kasey's next, and most ambitious, tour. This trek began 21 February and made twenty-eight stops before concluding in Chicago on 30 March. Working in tandem with Warner's Chris Palmer and Rabin, agent Bobby Cudd tried a different strategy, booking Kasey to open some dates for more established artists. Thus Kasey spent the first nine shows as support for rowdy Texan singer-songwriter Robert Earl Keen.

As in the November tour the entourage would venture coast-to-coast, this time completely via bus. The travelling squad was pared down for this run: Bill, Nash, B.J., James Gillard, Kym Warner and Worm joined road manager Greg Wilkinson, who was able to guide them again when his other main client, Patty Griffin, had her album release date postponed. The tour marked a return to many key markets and also their initial appearance in New Orleans, Washington DC, Norfolk, Ann Arbor, Atlanta, Tampa, Houston, Portland, Seattle and Minneapolis. Additionally, they were slated to kick off the release of *The Captain* in Canada with a high-profile show in Toronto.

Bobby Cudd also added a last-minute booking, securing them another Grand Ole Opry invitation, slated for 23 February. This time, however, the Opry was in its winter quarters at the Ryman Auditorium, its previous home from 1943–74. Thus the band performed on the very stage trod by such immortals as Hank Williams, Patsy Cline, Ernest Tubb, Marty Robbins, Buck Owens and the Carter Family—six of Bill's biggest influences. It

Bill and Kasey just after their Ryman Auditorium Grand Ole Opry performance. Drummer B. J. Barker bangs away in the background.

had been a huge thrill to play the Opry back in June but that was in the modern facility opened adjacent to the Opryland theme park in 1974. This time they sang at the famed Ryman itself, widely revered as 'the Mother Church of Country Music'.

Later in the tour they performed at South by Southwest (SXSW), the biggest, best and longest-lived of the regional music conferences. SXSW, now in its fifteenth year, has become one of the world's top music festivals, ranked with Midem in France, Popkomm in Germany and Manchester's 'In the City' events.

Given her success in Austin prior to SXSW, and the huge groundswell of media interest, Kasey was one of the highest profile performers—no small feat at an event that showcases over 1000 acts—hosted at over forty venues simultaneously—during four intense days and nights.

This time Kasey kept her voice throughout the tour and finished with a scintillating Schuba's performance which saw her and the band earn two encores. In addition to increased media attention and steady sales, the shows generated interest from a

*Nash lays down a solid groove in Nashville at 328 Performance Hall,
23 February 2001.*

most welcome quarter. Emmylou Harris had scheduled an April
Antipodean tour and her manager, Ken Levitan, contacted Gary
Rabin to see if Kasey could join the tour as support, performing
after a short set by Buddy Miller. Kasey got an even bigger
surprise just afterwards when Lucinda Williams' manager called to
say Lu had requested Kasey be *her* opening act in June. Lucinda
was poised to tour to promote *Essence*, follow-up release to *Car
Wheels On A Gravel Road*, her gold-selling, Grammy-winning 1998
album. Thus, in the space of a few weeks, Kasey received touring
offers from two of the world's premiere artists: both also major
influences on her own musical development.

This gratifying attention from fellow artists was com-
plemented by interest from one of the United States' top TV hits,
'The Sopranos'. A two-minute excerpt from 'The Captain' was
aired at the end and beneath the closing credits of an episode of
the show and the full track of 'The Captain' was chosen for the
second compilation album from the program. Kasey joined Bob

Dylan, the Rolling Stones, Frank Sinatra, Otis Redding and the Kinks on this CD, released in May as *The Sopranos: Peppers & Eggs.*

On the last day of March, after their triumphant return to Schuba's, Kasey, Bill, Nash, B.J., James, Kym and Worm bid adieu to the shiny white bus that had been their home for six weeks. As they climbed aboard the United 747 that would carry them home to Sydney's Kingsford Smith airport, they could reflect on thirty successful shows, an even more enhanced media profile and consistent sales. Kasey had passed the 40 000 sales mark in April; Warner Bros felt there was plenty of life left yet for her debut CD in the United States. They still believed Kasey was an artist destined to sell strongly in America and felt all their hard work in introducing *The Captain* would pay off by setting up *Barricades & Brickwalls* and Kasey's subsequent albums for platinum sales levels. Many in the company recalled k.d. Lang's records didn't start selling strongly until her third US album, *Absolute Torch and Twang*, in 1989.

As the band and crew flew back home high above the Pacific, they could look forward to a busy three months which would see them applying the finishing touches to *Barricades & Brickwalls*, touring with Emmylou Harris and Buddy Miller, kicking off the new album with key tour dates in Australia in May, then flying back to the United States to spend June opening seventeen shows on Lucinda Williams' summer tour.

As Bill, Nash and Kasey gazed down at the blue waters of the Pacific ten kilometres below them they could be excused for briefly basking in the glow of their achievements. They had truly come a long way. Nash and Kasey had spent over half their childhood years in the extreme outback of Australia, first joining their parents for 'serious' performances in the tiny town of Southend eleven years ago. Now they had become two of Australia's most promising young talents—Kasey as an award-winning singer-songwriter, Nash as an in-demand record producer and engineer, sought out by everyone from fifteen-year-old aspiring

Wistful thinking.

Newcastle country singer Catherine Britt to fifty-four-year-old pioneering rock legend Ross Wilson.

After gaining his original notice for his songwriting, Bill has now become one of the finest multi-instrumentalists in Australian music. Kasey's solo success has allowed him to step back into being the main 'picker' in her band, a much more comfortable role for him.

Diane continues to hold the family together on practical, emotional and spiritual fronts. She has also begun working to aid orphanages in several countries, assisting in numerous fundraising efforts aimed at helping those less fortunate.

Three ARIA statuettes stand in the trophy case in the Chambers Central Coast home, accompanied by five MO Awards and five Gold Guitars, thirteen tangible symbols that their fans and their peers deem them more than worthy competitors in the music world they have chosen.

Bill, Diane, Nash and Kasey Chambers have all survived, nay

thrived on an existence few of us could even contemplate, much less undertake, and complete. Those years on the Nullarbor and the quality time the family spent—and still spends—together have paid off by enabling them to survive twenty-five years of trials by fire, first in the hostile Nullarbor environment, then in the treacherous music business.

For most of that time they had been told they couldn't succeed at various musical endeavours. Yet, fuelled by determination, self-confidence and, as Bill says, 'naivety and pig-headedness', Dead Ringer Band aka the Chambers family had given it a go anyway and, surmounting every obstacle, have created music now heard around the world.

Kasey: I was exposed to a lifestyle that not many people get to be exposed to, which is pretty amazing. I think one of the main things about living out there was that we created a closeness in the family. And that's stayed ever since. Even through Mum and Dad breaking up, we still have a closeness in our family that I think a lot of families don't ever have and which we're lucky to have. And that closeness really affects my songwriting, too. There's a mention of someone in my family in nearly every one of my songs.

Diane: There was a strength brought through which I feel is with all of us even today, a closeness and a family bond. Even though Bill and I are parted, I still think we have that in a different role. I know the kids and I have that very strongly, and I believe the kids have it with Bill, also. Instead of being one unit, we're kind of two units, but somehow we've still sort of got one circle around us.

Kasey: Musically, I think that the biggest influence wasn't really the actual environment that I was in—although I think that had an effect too—but the music I was exposed to out there. I wasn't just hanging around with a whole lot of friends that all listened to the Top 40—I went through that stage as well, but the first ten years of my life, I was only exposed to the music that my dad liked. I consider myself pretty lucky to be one of those few people out there who were brought up on Emmylou Harris instead of Tina Turner. In a way I've got to thank my grandparents for that, for bringing my dad up on Jimmie Rodgers and the Carter Family and Hank Williams, which made him bring me and Nash up on that sort of music. Being out there, there wasn't a way of just walking into the shop and buying the latest record.

Nash: I think the Nullarbor helped give me and Kasey a grounding as decent people with decent family values, qualities which are seldom found in this industry. I think it was just a great grounding in life, because we'd travelled all around Australia before I even started high school. It's just great experiences—it's fantastic to look back on them, to have them as memories. I know we couldn't go back and live like that now. It really helped us as people, to just sort of ground ourselves. I don't know if we'd be able to cope with what we're doing now, although it's a long way from what we were doing then. I think the Nullarbor was a great thing to have as our childhood home. I wouldn't change it for the world.

Diane: When we first started going into the outback, both of our families said, 'You'll never get Bill past the first turn, the Chambers have been here for five generations,' how the Chambers aren't known for stretching out in society, that sort of thing. They've always sort of clung to themselves and Bill was always a very quiet kind of guy.

We must have always had some sort of a survival spirit in us, a challenging spirit, an adventure spirit in us to be able to keep overcoming obstacles. Mind you, we've been blessed with an amazing amount of support and help from family and friends, financially and emotionally. Both my family and Bill's family have always stuck with us and believed in us, whatever we've done.

But right from the very start, as time went by, we bonded together as a foursome so that we lost the role of parent/children and we became old buddies, all on one level. That's another reason why things worked during our touring together. Life wasn't always rosy; there were times when we had family fights, arguments and hiccups like anybody else, but we did always seem to pull through and strive on to the next stage.

I believe we've been guided—you can put your own interpretation on that, whether by a god or a universe. People can sum that up with their own beliefs, but I believe we've been guided right throughout our life, leading to a point. That point is almost where we are now, we're not there yet. We seem to have had someone at our home guiding us and leading us through the tough times, the hard times, the no money times; it's all been to strengthen us, to nurture and mature us in all our different roles.

Epilogue

The sound of kookaburras greeted the fifty-year-old woman as she awakened in her Central Coast home, high above the Pacific waters. She yawned then stretched as she set the coffee to boil on the stove, moving quietly so she wouldn't wake Nash, who had just returned from six weeks of US touring. Outside was a vista of lush green shrubbery, tall tan trees and birds of every colour. If she listened closely she could hear the faint sounds of the blue-green surf rising and falling on the sloped beach below her.

Had it really been nearly twenty-five years since she and Bill had taken toddler Nash and newborn Kasey into the heart of the Nullarbor? She thought back to her first night on the Plain. She had cried for hours, wondering if they would ever survive living in that inhospitable place.

She thought back to those times, to the happy hours spent singing around the campfire, to the peaceful solitude and incredible beauty of outback sunsets, to the closeness they had shared as a family unit—a mother, father and two kids against the world.

Everyone had said they were crazy to try to live on the Plain and incredibly irresponsible to bring two small children into that life with them. Yet they had overcome every peril the Nullarbor presented and survived, all four of them, armed with lessons and memories she wouldn't trade for anything.

On this warm April morning Diane reflected upon her many blessings. She shared a comfortable home with her son, Nash.

Her daughter Kasey lived just down the road with Worm, their long-time South Australian friend who had been like a second son to her. She thought about her two healthy children who, though still in their twenties, had established international reputations in the world of popular music.

Though her marriage to Bill had ended she was well past the pain of their parting and could instead remember the good times they had shared and take pride in the children they had raised together.

The cool southern breeze began to rustle the trees, reminding her that there was still breakfast to fix and merchandising business to complete. Soon they would start another tour, this time with Kasey as support act for Emmylou Harris, one of the artists whose tapes had helped them get through those years on the Nullarbor.

If anyone had walked up to her years ago on the Plain and told her what would happen to them in the next twenty or so years, she would have laughed them off as insane fools.

It had been an incredible life so far and, as the coffee pot started singing, Diane reflected that if her life ended tomorrow she could truthfully say she'd been served extra helpings of love and fulfilment. She faintly heard the sound of a radio from a car passing on the nearby road:

> . . . And after all that I have done
> I'm not half what I hoped that I'd become
> There's still a long way to go.

Appendix A
Initial Correspondence

The Dead Ringer Band
Avoca Beach, NSW
Australia

25 March 1996

Hello Folks,

Greetings and best wishes from Nashville! Before going further let me say that I enjoy your *Home Fires* album very, very much. It's a remarkable record, as country as hay bales in the barn, with exemplary picking, fine songs, superb harmonies and Kasey's exceptional voice. Thanks for making *Home Fires*, it's already given me a lot of pleasure and I've also had the joy of turning others on to it, so far just my wife, daughter and two friends, but there will be others. Many others if the Lord is willing and the creeks don't rise.

Laurie faxed me earlier today to let me know he has kept you informed of my intent to explore opportunities here. I have several targets in mind and will be making appointments Monday to play the album for a few labels and a publisher later in the week. I know it's a long shot—James Blundell is the only Aussie recently to have a deal up here and as you know he didn't do well. I've heard Keith Urban has signed with Warners but he's been here for a couple of years. However, stranger things have happened, who would have thought Shania Twain would sell over 5 million albums or that Allison Krauss would be closing in on half that? And with CMT now set up 'down under' perhaps that will open a new window of opportunity for you and other Australian country artists . . .

I feel honored to have the chance to play the album for some carefully chosen label and publishing execs and will do my dead level best to sell this most extraordinary record to them. Nashville music has become so plastic and is so lacking in soul that this record, so filled with heart and so unmistakably *country*, may well have a good shot at attracting serious attention.

I will keep you informed about my progress in pitching this very exciting project! And again, thanks for making a brilliant record, I really, really love it!

Sincerely yours,
John Lomax III

cc: Laurie Dunn

P.S. I've appended my résumé in case you are curious about my background and experience.

25 March 1996

Hi John,

Laurie has kept us to date with our faxes and we were thrilled to hear from you personally.

We would certainly appreciate any help you can give us regarding a recording deal or publishing in the US, and even if nothing else happens, we are glad you like *Home Fires*.

I guess Laurie has told you we are a family which means we are pretty much self-contained and ready to have a shot at anything that may further our career. We have a great relationship with Laurie and Massive, so we are happy for any negotiations to come via Laurie. All we ask is to be kept up to date as to any progress, and we know that you and Laurie will see to that.

WOW!! You certainly have been involved in almost every

part of the Country Music Industry. Steve Earle and Townes Van
Zandt happen to be two of our favourite singer/songwriters . . .
      . . . Looking forward to hearing from you again and hope
to meet you someday soon.

Regards,
Dead Ringer Band

Appendix B
A Brief History of Country Music in Australia

Given the shared ethnic influences, the colonisation of hitherto sparsely populated continents and mutual wide open environments, one could assume there are more similarities than differences in the evolution of the rural based music we call 'country' as they developed in the bustling new world of North America and the strange isolated island continent, the Great Southern Land, *Terra Australis*.

You'd be half right.

The English, Scottish and Irish convicts and free settlers brought their folk music to Australia, just as they did spreading westward from the east coast of the original American thirteen states and above, in the colony of Canada.

In the northern hemisphere other influences came into play. The field hollers and rhythms of African black slave labour and the substantial continental European immigrant group from Germany, Austria, France, Switzerland and elsewhere added their own flavours, and in places melded with the 'south of the border' sounds of Mexican/Spanish heritage.

In Australia, the harsh reality of a continent starved of water and isolated from easy transportation in the eighteenth and ninteenth centuries created a distinct and rugged 'bush' culture, one based squarely on the predominate Anglo-Saxon and Celtic heritage. This view was propagated and supported by city-based sympathisers such as Banjo Paterson and Henry Lawson, the twin giants in the consolidation of a truly Australian literature, both prose and poetry.

Similarly, the early history of music that can be considered country is dominated by three men, Tex Morton, Buddy Williams and Slim Dusty, each of whom made career breakthroughs in the middle years of the twentieth century.

Morton, a native New Zealander, was a brilliant showman but a total enigma. He recorded his first songs on an aluminum disc process while still in Wellington, New Zealand in 1932. The approximately twenty sides were played widely on radio and each disc was copied from the one preceding it, which makes them exceedingly rare today. He came to Australia as a 'jack of all trades' entertainer, but his eventual recording at EMI's Homebush studio on 25 February 1936 set in motion an ongoing musical influence. Tex sang two American songs that day, 'Texas in the Spring' and 'Going Back to Texas', but he also performed his own 'Swiss Sweetheart' and 'Happy Yodeller', thus encapsulating the schizophrenic nature of Australian country music at the very moment of its creation.

Present on that recording is the personality of a great artist, only nineteen years of age, who had managed to assimilate the influences of Jimmie Rodgers and Goebbel Reeves (little known in the United States but a huge influence on Australian country, particularly in his yodelling style) and make them his own. Success came quickly: as a result, Tex Morton became the biggest influence on the artists who followed, most listening in far flung and mainly outback regions. Favour with the establishment was harder to attain: in spite of huge record sales and barnstorming tours, Morton was deemed a 'hillbilly' by the big city industry— their philosophy was to record him as quickly and cheaply as possible. Despite these hurdles, by mid-1937 among the many tunes Tex had recorded were 'The Yodelling Bag Man', a song historian Eric Watson tags as 'the first thoroughly authentic Australian country song', as well as Morton's all time best seller, 'The Black Sheep'. His prolific period of recording and performing by the early 1940s alone makes Tex Morton's career every bit as interesting as the greatest of the American country artists of this period. He went on to separate careers as a hypnotist (The Great

Morton), and as a film and TV character actor in Hollywood, resuming recording in the 1960s and 1970s, even adding another hit to his name with 'The Goondiwindi Grey' in 1973.

In the midst of this first flush of Morton-mania, another colossus appeared. Buddy Williams was a truly home-grown product, again deeply indebted to Rodgers and Reeves as well as Morton and Alberta-based cowboy singer Wilf Carter, also known south of the Canadian border as Montana Slim.

Williams was born in Sydney in 1918 and spent his first seven years in an orphanage before being farmed out to a family in Dorrigo, on the north coast of New South Wales. There he was treated as cheap labour for a dairy farm but his early years of isolation cemented the love for the land which later permeated his music. After running away from home and scratching for a living during the Depression, Williams turned to music as the way out and began busking up and down the coast, eventually gaining an audition with EMI A&R man Arch Kerr. He was first recorded on 7 September 1939, two days after his twenty-first birthday. With 'That Dappled Grey Bronco of Mine' and 'They Call Me the Rambling Yodeller', we finally have, as Watson remarks, 'an Australian singing first-hand of his experiences'. Buddy is the pivotal artist in Australian country music's development. Although enlisting during World War II, he continued to record and fashioned most of his classic songs such as 'Where the White Faced Cattle Roam' and 'The Overlander Trail' during the 1940s.

The third Australian country giant emerged right at the end of the war. Slim Dusty first journeyed down to Sydney to record some custom releases in 1945 but in the following year he recorded a song that remains a milestone in Australian country. Inspired by the floods around Kempsey and his little town of Nulla Nulla Creek, 'The Rain Tumbles Down in July' remains an acutely observed concise piece that is as classic and meaningful today as when David Gordon 'Slim Dusty' Kirkpatrick wrote it. Countless classics have flowed from Dusty's pen since then, all released by EMI on over 100 albums, beginning in 1946. His songs, recordings and very bearing defined the 'bush ballad' form many consider the only true original style music of European settlement in Australia.

Dusty also found other writers to aid him in the execution and preservation of the form, like his childhood friend Shorty Ranger ('Winter Winds'), Gordon Parsons ('The Pub with No Beer)', Joe Daley ('Trumby') and most prolifically, Stan Coster ('A Fire of Gidgee Coal', 'Cunnamulla Feller'). Slim Dusty has bent with the times but never changed; he has fashioned the words of Banjo Paterson and Henry Lawson into song and performed with most of the 'new breed' of artists to emerge during his half-century reign as the King of Australian country music. He has received every award and accolade possible and most importantly has been blessed with a wonderful family life. Wife Joy McKean came to prominence as one of the McKean Sisters and has gone on to become an outstanding country songwriter herself ('The Lights on the Hill', 'The Biggest Disappointment'). Daughter Anne Kirkpatrick is a highly regarded singer and son David also sings, but became a doctor by profession.

If by 1950 Tex, Buddy and Slim had set the rules and put the train in motion, they were aided by a groundswell of artists such as Smoky Dawson, who early on put his own style on cowboy and bushranger songs and as a familiar popular personality remains an icon. Shirley Thoms and June Holms never had the same opportunities as the men, but they nonetheless created memorable and meaningful recordings from a feminine perspective. A slew of lesser known, though talented folks added to the form, all lacking only the opportunity to make their mark: Dusty Rankin, Tim McNamara, the aforementioned Shorty Ranger and Gordon Parsons, a man who just lacked the drive and gave it all away.

The early 1950s represented a high point of country music activity with caravans of country and variety performers crisscrossing the land in search of a town where they could 'put on a show'. Once again, Slim led the way, but troupes like that of Rick and Thel Carey, who initially toured with Dusty, became a staple in the bush even after the introduction of television had eroded the audience. This spirit of rugged individualism and battling against the odds continues to this day in the far outback tours led by veteran Brian Young. Many up and coming performers consider it a badge of honour to go on at least one of these treks. In many places, Young's audience comprises mainly Indigenous Australians. The Aboriginal people have a long tradition of appreciating country music and have provided some great exponents of their own to the form. Top Aboriginal artists range from the pop stylings of Jimmie Little, who emerged in the 1950s and has lately revitalised his career, to the Lefty Frizzell-influenced modern sounds of current country superstar Troy Cassar-Daley. Just to the north of Australia in Papua New Guinea, country music is simply known as 'Slim Dusty Music', such is 'The King's' influence in this region.

In a curious switch, the ground-breaking research of Sydney-based folk/hillbilly enthusiast and collector John Edwards led to a new American awareness of the importance of The Carter Family, Jimmie Rodgers and many other pioneering stateside artists. Edwards corresponded with like-minded collectors worldwide, as well as the surviving artists and their families, from 1953 until his premature death in 1960, at the age of twenty-nine. He instigated discographical documentation of southern folk/hillbilly artists and wrote articles in magazines internationally, fostering new awareness of their importance. An automobile accident ended his life, but Edwards' will provided for the shipment of his entire collection of 2500 records and tapes and his extensive correspondence to UCLA in Southern California. There, under the care of fellow collector Eugene Earle and others, Edwards' collection was eventually expanded tenfold. In 1978 these vital archives were purchased by The University of North Carolina in Chapel Hill, where they were integrated into The Southern Folklife Collection. Sadly, John Edwards never visited the country that originated the music he loved.

Due to the dominance of Top 40 radio, television shows and the media attention given to the big overseas names, the greater part of the 1950s through to the 1970s found Australian country coming to grips with an increasing contemporary US influence. It is fair to say that only two artists emerged during this period who created their own completely different styles, one by outright rejection of the American model, the other by being so unique he defies comparison!

The latter is 'The Sheik Of Scrubby Creek', Chad Morgan. Born in Wondai, Queensland in 1933, the self-deprecation so apparent in his signature song and many others was concocted because as a lad he was sensitive about his appearance and mostly struck out with 'the sheilas'. He transformed these mishaps into a persona, recording his aforementioned hit in 1952. Alas, Morgan was still shy and not prepared for fame; self-doubt, alcohol and health problems plagued him following his breakthrough. Still, in the annals of country music, his laconic, humorous style is totally individual and he remains a popular performer.

John Williamson, on the other hand, emerged from a background of comparative privilege. The boy from Victoria's Mallee area gained his education at an exclusive private boarding school in Melbourne. Back home, the vagaries of farm life encouraged him to seek a career in music and the folk/pop style of his early 1970s novelty hit 'Old Man Emu' led to some floundering around before he perfected his take on an Australian music form that consciously rejects direct American influence. At one time, the performer even decreed that 'our' music should not have any 'blues' influence! At that stage, Buddy Williams had already long ago recorded an entire album dedicated to the songs of 'The Blue Yodeller', Jimmie Rodgers, someone clearly influenced by black music!

Nevertheless, Williamson has provided a rallying point for those concerned Australian country music was heading too far down a path of singing songs about San Antonio in a pseudo American accent. For a while, the anti-Nashville movement took on the distinct tone of a para-military thought police. Now some semblance of sanity has returned with artists able to assimilate their influences as found in the current work of Cassar-Daley, the middle-of-the-road fare of current Country Queen Gina Jeffreys and the mix of Garth Brooks and Slim Dusty that 'The Boy from the Bush', Lee Kernaghan, has taken to amazing concert and record sales success.

If there seems to be a gaping hole in this potted history around the 1960s to the mid-1970s, that is because very few artists peculiar to this era created anything of lasting artistic value. Reg Lindsay had a television show of some influence but it wasted the opportunity to promote much good music. Instead, the show reinforced the 'hick' stereotypes of earlier radio shows such as *Bonnington's Bunkhouse* in fabricating a rural authenticity. The concept of the New South Wales town Tamworth as the nation's 'Country Music Capital' came to be, and has remained, a great focal point for two weeks every year, but the vast majority of country music activity occurs elsewhere during the remainder. Sydney was the true early country music centre; it remains the hub of record and publishing companies and is the site of the bulk of contemporary recording.

The Hawking Brothers sprang from the ranks of Melbourne's 'Australian Hillbilly Club' and the loosely knit group The Trailblazers. Highly successful on the live circuit, the brothers oscillated between recording contemporary American and traditional Australian folk songs, while a decade later The Flying Emus similarly strived for new ways to marry bluegrass and Australian themes. Ex-rocker Johnny Chester created country pop hits, as had English immigrant Frank Ifield in an earlier era. One-off hit artists like Slim Newton ('Redback on the Toilet Seat'), Johnny Ashcroft ('Little Boy Lost') and Lionel Rose ('Thank You'), relied on bad taste, opportunism or celebrity in another area for a hit.

Expatriate Olivia Newton-John recorded a string of surprise pop-flavoured US country chart hits in England, raising the hackles of many Nashville artists. On arriving in Tennessee for the first time, she supposedly expressed a desire to meet Hank Williams! Meanwhile Victorian-born jazz/cabaret singer Diana Trask had 'gone country' only once. She made it to Dixie but nevertheless released a number of well-received albums and had some moderate hits, also during the first half of the 1970s. Her release, 'Lean it All on Me', reached number 13 on the *Billboard* country singles list in 1974 and that was the high-water mark for Australian artists on that chart for twenty-six years (see Appendix D).

Strangely enough, a few early 1970s country-rock bands operating in the main outside the established country circuit came to impart more influence over future trends than the majority of established country artists. Groups such as Melbourne's Dingoes, who were at one stage signed to A&M Records in the United States, Victoria-based Saltbush, Adelaide's Stars and Sydney's Goldrush were pointers to the 1990s, while the phenomenally successful Daddy Cool joined them in providing songs that would later be regarded as country. In the late 1980s, James Blundell wrestled with the vision of a kind of bush/rock hybrid, was signed briefly to Capitol in the United States but eventually lost his way. His influence on a younger generation, however, should not be under-estimated. Similarly, Graeme Connors brought a new literacy to countrified songwriting, if not always operating strictly within the confines of the genre. Fellow travellers Eric Bogle, Paul Kelly and others could be added to that list.

Through it all, Slim Dusty soldiered on and today can reflect on the industry he has largely created. While he goes on from strength to strength, his daughter Anne delivered her best-ever albums in the 1990s. Artists such as Shanley Del, Gina Jeffreys and Melinda Schneider regularly travel to Nashville to write and record while precocious talent Keith Urban has stuck it out 'over there' for most of the last decade to finally post a US Top 20 chart hit early in 2000. The other antipodean with a recent American recording contract, Sherrié Austin, bypassed the Australian training ground altogether.

Back home, young hopeful Adam Brand came from nowhere to snatch three Golden Guitars and reach gold record status for his first release in 1999 while Kasey Chambers has shattered the mystical barrier between rock and country to gain accolades in both camps without changing her musical style one bit.

Keith Glass

Postscript

As this book goes to press, four Australians are in the US Country album charts: Sherrié Austin, Jamie O'Neil (who, like Sherrié, bypassed local country music involvement), Keith Urban (who has achieved a gold-certified album with several hit US country chart singles and a grammy nomination), and Kasey Chambers. Kasey's debut album had registered twelve weeks on the chart by July, despite not being actively promoted to country radio.

References

Catalogue of Recorded Music In Australia, 1942 edition.

Latta, David (1991) *Australian Country Music*, Random House.

Minson, John and Ellis, Max (2000) *Country Music Through the Years*, chronological entries from *Directory of Australian Country Music*, No. 5, CMAA, Tamworth.

Smith, Jazzer and Blinman, Keith (1985) *Book of Australian Country Music*, Berghouse, Floyd, Tuckey Publishing.

Watson, Eric (1975 and 1983) *Eric Watson's Country Music in Australia*, Volumes 1&2, Cornstalk.

Appendix C
Chambers Discography
(excluding singles)

Year	Title	Label and record no.	Comments
1987	*Sea Eagle*	Privately issued cassette	Bill Chambers
1991	*Kindred Spirit*	Privately issued cassette	Bill Chambers
1992	*A Matter of Time*	Dead Ringer Band/none	Four-song EP
1993	*Red Desert Sky*	Larrikin/LRF 302	First full album
1994	*Nu-Music Sampler #10*	Studio 52/52 CD100#10	One cut
1994	Compilation	Gympie Muster	One cut
1995	Compilation	Gympie Muster	One cut
1995	*Home Fires*	Massive/7310752	ARIA winner
1997	*Living in the Circle*	Massive/7320762	ARIA nominee
1998	*Hopeville*	Massive/7321962	Covers album
1998	*Not So Dusty*	EMI/7243 4 96406 2 7	One cut
1998	*Looking Back to See*	Reck 001	Bill and Audrey album Produced by Bill, Nash and Audrey
1999	*The Captain* (Australian release)	EMI/7243 5 20355 2 6	Kasey Chambers ARIA Winner
1999	The Sparnetts	ACMEC	Produced by Nash CMAA Winner

2000	*Till Now—Best of DRB*	Massive 7322882	18 tracks
2000	*The Captain* (UK release)	CD VIR 101	Kasey Chambers
2000	*The Captain* (US only)	Asylum Nashville (no number)	Fan Fair Special Invitation
2000	*The Captain* (US release)	Asylum/Warner Bros. 9 47823-2	Kasey Chambers
2000	*The Captain* Special Bonus Edition (Australia only)	EMI 7243 5 29281 2 5	Kasey Chambers
2000	*On The Road with Kasey Chambers* (US Promo only)	PRO-CD-100573	Kasey Chambers
2001	*Barricades & Brickwalls* (Australian release)	EMI	Kasey Chambers Issued in August

Appendix D
US Country Singles Chart Performance
(artists born in Australia, England or New Zealand)

Australian-born performers

Year	Act	Chart singles	Best performance
1968–75, 1981	Diana Trask	18	#13
1977	Helen Reddy	1	#98
1978–79	Arthur Blanch	2	#73
1978–79	Jewel Blanch	2	#33
1979	Helen Hudson	1	#91
1978–80, 1988	LeGarde Twins	4	#82
1997–2001	Sherrié Austin	7	#34
1997–1998	The Ranch+	2	#50
2000–2001	Jamie Oneal	2	#1

English-born performers

Year	Act	Chart singles	Best performance
1962	Springfields	1	#16
1966–68	Frank Ifield	4	#28
1968, 1970, 1975	Leapy Lee	3	#11
1973–79, 1998	Olivia Newton-John*	16	#2
1974	Paul McCartney (and Wings)	1	#51

1974	Peters and Lee	1	#79
1978	Eric Clapton	2	#26
1978	Bee Gees*	1	#39
1978	Leo Sayer	1	#63
1978	Poacher	1	#86
1982	Petula Clark	1	#20
1985	Simon & Verity	2	#78
1988–89	Jon Washington	2	#73
1989	Fairground Attraction#	1	#85

New Zealand-born performers

Year	Act	Chart singles	Best performance
1964	Gale Garnett	1	#43
1999–2001	Keith Urban	4	#1

Notes + Peter Clarke was born in Australia, Keith Urban in New Zealand, Jerry Flowers in the United States. * Olivia Newton-John and the Bee Gees both lived in Australia for a number of years. # Fairground Attraction was a mixed English-Scottish group.

Sources: Original research by John Lomax III based on: *Joel Whitburn's Top Country Singles: 1944–1993*, Billboard Publications, 1994; *Joel Whitburn's Annual*, 1994, 1995; and 1996–2000 weekly *Billboard* charts.

Appendix E
Awards

Dead Ringer Band

ARIA	Best Country Album: Winner 1996; Finalist 1997
Toyota/CMAA Country Music Awards of Australia	Vocal Group/Duo: Winner 1995, 1998, 1999; Finalist 1996, 1997 Vocal Collaboration: Winner (with others) 1995*
APRA Song of the Year	'Living in the Circle', 1998 Written by Richard Porteous, sung by Dead Ringer Band
MO Awards	Best Country Group: Winner 1996, 1997, 1998, 1999; Finalist 1994, 1995, 2000
Victorian Country Music Awards	Best Group/Duo: Winner 1996, 1997, 1998, 1999
Songwriter's Award	Finalist 1996
South Australia Music Industry Award	Outstanding Contribution to Country Music, 1994
People's Choice Award	Australia's Most Popular Country Group, 1993**

Bill Chambers

APRA Song of the Year	'Things Are Not the Same on the Land', 1992; written by Bill Chambers, sung by Slim Dusty

Kasey Chambers

ARIA

Best Country Album: Winner 1999
Best Female Vocalist: Finalist 1999
Best Female Artist: Winner 2000
Record of the Year: Finalist 2000

Toyota/CMAA Country Music
Awards of Australia

Album (of the Year): Winner 2000
Female Vocalist: Winner 2000
Song: Finalist 2000
Video: Finalist 2000
Entertainer: Finalist 2000
Collaboration: Finalist 2000
Video: Finalist 2001
Bestselling album: Finalist 2001

MO Awards

Best Female Country Artist: Winner
2000

APRA

Song of the Year: 'Cry Like A Baby'
Finalist 2000; 'The Captain', Finalist
2001
Country Work of the Year: 'The
Captain', Winner 2001; 'Cry Like A
Baby', Finalist 2000

Nash Chambers

Toyota/CMAA Country Music
Awards of Australia

Producer (of the Year): Winner
2000; Finalist 1999, 1998

Notes: * awarded for 'Bridge of Love', credited to 'Family of Country Music'
(numerous artists participated); ** award discontinued in 1994.

Illustration Sources

133 Beth Gwinn photo
137 Courtesy Chambers family
138 John Montgomery photo
142 Courtesy John Lomax III
143 John Montgomery photo
144 John Montgomery photo
146 Festival/Mushroom Records Archives;
     courtesy Martin Delcanho
156 Courtesy Chambers family
158 John Lomax III Archives; courtesy The Road Mangler
170 John Lomax III Archives; courtesy Massive Records
175 Courtesy Chambers family
192 John Montgomery photo
194 John Montgomery photo
201 John Lomax III Archives;
     courtesy EMI Music/Melita Hodge
202 John Lomax III Archives;
     courtesy EMI Music/Melita Hodge
206 John Lomax III Archives; courtesy EMI Music
212 John Lomax III Archives; courtesy EMI Music
221 John Lomax III Archives; courtesy EMI Music
226 John Lomax III Archives;
     courtesy EMI Music/Melita Hodge
229 John Lomax III Archives;
     courtesy EMI Music/Melita Hodge
265 John Montgomery photo
266 John Montgomery photo
268 John Lomax III Archives;
     courtesy EMI Music/Melita Hodge